W9-BUF-879

The Fly-Tyer's Almanac

The Fly-Tyer's Almanac

Robert H. Boyle • Dave Whitlock

Fully Illustrated

Crown Publishers, Inc., New York

Printed in the United States of America
Published simultaneously in Canada by General Publishing Company Limited

Designed by Leonard Telesca

Library of Congress Cataloging in Publication Data
Main entry under title:

The Fly-tyer's almanac.

Bibliography: p.
Includes index.
1. Fly tying. 2. Insects, Aquatic.
I. Boyle, Robert H. II. Whitlock, Dave.
SH451.F57 1975 688.7'9 75-29433
ISBN 0-517-52372-8

Acknowledgments

We would like to express our thanks and appreciation to the following for permission to excerpt material for this book:

The Connecticut State Geological and Natural History Survey for text and illustrations from Philip Garman, "The Odonata or Dragonflies of Connecticut," *State Geological and Natural History Survey Bulletin,* No. 39 (Hartford, 1927).

The Duke University Press for illustrations from G. S. Dodds and F. L. Hisaw, "Ecological Studies on Aquatic Insects. III. Adaptations of Caddis Fly Larvae to Swift Streams," *Ecology,* Vol. 6 (1925).

The Entomological Society of America for drawings from Winston A. Elkins, "The Immature Stages of Some Minnesota Trichoptera," *Annals Entomological Society of America,* Vol. 29 (1936).

The Illinois Natural History Survey for text and illustrations from Herbert H. Ross, "The Caddis Flies, or Trichoptera, of Illinois," *Bulletin of the Illinois Natural History Survey,* Vol. 23 (1944).

The Lloyd Library and Museum for illustrations from J. T. Lloyd, "The Biology of North American Caddis Fly Larvae," *Bulletin of the Lloyd Library of Botany, Pharmacy, and Materia Medica,* Vol. 21, Entomological Series, No. 1 (1921).

The National Museum of Natural History, Smithsonian Institution, for illustrations from Clarence Hamilton Kennedy, "Notes on the Life History and Ecology of the Dragonflies (Odonata) of Washington and Oregon," *Proceedings of the United States National Museum,* Vol. 49, Washington, D.C., 1915, and same author, "Notes on the Life History and Ecology of the Dragonflies (Odonata) of Central California and Nevada," *Proceedings of the United States National Museum,* Vol. 52, Washington, D.C., 1917.

The New York Entomological Society for the illustrations adapted from Charles E. Sleight, "Relations of Trichoptera to Their Environment," *Journal of the New York Entomological Society,* Vol. 21 (1913).

The New York State Museum and Science Service for illustrations from Cornelius Betten, "The Caddis Flies or Trichoptera of New York State," *New York State Museum Bulletin,* No. 292 (1934).

The Theodore Gordon Flyfishers, Inc. for text from Larry Solomon, "The Caddis Dry Fly," *Random Casts,* No. 6 (1973).

Mrs. Helen Peterson for illustrations from Alvah Peterson, *Larvae of Insects,* Part 2 (Columbus, Ohio; privately printed, 1960).

Sports Illustrated for "The East: Elsie and Harry Darbee," adapted and reprinted from the June 29, 1964, article, "He Deftly Ties the World's Fanciest Flies." Copyright © 1964 Time Inc.

We wish to thank Nick Lyons and Jerry Hoffnagle, Jr., of Crown for editorial assistance above and beyond the call of duty in the profession of publishing. At a very critical time, they voluntarily came forward to assume burdensome editorial and organizational chores to enable the book to meet its deadline. We cannot thank Nick and Jerry enough for their efforts.

We would also like to thank Dr. C. O. Berg of Cornell University for his entomological guidance, so freely and generously given, and the staff of the Croton Free Library.

We thank all our contributors, and we offer special thanks to Joan Whitlock, Stephanie Boyle, and, with cherished memory, the late Jane Sanger Boyle.

ROBERT H. BOYLE and DAVE WHITLOCK

To Dominick J. Pirone, Ph.D., entomologist, fisherman, friend and fighter for the Hudson River; Dr. Herbert H. Ross of the University of Georgia, formerly of the Illinois Natural History Survey; and to the memories of the late Cornelius Betten, Philip Garman, J. T. Lloyd, and Alvah Peterson for their studies in aquatic entomology; and to all the flytyers who contributed their ideas, talents, and time to make this book more useful.

Contents

Introduction

Fly-tying has grown tremendously in popularity in recent years. There are now something on the order of two hundred thousand flytyers in the United States, and the number is increasing with no sign of surcease, thank God.

The appeals of fly-tying are numerous and varied. There is a distinct sense of achievement taking a fish on a fly the angler has tied himself. For another, an angler who ties has a sturdy sense of independence that nonflytyers lack. Instead of having to rely on store-bought flies (often of inferior quality) or wait for a professional to fill an order, a flytyer can quickly match the hatch with appropriate fur and feathers or, if required, alter a pattern or devise a new one to answer the specific needs of the moment. Inasmuch as a good flytyer is usually a thoughtful student of aquatic life, he is better prepared to catch fish than an angler who might think a nymph is the White Rock girl.

Above all, fly-tying is immensely enjoyable as a creative activity, conferring aesthetic bliss upon even minimal manual skill. Great satisfaction is to be had simply by storing up materials, preparing dye baths, dubbing fur, clipping deer hair, folding wing cases, winding hackle, and performing all the pleasant little tasks associated with this most engaging pastime. Perhaps tying flies is the closest any of us get to playing God.

As fly-fishing has spread from trout stream and bass pond to salt water, so fly-tying has burgeoned, and new materials and techniques appear with amazing rapidity. There has been a spate of books on the subject, ranging from new editions of the Marinaro and Flick classics to such new works as Schwiebert's *Nymphs* and Leiser's *Fly-Tying Materials.* Yet for all the books, a key element has been lacking until now. There has been no regular book of record to note advances, describe new patterns, or cite important scientific studies upon which much of fly-tying is based. *The Fly-Ty-*

er's Almanac has been published to serve just that purpose. The volume in hand is the first of a series of *Almanacs* that will appear every two years to note new patterns, materials, techniques, tools, and other information of value and pertinence; readers interested in contributing to the next edition should query the editors, enclosing a self-addressed stamped envelope. If *The Fly-Tyer's Almanac* is truly to achieve its stated purpose of serving as a book of record, it must involve those flytyers who are doing so much to break new ground. In that sense, this book and those that follow in this series are as much yours as ours.

One of the aims of *The Fly-Tyer's Almanac* is to focus attention on flytyers who have made important contributions to the field. Profiles of flytyers are to be a regular feature of *The Fly-Tyer's Almanac,* and we have led off Part I of this first effort with pieces on two husband-and-wife teams of professionals who exemplify the best of East and West: Harry and Elsie Darbee of the Catskills, and René and Bonnie Harrop of St. Anthony, Idaho. The Harrops contribute two mayfly patterns, and Harry Darbee offers an unusual but successful tie for Atlantic salmon, the Horrible Matuka, a fitting name for a fly from the man who co-devised the Rat-Faced MacDougall.

Special attention is next given in Parts II and III to two orders of insects that have been somewhat ignored in fly-tying literature, the Trichoptera (caddis) and the Odonata (damselflies and dragonflies). In the caddis, Raleigh Boaze, Jr., uses dental latex for the larval and pupal forms, and Larry Solomon deals at length with caddis drys. Russ Thomas, Whygin Argus, and the coeditors offer patterns for both nymphs and adults of damselflies and dragonflies.

To give readers extra insight into the Trichoptera and Odonata, we have in Part VII, to leap ahead in the book, reprinted extracts from two very important studies on these orders by Dr. Herbert H. Ross and the late Philip Garman, studies that would ordinarily escape the eyes of anyone not an entomological zealot. Appended to this are anatomical drawings and sketches of individual species taken from a number of works, a Glossary of Entomology, and a Bibliography of Basic Scientific Books for those who wish to pursue matters in more detail.

New saltwater and steelhead patterns are dealt with in Part IV by West Coasters Dan Blanton and Darwin Atkin respectively, and Part V presents a variety of unique flies, from the Four-Phase Polymidge to the Eelworm Streamer. There are variations on two bass bugs, and several flies—Thom Green's Leech, the Quill-bodied Mylar Minnow, and the Transparent Shrimp—should prove successful in both fresh and salt water for a variety of species.

Part VI is given over to the materials of the art. T. Donald Overfield, the well-known English angling writer, discusses the evolution of the new mayfly or dayfly hook with extended shank; Bill Charles writes on how to make liquid-latex bodies, and coeditor Whitlock deals with numerous new materials and tools.

There is all this and much more, as readers can see from an inspection of the table of contents. We hope that the concept of *The Fly-Tyer's Almanac* wins the approbation of readers, and we look forward to receiving criticisms, suggestions, and ideas to make successor volumes even better.

Robert H. Boyle
Dave Whitlock

I

Flytyers - East and West

1

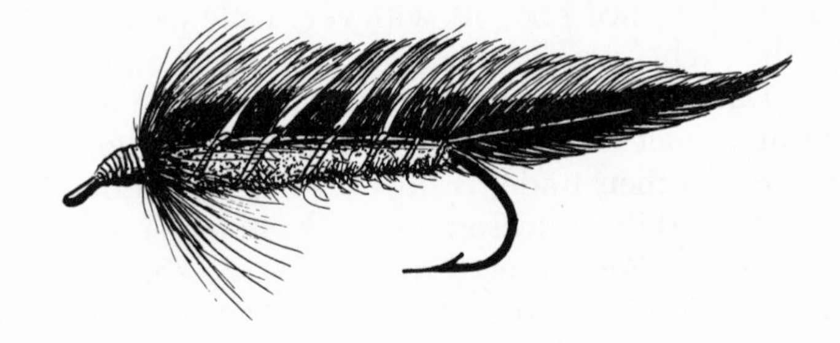

The East: Elsie and Harry Darbee

by Robert H. Boyle

If it were somehow possible in this age of gene banks, artificial insemination, and freeze-dry cadavers to cross Henry David Thoreau with H. L. Mencken, the result might be someone very much like Harry Darbee of Roscoe, New York. To many flytyers and fly-fishermen, Harry Darbee and his wife, Elsie, are figures of veneration.

For one thing, the Darbees exhibit a terrierlike ferocity and tenacity should they learn of a threat to stream or forest, and they have been known to show up at a legislative hearing far from home "just in case," as Harry once put it, "you striped-bass people need a hand." For another, innumerable fly-fishermen have stood in line waiting for Darbee flies over the years. The best-known husband-and-wife team of professional tyers, they work at adjoining desks in the front parlor of their home, and their ties are so similar they have even argued between themselves as to who tied what. In recent years the Darbees haven't done as much tying as they did in the past. Much of their time is taken up selling materials and tackle. Elsie has been especially busy handling a stock of out-of-print books on angling, and Harry is working on a book about his life and fly-tying. When the Darbees do tie, it is usually in the evening. Elsie ties trout flies for old and favored customers while Harry specializes in salmon patterns.

For all the pressure and tedium that can be a part of professional tying, Harry has always been very imaginative. Among his creations are Darbee's Green Egg Sac, Darbee's Spate, Darbee's Crane Fly, and a large imitation of a mayfly that is a cross between a bass bug and a trout fly and thus is named the Beaverkill Bastard. With the late Percy Jennings, Harry devised a dry fly that is not an imitation of any insect at all and is called, simply because a girl happened to name it so, the Rat-Faced MacDougall. Another of Harry's creations is Darbee's Two-Feather Mayfly, which uses one feather for the tails, body, and wing and another for the hackle. The ingenious part is the use of the first feather. Asked how he happened upon the idea, Darbee said, "I wanted a detached-body fly with very little weight. I picked up a feather and said to myself, 'It's right here.'"

The Darbee home, a cozy seven-room house marked outside by a large wooden carving of a trout and cluttered inside with feathers, fur, hair, hooks, and other appurtenances of their trade, is only a long cast above the Willowemoc just before it joins the Beaverkill. In season or out, the house serves as a gathering point for anglers, local characters, Wall Street brokers seeking solace, fishery biologists, curious tourists, and wandering oddballs who come to hear Harry hold forth on all sorts of subjects, sometimes until dawn. As an old friend said, "Harry does the talking while Elsie does the tying." Whatever the case, the atmosphere is Cannery Row out of Abercrombie & Fitch.

Darbee's conversation takes in the entire field of natural history. Apart from his deep and wide knowledge of stream life, he is a self-taught botanist with a marked fondness for edible nettles, and as a confirmed mycologist, he has eaten his way through thirty-five species of mushrooms lurking in the Catskill Forest Preserve. In his years as a trapper—and he was one of the most successful in the mountains, taking as many as one hundred foxes in a winter when a good pelt brought twenty-five dollars—he used to dine on such gamy fare as infant porcupine, parboiled raccoon, fried muskrat, boiled crayfish, and sauteed gray squirrel. In much the same way that he might devise a new fly to catch a wise brown, Harry as a trapper would experiment with baits. Field mice, their bodies aged in a manure pile, were very productive. "Sometimes there was nothing like a high mouse," he sighs.

To seekers of hackle, Darbee is best known for his chickens. He has had the flock for fifty years. He started with Andalusians, but then, he says, "I got disillusioned with Andalusians. I needed a narrower and longer hackle and a smaller hackle with an absence of web. I want a flexible quill, not too coarse, not too brittle."

In his quest for ideal hackle, Darbee began introducing other strains of chickens much in the manner of a chef adding ingredients to a stew. "I haven't been very scientific about it," he says. "I added three or four breeds of Cochins, several leghorns, buff, brown, and white leghorn, several shades of old English game and Rose Comb bantams. I also used Dominiques and Plymouth Rocks. Oh yes, and several breeds of game chickens, including Aseels and black-breasted reds." Unfortunately, the game chickens imparted to the flock pugnacious qualities that took ten years to eliminate. The most chickens Darbee has ever had was 980; the fewest, a foundation stock of twenty that Elsie and her mother looked after while Harry was in the navy in World War II.

The Darbee chickens live outdoors and are a vigorous lot with less than 1 percent lost to disease. It costs fifteen to twenty dollars a year to feed each chicken a high-protein diet of small grains, oats, and turkey-grower pellets. Darbee raises about one hundred new birds a year, and has to wait until they are nine to twelve months old and have adult plumage to check on quality. "That's what costs money, keeping birds that don't pan out," he says. "It's more expensive raising birds than buying hackle." Then why does he do it? "Nobody's got 'em," he says with a smile. The chickens that don't pan out are eaten—they are superb smoked—and the chickens that have quality hackle get to live and breed until they are three. While they are strutting around the yard, Darbee plucks hackle from them when needed, and since they replace the missing feathers, he has a full neck when a bird is killed for soup or stew.

Elsie and Harry Darbee. *Photo by F. W. Davis*

The genetics of fowl are such that no one has ever been able to get a true-breeding blue dun. A blue rooster bred to a blue hen will in theory produce two blues, one black and a blue–splashed white chick. However, if blue is bred to blue consistently, the offspring will throw back to white and other colors, and Darbee, who keeps his breeding program in his head, is constantly thinking of new ways to get blue in the offspring. Last year in a shotgun approach he introduced a dozen buff leghorn roosters (which carry the gene for black) into a harem of one hundred blue-splashed hens in the hope that the offspring would be blue, since black to blue-splashed will, theoretically, produce blue. "I got a whole lot of red-splashed chickens," he said. "I did it again this year and this time I got a whole lot of nice duns of various shades." For all the difficulties and expense, Darbee perseveres. He has sent a number of hatching eggs to Dennis Dodson in Laingsburg, Michigan, who is hopeful of raising blue duns commercially.

For years, Darbee photo-dyed necks, but he never said anything to anyone "because nobody asked me." According to Darbee, the late Edward Ringwood Hewitt might have had something to do with developing the technique. "Hewitt used silver nitrate on his leaders," Darbee says. "He sold $6,000 worth of leaders in England in one year, and he was more proud of that than anything he did in his life. He was when he told me about it, that's for sure."

Darbee is of medium height and has a snub nose, a high forehead, and a white pompadour that gives him the look of a pre-Revolutionary Russian playwright. On both sides he is of Connecticut Yankee stock. Now sixty-nine, he was born in Roscoe, the oldest of five children. He passed the formative years of his childhood near West Park on the Hudson River, where his father worked for the West Shore Railroad. When he was ten years old, the family moved back to Roscoe, and except for a year spent in Wisconsin laying track and fishing, and a hitch in the navy as a hospital corpsman during World War II, he has always lived in the Catskills. He derived his approach to nature, which he sums up as "Leave it the hell alone," from John Burroughs, the bearded sage who was a neighbor in West Park. Burroughs was then in his seventies, and young Darbee used to accompany him through the woods in search of bird nests.

A chronic truant from school, Darbee started fishing seriously when he was ten. By twelve, he was tying his own flies and guiding anglers. Upon leaving high school he immersed himself in the outdoors. He spent an entire summer hunting ginseng root. "After I came out, I had, oh, cleared about $10," he says, "but I had lived in the woods all summer."

In 1928 Darbee began tying flies professionally. He and Elsie, whom he married in 1933 after she came to work as an assistant, weathered the depression easily since the Big Rich tightened their budgets by trouting instead of larking off to Europe for vacations. Still, there were some customers who wondered how the Darbees could manage. One of them, the late J. P. Knapp, chairman of the board of Publication Corp., felt such pity that he gave Darbee a standing order to tie flies whenever he hit a slack period. At one time Knapp had some quarter of a million flies in the house. "Knapp," explains Darbee, "used to say, 'When I get a good fly, I like to keep it around.'"

The idea that he is an artist makes Darbee choleric. "The flytyer is an artisan 98 percent of the time and perhaps an artist the other 2 percent," he once wrote. "When creating a pattern or inventing a style or type of fly not heretofore known or maybe in adapting new techniques to old fly-tying problems, a tyer could be called, temporarily at least, an artist. But to place an artistic label on the humdrum process of repeating a pattern day after day, as any professional tyer must to earn his dinner, is stretching the word artist beyond its meaning."

Still, if Darbee does not consider a tyer an artist, "I can," he says, "certainly proclaim him an individualist in the full sense of the term. To me, fly-tying represents a way of life quite as much as a means of livelihood. Tying flies along the banks of a beloved stream, away from the bustle and stench of a city, is my idea of the ultimate in occupations. Tying flies for a living has enabled us to enjoy a certain independence of action and thought not easily come by in these days of mass production and time-clock-dominated lives."

Every fall the Darbees go to Nova Scotia to fish the Margaree for salmon. The patterns that have worked for him and other anglers on the Margaree would make traditionalists flip out. For a while, he was fond of the saltwater Blonde series devised by the late Joe Brooks. "Some anglers are so partial to them they'll use the horrible saltwater hook with the straight eye," he says. "For late fish we sometimes use the Platinum Blonde, but the Strawberry Blonde is the best of the lot." On his trip to the Margaree in 1974, Darbee killed two fish on what he called "a horrible concoction." What was it? He shudders. "A variation of a Matuka streamer from New Zealand," he says.

"I call it the Horrible Matuka, and I think it's going to be a great fly for Atlantic salmon."

The Horrible Matuka

Hook:	No. 2 salmon low water
Tying thread:	any strong thread
Body:	fluorescent orange chenille
Ribbing:	oval silver tinsel
Wing or Shoulder:	two saddle hackle, dyed reddish orange, lower fibers stripped from the quills the length of the body
Tail:	the unstripped tips, about an inch long, of the two saddle hackles used for the wing or shoulder
Hackle:	two short badger hackles dyed reddish orange
Head:	black lacquer

Tying Steps:

1. Place the hook in the vise, secure the tying thread to the hook, and bind in the oval silver tinsel ribbing just before the bend. Wrap two turns of tinsel around the hook near the bend, then hang it in place with hackle pliers.

2. Tie in the fluorescent orange chenille before the bend, move the tying thread forward to the shoulder, follow with the chenille, then secure the chenille in place with the thread. Trim excess chenille.

3. Take two saddle hackles, dyed reddish orange, and starting an inch from the tips, strip the fibers from the bottom of the quills where they will be tied in on top of the chenille body. Strip fibers from the tops of the quills where these two feathers will be tied in at the shoulder.

4. With your left hand hold the tips or tails so they project straight out from the body. With your right hand, take one turn of the tinsel to secure the tails in place. Now continue to wind the tinsel forward, securing the wings so that the fibers stand upright from the body. Separate the fibers to allow the tinsel to pass through. Five to seven wraps of the tinsel should carry it to the shoulder where it can be secured with the tying thread and the excess can be trimmed.

5. Tie in two short badger hackles dyed reddish orange, wind three or four times each, tie off, and finish the head with cement and black lacquer.

Readers are advised to refer to the photographs accompanying the Matuka tie by Dave Whitlock. Although the Darbee and Whitlock ties are different, the basic winging principle is the same. Darbee says, "This gives you a streamerlike fly with a tail that does not catch under the bend of the hook when properly cast. I found the fly effective enough to take two salmon from the same location in a short time. The second salmon followed the first one all the way to shore during a five-minute fight. The second salmon then resumed his lie and within fifteen minutes I had him on the same fly."

2

The West: The House of Harrop

by Dave Whitlock

It was on a crisp summer evening at the Federation of Fly Fishermen's annual conclave in Sun Valley, Idaho, that I met René and Bonnie Harrop. For several years I had heard about this young couple, still in their twenties, whenever the subject of No-Hackle flies was discussed, and just a few minutes in their company confirmed my enthusiasm for what I had heard about them as people and their approach to professional fly-tying.

Since first meeting the Harrops I have had the privilege of seeing them often, and there is no doubt in my mind that this attractive couple will play a significant role in fly-tying and fly-fishing for many years to come.

Bonnie was born in St. Anthony, Idaho, and René in Los Angeles. He moved to the St. Anthony–Rexburg area ten years ago, and for a number of years he worked as a reclaimer and cutter at a local lumber mill, where he met and married Bonnie. Encouraged by Will Godfrey, they both began tying flies part time for Will's shop in Last Chance. The demand for the quality flies they tied was such that they both gave up their jobs at the mill to found the House of Harrop and tie flies full time in their two-story house outside St. Anthony. The second floor contains mostly tackle and materials and a room given over to adjacent tying benches. In truth, they do not tie together as often as they would like because Bonnie is usually downstairs looking after their children, attending to daily household demands, or answering the phone—which rings constantly with orders.

When Bonnie does find time to tie, she specializes in wet flies, nymphs, and spinners. At first, René specialized in standard western dry-fly patterns, but then he began tying the new No-Hackle patterns developed by Doug Swisher and Carl Richards. Swisher and Richards were so taken with his ties that they gave him a contract to supply their "Fly-Fisherman's Shoppe" with spinners and duns in their Super Hatch series. In fact, they were so eager to take all the flies René could tie that they practically swore me to secrecy on the identity of their source.

Nowadays, René and Bonnie, assisted by Roy Harrop, René's brother, and Mike Lawson, supply thousands of flies to a list of customers that includes some of the most famous anglers in the country and such corporate accounts as Orvis, Bud Lilly, and Gates Ausable Lodge. It is not easy to meet the demand, but it is a mark of the House of Harrop that both René and Bonnie insist that their flies use the best materials available.

As any professional flytyer knows, obtaining fine materials in bulk can be a problem. The Harrops do what they can to utilize the fur and feathers from local wild and domestic animals, but they also have to rely on suppliers for necks, quills, and furs. One night when René and I were discussing problems common to professional tyers, he remarked that in his opinion fly-tying materials are going through an even faster evolution than the development of new patterns, and that his and Bonnie's answer was to design stock patterns using synthetic or natural materials readily available. It is one thing for an amateur tyer to tie up a dozen Humpies, say, for his own use; it is something else again, René pointed out, when a professional gets an order for five hundred dozen flies of just one pattern. An order like that (and such orders are not uncommon) can put a terrific strain on a stock of materials, if not deplete it outright. This is a fact of life that every professional, or any hopeful amateur, must face, and they might have to face it with the next ring of the phone. As a result, the Harrops have been forced by necessity to design stock patterns with synthetic or natural materials that are readily available in bulk. For example, take the poly spinner fly. The standard pattern calls for a body of rabbit fur and beaver belly. Try getting beaver belly readily in large lots. The Harrops have overcome this hurdle by stocking large lots of polypropylene synthetic, and *mirabile dictu,* they have found that the pattern employing this synthetic is not only just as attractive to fish but holds up longer. But then necessity mothered another invention, and inventiveness and quality are House of Harrop staples.

René and Bonnie try to fish as often as they can and are fortunate that in winter when the weather is decent they can fish a day or two every week because nearby Henry's Fork is warmer than the average stream and hatches occur even in January and February. Casting a fly in midwinter is not only relaxing but it helps René and Bonnie in two other ways. For one, it breaks the monotony of tying flies—which can become sorely tedious—and for another, fishing gives them both perspective on good artificial-fly composition and design because they have a firsthand opportunity to observe the living insects artificials are supposed to represent. René and Bonnie are ardent believers in leaving the vise to fish the water and then returning to the vise with fresh insights and refreshed spirits. That may sound obvious, but such a procedure is most important for flytyers who wish to reach the top of this fascinating craft, and it is the first lesson René and Bonnie offer to a newcomer seeking advice on fly-tying: *Observe nature.*

Other advice from René and Bonnie to flytyers:

Learn the basic techniques of tying from a professional or a proficient friend. One hour at the bench with an experienced flytyer is worth hours of trying to figure out techniques from books. "Manuals are helpful," says René, "but they can never be as effective as a one-to-one tying session."

Obtain quality tools, hooks, and materials. Don't skimp unless you are absolutely

Bonnie and René Harrop

sure you know what you are doing. Buy a good pair of hackle pliers that won't slip rather than a cheaper pair that might.

Set aside a well-lit, comfortable area in which to tie. Place the vise so that it is at the easiest working level for you.

Buy and read good books on fly-tying and fishing. Books that René and Bonnie recommend are Eric Leiser's *Fly-Tying Materials*, Art Flick's *Master Fly-Tying Guide,* Edson Leonard's *Flies,* Doug Swisher and Carl Richards's *Selective Trout,* Ernest Schwiebert's *Nymphs,* and Joe Brooks's *Trout Fishing.*

Both proprietors of the House of Harrop were happy to contribute a pattern to this edition of the *Almanac.* René's choice is his own interesting variation of the Swisher and Richards Sidewinder Dun. Tied with double-segment duck wings, it is very durable and more effective than the single-wing sidewinder dun for most hatches.

Double-Wing Sidewinder

Hook:	Mustad 94840, fine wire
Thread:	Herb Howard 6/0
Tail:	very stiff hackle fibers or guard hair of mink tail
Wing:	four duck quill segments (dark gray)
Body:	blend of tan, brown, yellow, olive, or gray fur

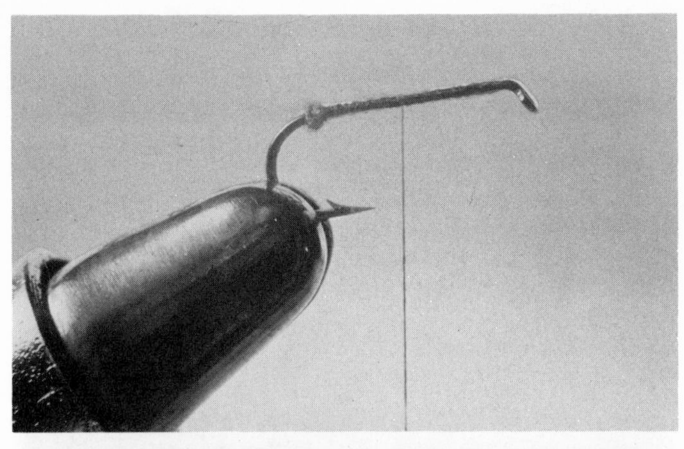

1. Place the hook firmly in the vise with the barb and point exposed. Attach tying thread at hook eye and wind the thread back along the shank to a point directly over the barb of the hook. Dub a small amount of fur onto the tying thread as shown. Wind the dubbed thread on the rear of the shank, forming a small fur ball, and then return the tying thread to the middle of the shank.

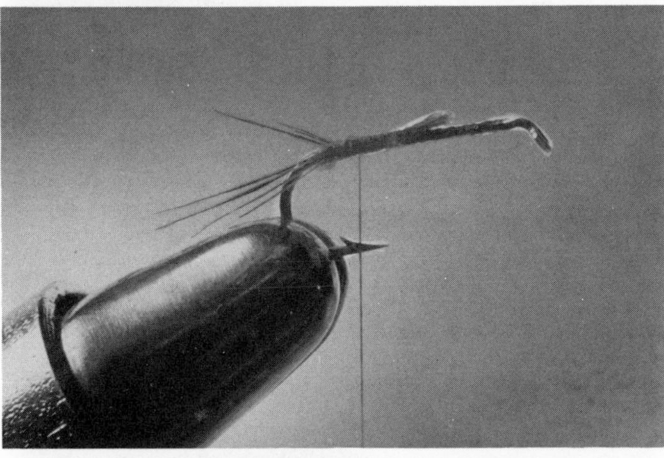

2. Select eight to ten stiff hackle fibers (or guard hairs). Tie in the hackle fibers (or guard hairs) and wind the thread back over them, dividing them equally around the fur ball so they divide into a wide "V" as shown in the close-up photograph.

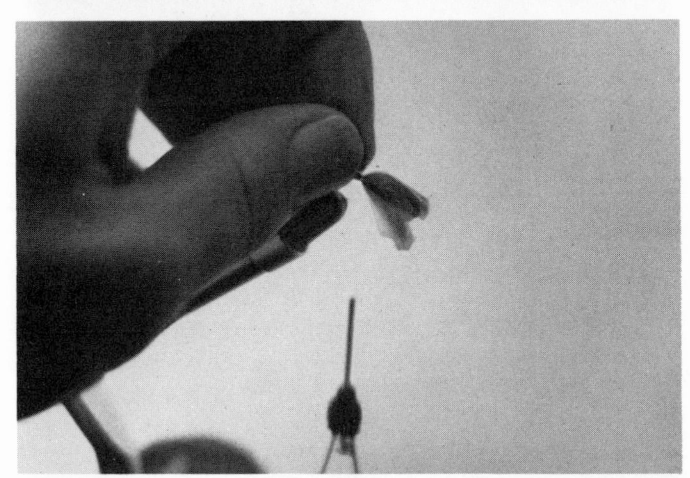

3. Select two dark-gray duck quills, one from each side of the duck. Cut two segments from each quill. The width of each segment should be at least one-third the length of the hook shank. Hold the wings by the tips between the thumb and forefinger.

4. Straddle the hook shank with the butt ends and wind them down tightly on the sides of the hook shank as shown.

5. Clip the wing butts close to the hook. Now divide the wings with figure-eight wraps of the tying thread.

6. Return the tying thread to the tail, dub on enough fur to form the body, and then wind forward to the wings. The dubbing is then wound forward of the wings to just behind the eye of the hook. Take care that the body is neat and slender.

7. Tie off the head and the Double-Wing Sidewinder is complete.

Bonnie's contribution is a variant of the above with wings of light-gray polypropylene yarn and a dubbed poly body.

Bonnie's Poly-Wing Spinner

Hook:	Mustad 94840 fine wire
Thread:	Herb Howard 6/0
Tail:	stiff hackle fibers or guard hair
Body:	reddish-brown poly dubbing
Wing:	light-gray Orvis poly-wing yarn

Steps 1–4 are the same as above for the Double-Wing Sidewinder except that poly dubbing is used instead of fur to make the ball that divides the tail.

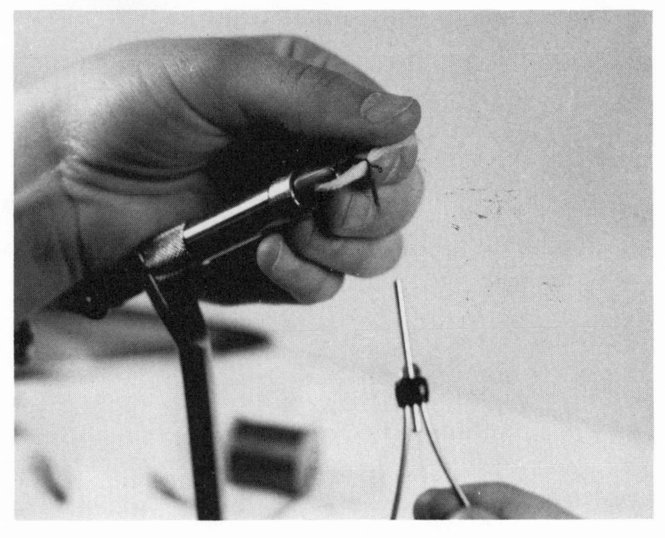

5. Cut off a section of light-gray poly yarn about an inch long and lay it across the shank as shown. Secure the wing in place with four or five figure eights of the tying thread.

6. Return the thread to the tail and dub enough reddish brown poly on the thread to form a neat, slender body. Crisscross the dubbing over the base of the wings. Continue to the eye, and whip-finish.

7. Clip the wings to shape. The completed fly is shown here.

II

Trichoptera - Caddis Flies

The caddis, or Trichoptera, are one of the most important but least understood orders of aquatic insects. In the pages that follow, Raleigh Boaze, Jr., and Larry Solomon deal with new and effective ties of the larva, pupa, and adult. In view of the importance of the order, the reader is also advised to consult the extract from Dr. Herbert H. Ross's classic study of caddis, the drawings of larvae, cases, and adults, and the appended Glossary of Entomology and the scientific bibliography, which lists further references.

3

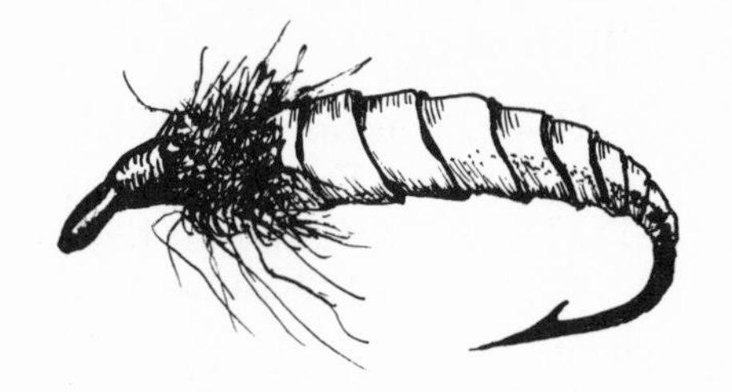

Caddis Larva and Pupa

by Raleigh Boaze, Jr.

The caddis larva and pupa that I tie were developed entirely by accident. I work as a research technician in a government laboratory, and while engaged in conversation at work one day, I picked up a strip of latex and without thinking wrapped it around a pencil. When I happened to look down at my absentminded fumbling, I noticed that it looked very much like a caddis larva; in fact, exactly like those that I'd extracted from cases while fishing for brook trout in mountain beaver ponds in West Virginia.

Later that week I tied several caddis larvae out of latex and placed them in my fly boxes. Shortly afterward, I was fishing a very productive stream in West Virginia with my friend Don Cooper. We hadn't had much luck, and after Don had a dark mayfly nymph refused three times by a good rainbow, he asked me to try my luck with the fish. I had a yellow stone nymph on at the time, and the rainbow also refused that after careful examination. Out of desperation I poked into my fly boxes, and just for the heck of it tied on one of the latex caddis larvae I had tied. I cast, and after only a six-inch drift I was fast to the rainbow. Don netted and measured the fish before release. The rainbow was sixteen inches long. Using the caddis larva, I fished the next six pools in succession. In each I was fast to a fish, and after I caught one from a pool I would move on to the next. Don measured each fish. The result was six trout in six pools, from sixteen to nineteen inches.

That day changed our lives. This may sound incredible, but since then Don and I have dominated every stream we have fished, regardless of water conditions. We have fished behind unsuccessful anglers and caught fish. We have been so successful that we have been accused of using live bait. Live latex is more like it. The latex larval or pupal caddis has a springy look and feel to it that is intriguing to both fish and fishermen. The ties are not only effective but simple. Here they are.

Ral's Caddis Larva

Hook:	hollow-point Mustad beak 9620, size 8, or Herter's No. 707 Old English Bait Hook, sizes 12 and 14. Because of the design of these bait hooks, the size differs from conventional hooks. A size 12 bait hook is equal to a size 8 or 10 conventional hook.
Underbody:	light-yellow nylon yarn
Outer body:	latex strip cut from a sheet used for a dental dam. This sheeting comes in cream and light tan.
Dubbing:	muskrat fur
Head:	dark brown or black thread used in tying

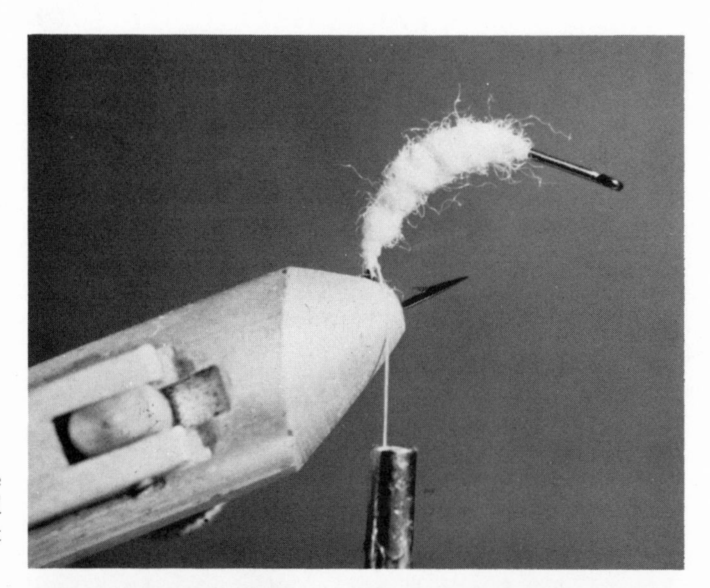

1. Tie in yarn down the bend of the hook near the gap. Wrap the yarn forward, building up a tapered underbody. The yarn is tied off at the bend where it was tied in.

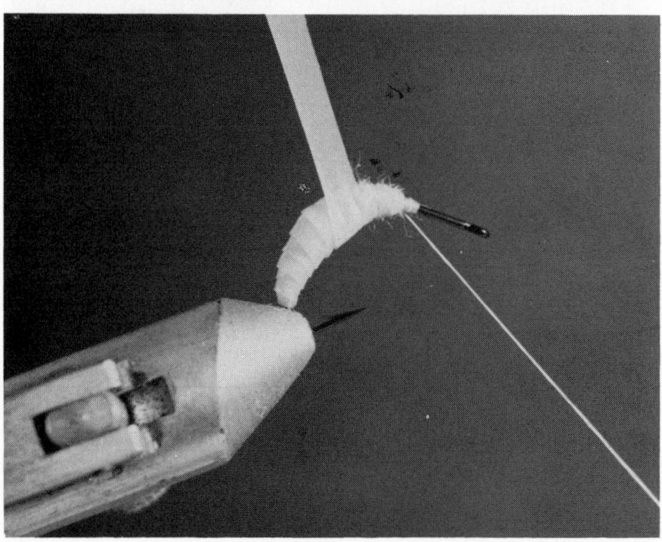

2. Tie in the latex strip and advance the tying thread forward to the area where the thorax will begin. After hitching the thread, start spiraling the latex forward, overlapping each previous wrap or spiral by half its width.

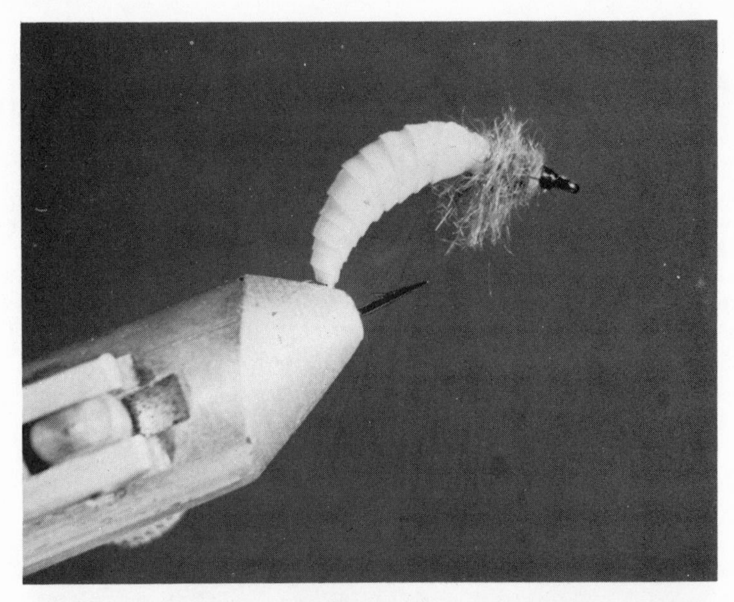

3. Tie off the latex and dub the thorax. Tie off, and lacquer for the finished larva.

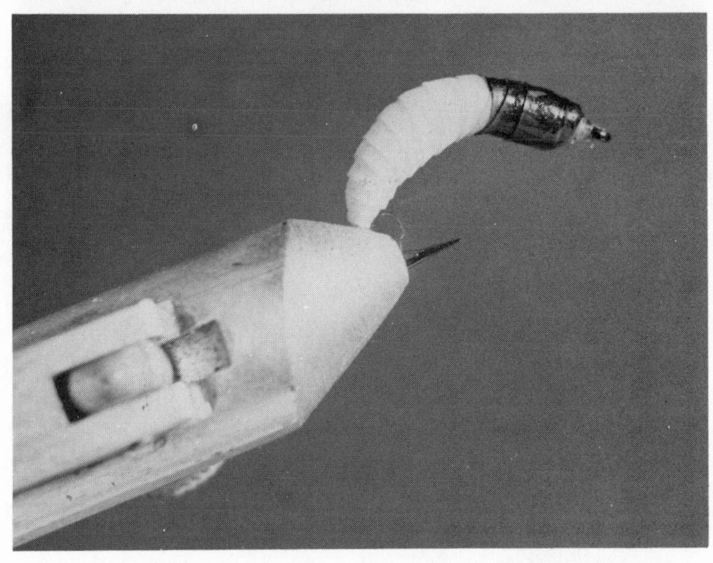

4. You can make a different type of thorax, just as effective as the dubbed, by coloring the underside of the latex with a waterproof felt-tip marking pen after you have completed the abdomen. Wrap the colored latex forward and tie off at the head to complete the larva as shown.

Ral's Caddis Pupa

Hook:	same as above
Underbody:	ditto
Outer body:	same as above, but colored green or brown, depending on species imitated, with a felt-tip marking pen
Wings:	slate-gray mallard primary
Legs:	grouse breast hackles
Head:	same as larva

5. The pupa is tied like the larva with the addition of wings and legs prior to dubbing the thorax.

Latex strip shaded on underside

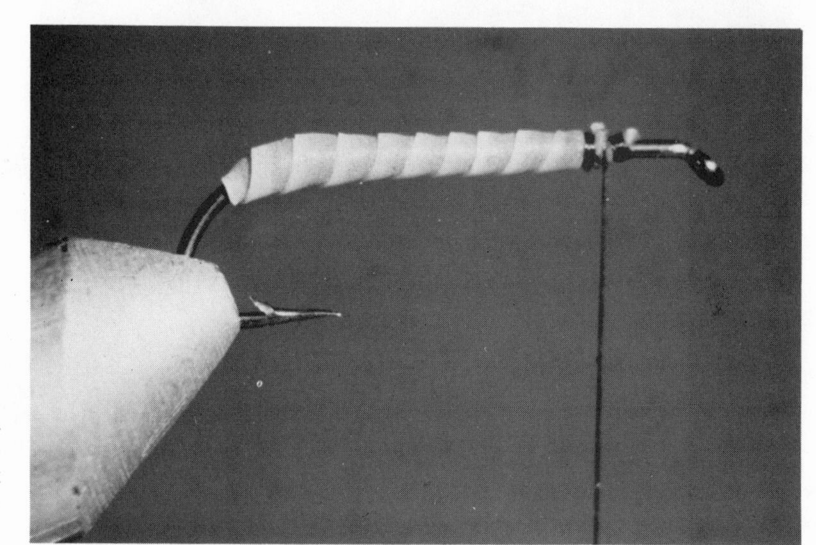

Banded or variegated bodies, like those found in stone flies and some mayfly nymphs, can be produced by shading all but a thin area along the latex strip's underside (any waterproof marker will do the job) and tying in an appropriate pattern.

Editor's Note: According to Dr. Oliver Flint of the National Museum of Natural History, Smithsonian Institution, a leading student of Trichoptera, the abdomens of case caddis larvae are off-white or cream in color "90 percent of the time." Green is the most common abdominal color the remaining 10 percent. Noncase makers have darker abdomens—dirty white, tan, and green.

The Horrible Matuka (Harry Darbee)

Left: Solomon's Hairwing Caddis;
Right: Delta-Wing Caddis (Larry Solomon)

René's Double-Wing Sidewinder (René Harrop)

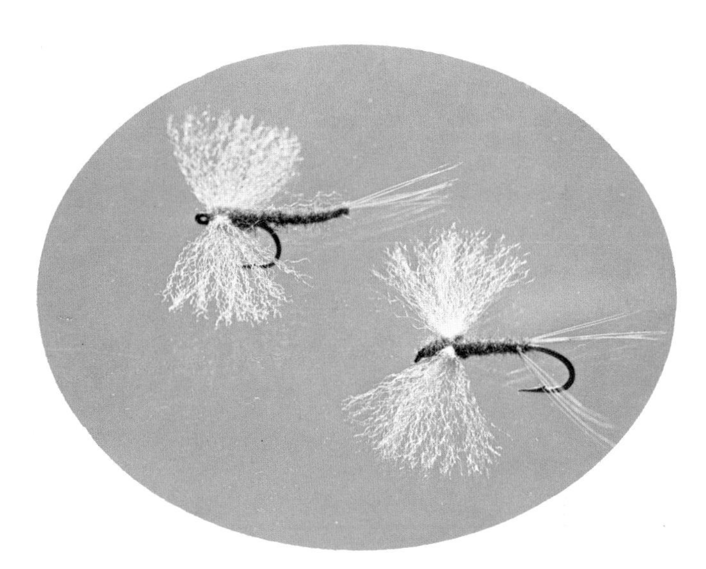

Bonnie's Polywing Spinner (Bonnie Harrop)

The Sar-Mul-Mac (Dan Blanton)

The Bay-Delta Eelet (Dan Blanton)

Russ's Adult Damselfly (Russ Thomas)

Ral's Caddis Larva (Raleigh Boaze, Jr.)

The Mari-Boos. *Top row:* Streaker, Pole-Kat, Daisy; *Middle:* Dark Ember, Bright Ember; *Bottom:* Chiquita, Bloody, Sun Burst (Darwin Atkin)

Old-Hat Dragonfly Nymph (Whygin Argus)

Adult Dragonfly Bass Bug (Bob Boyle)

4

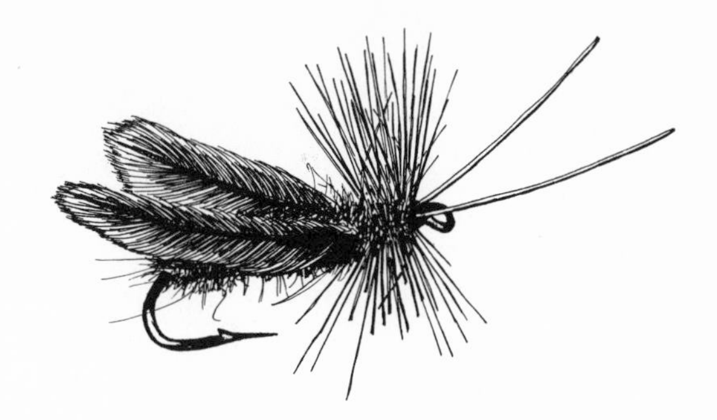

The Adult Caddis Dry Fly

by Larry Solomon

Only in recent years has the caddis begun to receive the attention and recognition it justly deserves. Most of the fly-fishing literature of the past has concentrated on the mayfly and its imitations. Leonard Wright's *Fishing the Dry Fly as a Living Insect* is a recent book that begins to place the caddis in proper perspective for anglers.

For those of you unfamiliar with the adult caddis, it is that crazy little fly you've seen bouncing around the surface like a miniature ping-pong ball. It differs from the mayfly in appearance, having a short body and long, down, tentlike wings that give it a mothlike resemblance. The mayfly has a more slender body and upright wings, making it appear like a miniature sailboat cruising along the water surface.

As a trout food, the caddis is nearly as important as the mayfly. Its larvae abound in streams and, even more important, in the stomachs of trout throughout the entire season. Moreover, gradual pollution of our rivers and streams over the years has increased the importance of the caddis. There are some one thousand species in America north of Mexico and they seem less vulnerable to pollution and drastic environmental changes; apparently they are able to thrive under conditions that have caused decline in many once-abundant mayfly hatches.

Since trout feed on caddis more frequently in larval and emerging pupal stages, good underwater imitations fished properly can be deadly, as Raleigh Boaze, Jr., has noted of his latex ties. However, it is one of the most exciting flies to fish in its adult stage as a dry fly because of the manner in which it is usually taken.

Caddis live on the stream bed under rocks and debris, in tiny stone-and-stick cases they build around themselves. At the proper moment, the pupa leaves its built-in home and rapidly ascends to the surface in a tiny air bubble it creates by the emission of gases. This emergence can be compared to holding an air-filled balloon at the bottom of a pool and letting it go. With some species, the caddis rockets to the surface and is airborne immediately. Other species ride the current for several minutes, drying and stretching their wings in the classic mayfly manner. Most of the time, the caddis does not fly directly away but bounces around a few times as if to gain stability. It is at this point that fishing a caddis dry fly becomes most exciting.

From the moment the caddis pupa catapults from the bottom until it finally wings away from the stream, it is a tantalizing target for the feeding trout. Because the fly is moving rapidly during this period, the trout must also move fast. This usually results in a very obvious and splashy rise form. There is exception to this, however (I'll come to that later), but usually the trout is rapid and persistent in his pursuit. It is this persistency that makes the fish so vulnerable to a cast fly at this time.

I'm sure many of you recall seeing a sharp rise followed by a caddis bouncing on the surface; then having the trout slash again at the fly he has just missed. He may miss again and turn to lunge once more if the fly obligingly sticks around. What has happened is that the trout, seeing the rapidly emerging pupa, gave chase but missed the elusive fly. Seeing the dancing caddis over him, he made another try. If he misses once more and the fly is still there, the trout will try again.

The best way to fish this rise was taught me by Ernie Maltz, who has been fishing caddis flies on Catskill waters for over thirty years. I learned from Ernie that if a fish is seen rising regularly, be ready to drop your fly on his nose. Even though the trout may have taken the natural, he'll turn sharply for your artificial if your aim has been good. His immediate reaction is probably "Ah, there's another one." In any case, he'll make a stab at your fly almost every time if you place it right.

Persistence in fishing the caddis is important to the fisherman. I have seen Maltz in the stream making ten, fifteen, twenty false casts at a time and I wondered if he were trying to hook a swallow. What he was doing was keeping his fly at the ready, searching for a target. When the rise came, he was ready to drop his fly on the trout's nose, resulting in a hooked fish and one more to release. When fishing by this method, Ernie advises, and I agree, use a relatively short line. I also agree with Wright that it's best to fish the fly down and across stream.

I mentioned earlier that most of the rise forms to caddis are obvious and splashy. This is true; but as with everything else, there *are* exceptions and one is when the trout are taking the caddis in the classic head-and-tail rise. On such occasions I have taken some large trout; the big fish don't like to move any faster than they have to. One of the known reasons for this kind of rise is that there is at least one variety of caddis that emerges from its pupal stage on the surface. In this instance, the fish has ample time to approach the insect and take it in the classic manner.

Another exception. During a caddis hatch some flies don't make it to the surface in prime condition because of an unopened or damaged wing. Inasmuch as it is impossible for the fly to leave the water immediately, it must remain in the surface film for a time. Again, this allows the trout to take the fly almost at leisure.

These exceptions led me to develop an artificial originally dubbed the Boeing Caddis because of its jetlike wings. This pattern supplemented an earlier design, the Hairwing Caddis, a dry pattern to imitate the emerged adult. Simple to tie and an excellent floater, the Hairwing works well under most conditions.

The Boeing, since renamed the Delta Wing, is designed to imitate a caddis in the surface film that is either partially emerged or disabled. The wings have a very lifelike action when twitched, giving the impression of a struggling insect. However, most of my success with the Delta Wing has been fishing it dead drift, both upstream and on a slack line downstream.

My first experience with the Delta Wing was in late May 1972. I was fishing below Painter's Bend on the Beaverkill and had noticed sporadic hatching of an amber caddis about size 16. I was able to pick up a few fish on various patterns, but nothing with any consistency. Rummaging through my fly boxes, I noticed an experimental Delta Wing tied the season before. With amber body, light rusty-dun wings, and brown hackle, it looked very much like the natural. In the next hour I took about fifteen trout until the wings came off the fly. After that I could only raise an occasional fish and with no regularity on any one pattern.

My next encounter with the Delta Wing came a week later on the Willowemoc. Jay Herbert, a Texas hunting and fishing companion, was in New York on business and wanted to spend a few days on Catskill waters. That week I had tied two or three Deltas to match a caddis hatch I knew was due. We were fishing the tail end of a Grey Fox hatch when the caddis appeared. I switched first to a Hairwing Caddis but failed to get the response I expected. The fish were working well, showing the classic head-and-tail rise. I spotted a very good fish feeding against the far bank, but could arouse no interest in it with the Hairwing. Remembering the previous week, I knotted on a Delta. But before attempting the big fish, I tested it on two smaller trout rising below me. Each one took immediately.

Fully confident now, I went after the big fish. The first two casts to the far bank were ignored. But as the third throw drifted over the lie, the big trout sucked in the fly and was hooked. It turned out to be a beautiful eighteen-inch brown. Jay took one look and demanded one of the flies I was using, "whatever it was." In the next hour we picked up ten trout, half of them twelve to fifteen inches. I was convinced I had a good thing in my strange little bug.

Throughout the season I enjoyed considerable success with the Delta during the majority of caddis hatches. Inevitably, however, there were times when it failed to produce at all. Experience leads me to believe the Delta's success is related to the manner in which a particular species of caddis emerges. My own experience, I have to add, has been somewhat limited, since this was my first season of experimentation with the Delta. On the other hand, most of the fly-fishers I've asked to try it report being successful with the Delta. My own observation suggests that the Delta Wing is most effective on two occasions: during an emergence period, and as a suggestive pattern in quiet periods when no hatching activity is apparent. Then, I believe, the fly should imitate a caddis that has recently hatched.

Although the experiences and observations I've described occurred on Catskill waters, caddis are just as plentiful on western streams and in most other parts of the country as well. In fact, almost any stream that holds trout will probably have a caddis population. Last July I spent two weeks fishing Montana and Idaho trout waters. Nearly half the fish I took on dry flies were taken on the Hairwing Caddis. Interestingly, I had less success with the Delta Wing.

Most western fishermen, I found, do not fish caddis flies, relying instead chiefly on large mayfly and stonefly imitatons. The one angler I met who fished caddis with any regularity spends his summers in West Yellowstone, Montana, but lives in the East. His feelings were much the same as mine: that westerners are missing the boat. Many of their caddis hatches are extremely heavy; and what's equally important is that trout take them avidly.

East or west, however, it's important to capture specimens of flies the fish are feeding on. Caddis always appear larger in the air than they actually are and it's almost impossible to tell the color of the body unless you examine one closely. For this reason, a tropical-fish-tank net is a valuable item on the stream. I stow one in my front wader pocket for immediate access. If you've ever tried catching a flying caddis with your hands you'll understand the reason for the net. Another sensible item of stream equipment is a piece of fine netting or screen about one-by-two feet. Held partially submerged, you'll find it handy for scooping up nymphs, emerging insects, and whatever else in the surface film. Bear in mind that it's extremely important to determine just what fly and in what stage the trout are *taking*, not simply what fly you see in the air or on the surface. At times three or four different flies may be on the water at the same time, yet the selective trout may be feeding on only one of them. That's when it pays to have a variety of mayfly and caddis patterns in both nymph and dry stages in your fly boxes.

No one should question the importance of caddis as a major food supply for trout. More attention needs to be given to the development of effective imitations and their use. Larva and pupa imitations fished with skill can be deadly and will take a lot of trout. But if you want to add a new dimension and excitement to your fly-fishing, the caddis dry fly might just possibly open a whole new world for you.

Solomon's Hairwing Caddis

Hook: sizes 14–22 light wire
Body: dubbing, various shades as indicated in seasonal chart
Wing: deer *body* hair, various colors as indicated in chart. Note again that the wing is deer *body* hair, not bucktail. Some flytyers are now using mink tail hair, but in my opinion the deer body hair is to be preferred.
Thread: Herb Howard's prewaxed, various colors

1. Wrap tying thread along entire hook shank. Wind on the fur dubbing two-thirds the length of hook shank so that it has a full body silhouette. The body should be shaped so that it is fat at the tail and then tapers down to the bare hook as shown. This is important because it allows the wing to lie flat on the body.

2. Arrange the deer-body hairwing as follows: Place the needed amount of body hair in an empty lipstick tube or cartridge case with the tip ends down. Tap the case on the table so that the tip ends are even with each other.

3. After trimming the butts of the hair to the proper length, lash them onto the shank behind the eye of the hook with two or three tight turns. Now follow with four or five *loose* turns back toward the bend and then wind forward again. The loose turns prevent the hair from flaring. Wind those loose turns about one-third of the hook length back to ensure a compact wing as shown. Put a drop of lacquer on those loose turns.

4. Tie in one or two hackles just behind the hook eye as shown and wind over the tied-down deer-body hair.

5. Tie off the head, and lacquer.

Solomon's Delta-Wing Caddis

Hook:	sizes 14–22 light wire
Body:	fur dubbing, various shades
Wing:	two hackle points, color as required
Thread:	Herb Howard's prewaxed

1. Wrap tying silk along the shank and wind on the fur dubbing two-thirds the length of the shank. However, unlike the body for the Hairwing Caddis, the delta-wing body is not tapered, as shown.

2. Select two hackle points and tie one on each side of the body so they each stand out at about a 45° angle. The tips of the wings should extend slightly beyond the bend of the hook as shown.

3. Tie in the stem of a single hackle feather just in front of the wings as shown here. Before you wind on the hackle, add a bit more dubbing in front of the wings to make a full-thorax silhouette.

4. Wind the hackle over the dubbed thorax, tie off and lacquer. Usually I like to trim the bottom of the hackle on the Delta-Wing Caddis so the fly sits flat on the surface film of the stream.

5. The completed Delta-Wing Caddis from the top.

Here are the patterns I have tied in season imitation of caddis adults on New York streams.

Period of emergence	Fur body	Deer-body Hairwing	Hackle shade	Hook size
April–early May	charcoal gray	tannish gray	light bronze dun	16
Early–mid-May	dark olive	medium brown	medium brown	16
Early–mid-May	light green	tan	light ginger	16
Mid–late May	amber	tannish gray	medium brown	18
Mid–late May	brown/gray	brown/gray	brown	18
Mid–late May	grayish olive	tan	ginger	18
Late May*	dark green	brown/gray	medium ginger	18
Late May–early June	brown/gray	tannish gray	dark brown	16 and 18
Early June	light olive	tan	ginger	18
Early June	dark gray	dark gray	dark blue dun	20
Early June	brown/gray	brown/gray	dark bronze/brown	16 and 18
Early June	Kelly green	brown/gray	bronze dun	22
Early–mid-June	grayish rustry cream	charcoal gray	light rusty dun	16
Early–mid-June	charcoal gray	charcoal gray	dark gray dun	14
Mid-June	dark brown	brown	brown	16 and 18
Mid-June	grayish olive	tannish gray	dark ginger	18
Mid-June	brown/gray	gray	dark brown	20
Mid-June	grayish olive	tannish gray	rusty dun	18
Early–mid-August	pale olive	light cream	cream	22
Late September	dark green	brown/gray	brown	18

*This is one variety that was seen emerging on the surface. I'm sure there are others.

III

Odonata - Damselflies and Dragonflies

Damselflies and dragonflies of the order Odonata are among the most beautiful insects on earth. They are aquatic in origin, but despite their presence—at times abundance—around water as flying adults, they have been largely ignored by both the fly-fisherman and the flytyer. If angling is, as someone once said, applied natural history, study of this order would more than repay the largemouth bass bugger and the big-trout addict of western rivers.

Damselflies belong to the suborder Zygoptera. They are slender, delicate creatures, mostly weak flyers that rest with their wings folded behind their backs. Dragonflies belong to the suborder Anisoptera. For the most part, they are stout-bodied and strong flyers, and rest with their wings outspread. The nymphs of the two suborders are equally different. The Zygoptera are slender with tracheal gills that look like three small feathers projecting from their rear ends. They move about by either walking or by wriggling their bodies. The Anisoptera are stout, ugly creatures that give no hint of the beauty of the adult. They can move through the water literally jet propelled by expelling water from their backsides. Depending upon their species, some nymphs camouflage themselves in weeds, others bury themselves in muck, and still others adhere to the stems of plants. Whatever the species, they feed by ambushing smaller creatures with a unique anatomical device, a pinching lower lip that can shoot out faster than the eye can see.

Readers interested in knowing more about the entire order are advised to consult the extract from the late Philip Garman's detailed study, "The Odonata or Dragonflies of Connecticut," reprinted in the Scientific Papers section at the end of this book.

5

The Damselfly Nymph
by Dave Whitlock

Damselflies have entertained me since I was a six-year-old fishing for sunfish with a cane pole, line, bobber, hook, and red worm. I remember how they would chase each other here and there over the water's surface or sometimes alight on my pole. Most damsels were green or blue, but I remember two deep-metallic green-and-red ones with inky black wings (possibly of the genus *Agrion*) that fluttered over some very beautiful smallmouth streams I used to fish near Dayton, Tennessee, when my Dad worked on TVA lake dams in the early 1940s. Not too long ago I discovered those same beautiful species one early summer afternoon here in Oklahoma over our own Spring Creek.

For the last six years, I have tied imitations of the nymph and adult stages for trout. In particular, the nymph pattern has triggered feeding sprees as fabulous as the celebrated stone fly, or "salmon fly," hatches of the West.

Most damselfly nymphs are unusual swimmers, actually appearing minnowlike in their movements and speed in the water. They wiggle much like fish to propel themselves along the bottom, in and out of vegetation or toward the water surface to "hatch" into adults. This wiggling action can be very difficult to imitate when tying or fishing a damselfly imitation. Therefore, much more thought has to be given to tying a damsel nymph than, say, a less energetic stone fly or caddis.

A very simple small marabou streamer of olive or brown is a fairish imitation of a swimming damsel nymph, and does catch trout in lakes that are noted for their abundance of damsels. My version, however, is more involved, but it is well worth tying because it brings the wiggle to the nymph, a task thought impossible, if memory serves, by that late great master of nymph fishing, G. E. M. Skues. In all candor, my damsel wriggle nymph incorporates the ideas, materials, and designs of other flytyers, such as Polly Rosborough's use of marabou for the triple tails or gills, Swisher and

Richards's thorax design, and Ernie Schwiebert's idea for a detached-bodied damsel suggested in his book *Nymphs.* I think of my inventive friend Jack Hutchinson of Everett, Washington, who sent me a beautiful and delicately realistic detached-bodied damsel nymph that further contributed to the design of my pattern. I think also of Billy Butts, Jr., Thom Green, Bob Spear, and other fly-tying friends who have shared their ideas with me on damsel nymphs. This nymph is a success because of these many talented friends.

My pattern philosophy is to use turkey marabou fibers for the gills (tail) to give good lifelike breathing and swimming action. The abdomen is dubbed to simulate best the lifelike body, with tinsel to add more life. The hinge between the abdomen and thorax further enhances the nymph's action and shape. The thorax is weighted with lead wraps and bead-chain eyes to assist not only in sinking the nymph but in allowing a wiggle-jig action during an erratically controlled retrieve. The thorax is also fur dubbed, and the legs are soft hackles to add further action and eye appeal. The nymph's action is very important, but it must also give the illusion of being slender and delicate. When actually swimming, the legs are folded back and the nymph looks streamlined and slender, much like a tiny minnow. The light-olive and golden-brown colors suggested as the tying materials are the two most common successful colors according to most damselfly nymphers across this country. Body proportions are:

Thorax: ⅜ of total length
Abdomen: ⅝ of total length
Tail (gills): ½ of length of abdomen
Legs: ½ of length of body

Damsel Wiggle Nymph

Hooks:	abdomen, Mustad Aberdeen 3261, sizes 8–10–12 thorax, Mustad 7957B or 3906, sizes 8–10–12–14
Thread:	Herb Howard's tan or olive prewaxed 6/0 nylon
Thorax weight:	lead wire
Hinge:	.010″ to .012″ piano wire
Tail (gills):	turkey marabou dyed light olive or golden brown
Abdomen rib:	size 18 gold oval tinsel
Wing case:	speckled turkey quill dyed light olive or dark golden brown
Abdomen and thorax dubbings:	50-50 blend of beaver belly fur and Orlon wool of light olive or golden brown
Legs:	pheasant or partridge hackle tinted light olive or light golden brown
Eyes:	small pair of attached bead chain or similar-sized attached plastic beads painted flat olive or brown (I use Hyplar paint)
Cement:	Pliobond thinned 50 percent with acetone and Herter's fly head varnish

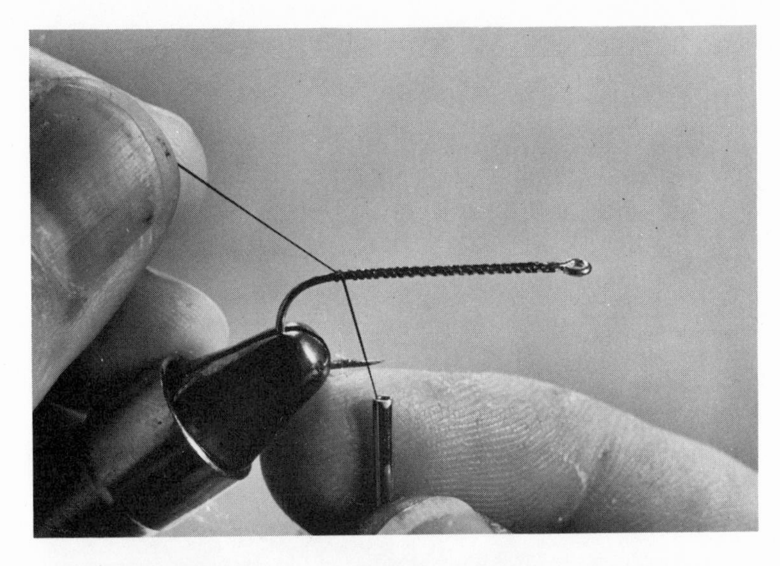

1. Abdomen hook: Place a No. 3261 hook in vise. Attach tying thread to shank and wrap entire length of shank with thread.

2. Tail (gills): Select a short-fibered turkey marabou feather and trim off six or eight fibers. Attach these to hook's shank at bend. These should lie parallel to shank and be one-half to two-thirds as long as hook's shank.

3. Abdomen rib: Cut a three-inch length of size 18 gold oval tinsel and tie it directly over the tail tiedown at rear end of shank. Clip tinsel loose end in vise's material spring clip. Coat the entire hook shank generously with thinned Pliobond to seal wraps and tiedowns and also to provide a sticky receptive surface for dubbing.

4. Abdomen ribbing: Thread should be at the back of the shank as you spin on a pinch of fur dubbing. Wrap the shank, forming a thinly dubbed body gradually tapering toward the hook's eye. Stop dubbing immediately at hook's eye.

5. Abdomen rib: Remove oval tinsel from clip and carefully make a spiraling rib over the abdomen dubbing. Each turn should be tight and slightly buried into the dubbing. At hook's eye stop and tie down. Trim away unused section of tinsel. Here I will again dub just a tiny bit of fur over this area and then whip-finish into the dubbing to provide a full-length dubbed abdomen. Remove abdomen from vise. Put just a tiny bit of varnish over whip finish. With a pair of dikes clip off the hook just below the tail.

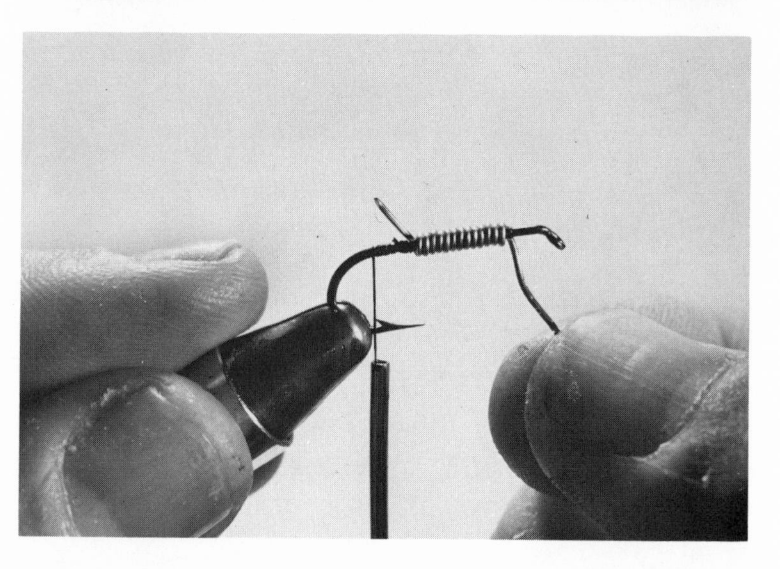

6. Thorax hook: Place the No. 7957B or 3906 hook in vise. Attach tying thread and wrap, covering the entire shank length. Over the midshank wrap ten to fifteen turns of lead wire, tapering both ends as you trim excess.

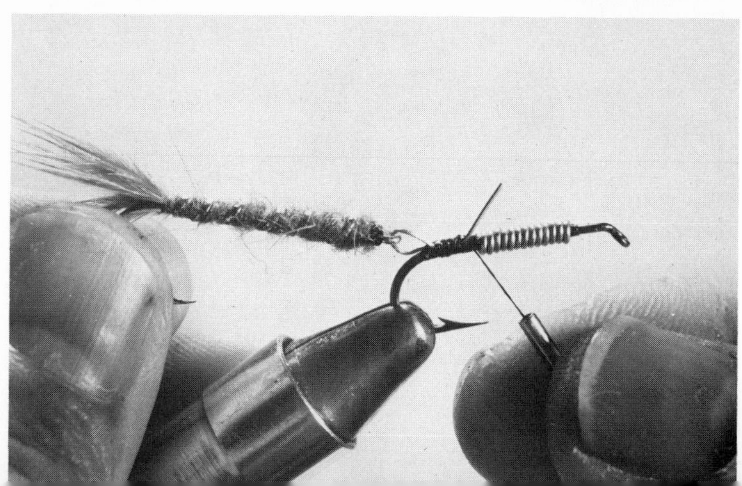

7. Wiggle hinge: Cut a one-and-a-half-inch length of piano wire and bend to form a loop with it. Pass abdomen's hook eye through loop. Now with pliers form a small closed loop eye containing the abdomen. Continue to twist the wire together. Trim all but one-eighth inch to one-quarter inch of hinge foot away. Directly over the rear hook shank in the vise, wrap the hinge foot to it with tying thread. Hinge loop should be at 90° angle to shank and be positioned at exactly the beginning of the hook's bend. Be positive that thread holds hinge shank firmly in position. Coat the entire thorax hook shank with Pliobond including the hinge foot tiedown area.

8. Thorax dubbing: A. Directly over the hinge foot, dub fur blend on loosely, a little larger than front of abdomen. Just cover the foot hinge area.

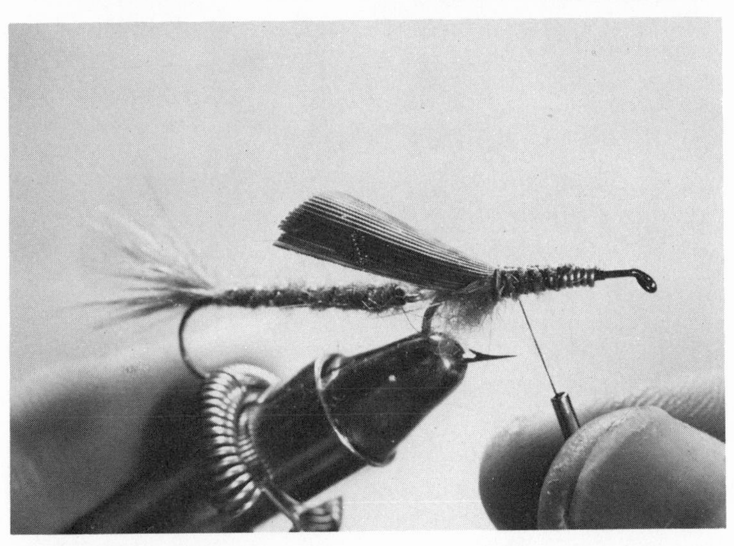

9. Wing case: A. From a turkey wing quill cut two sections of approximately three-eighths inch in width. Place one over the other, then tie their ends directly to the top of abdomen shank in front of the hinge.

10. Thorax dubbing: B. Spin a pinch of fur dubbing on thread and wrap over wing case tiedown, advancing to just past mid-shank.

11. Legs: Select a soft hackle that will have spines about equal to the thorax's total length or slightly longer. Attach it bright side facing you to the hook by its *stem tip,* not the butt! Make one or two turns around shank, then tie down and trim excess butt stem away. Also trim off all top and bottom spines, leaving just a few to each side.

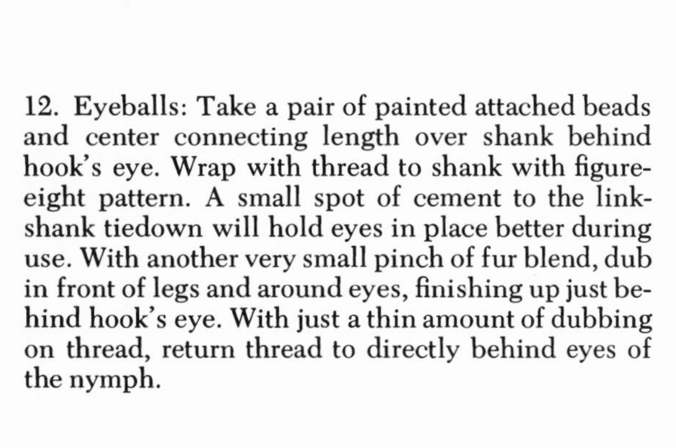

12. Eyeballs: Take a pair of painted attached beads and center connecting length over shank behind hook's eye. Wrap with thread to shank with figure-eight pattern. A small spot of cement to the link-shank tiedown will hold eyes in place better during use. With another very small pinch of fur blend, dub in front of legs and around eyes, finishing up just behind hook's eye. With just a thin amount of dubbing on thread, return thread to directly behind eyes of the nymph.

13. Wing case: B.Grasp wing case sections and bend forward and down over thorax with index finger to form encased nymph wings. With tying thread wrap over wing-case sections, binding them down tightly over dorsal thorax. Then advance tying thread to hook's eye and again over and around turkey quill sections to form a second small hump in the head. Trim away excess quill section past hook's eye.

14. Whip-finish at hook's eye. Cut away tying thread and add a small drop of varnish to whip-finish area. Hold nymph to a bright light and clip any excessively long fibers of dubbing off to facilitate sinking. Check hinge to see that it works freely. With a bodkin point or needle point, pick out rear thorax, dubbing some to conceal waist hinge better.

Damsel nymphs have a fairly wide color and size range. The light olive and golden brown I use are fairly standard—or most common. However, I have seen them very dark olives, browns, and blacks, and several creamy tans and greens. Ernie Schwiebert's *Nymphs* contains an unusually good color plate (opposite page 151) of the more common and useful damsel nymphs.

They generally run from ½ to 1½″ in length, an inch being the most common length I've observed. This would mean the wiggle version would use hook sizes about 8 through 14, with size 10 being a good average. Nothing beats on-the-spot observation and study to determine deadly wiggle-nymph patterns for your area.

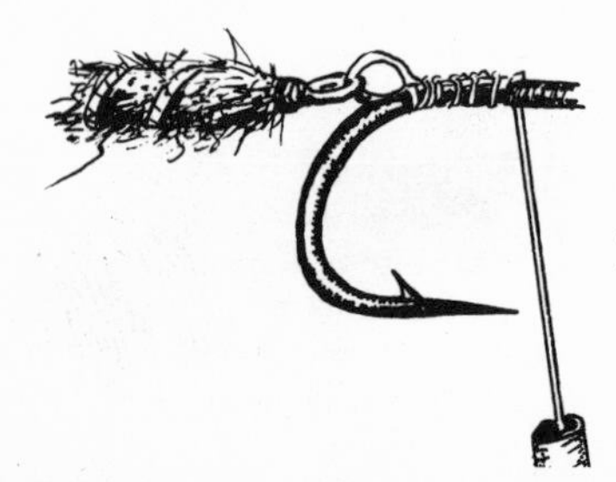

Dave's Wiggle Nymph—hinge detail

6

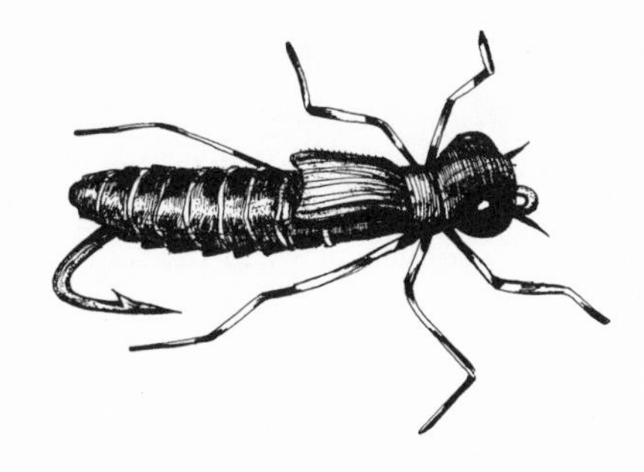

The Old Hat Dragonfly Nymph

by Whygin Argus

Though this pattern is new, it is literally old hat. Take an old fedora and cut pieces of felt from the brim and crown to a nymph shape. Purists who wish to play the game straight are advised to use the olive-brown fedoras made by Lock & Co. in England for Brooks Brothers. Dealers in fly-tying materials do not offer these hats for sale, but they can be found in unattended cloak rooms at almost any Manhattan men's club during the luncheon hour. Doubtless the Old Hat Dragonfly Nymph would have appealed to the late John O'Hara:

> When Quentin left St. Paul's after his father died, he attended the local high school and then went to Lehigh where he majored in blasting. He did well in the quarry business, but somehow he sensed he had never made it in Gibbsville society, and he felt this most keenly one summer while fishing the Ausable. The stockbroker from Princeton kept catching and releasing trout on an Old Hat Dragonfly Nymph while Quentin's turnip-flavored, two-tailed plastic worm, specially molded for twenty-pound-test spin-casting in the basement of Al and Chuck's Sports Emporium, attracted only sneers from the other men at camp, one of whom was senior warden at the church back home and about to let a contract for new granite steps.

The Old Hat Dragonfly Nymph

Hook: size 8 streamer
Tying thread: Herb Howard's prewaxed olive at first, then transparent, dark Dyno sewing thread

Body: Brooks Brothers' hat felt trimmed to shape
Segmentation: fine strand of gold mylar
Wing cases: quill sheathing dyed olive, or turkey feather
Head: hat felt built up with lacquer
Legs: javelina, hackle, or fine dark rubber

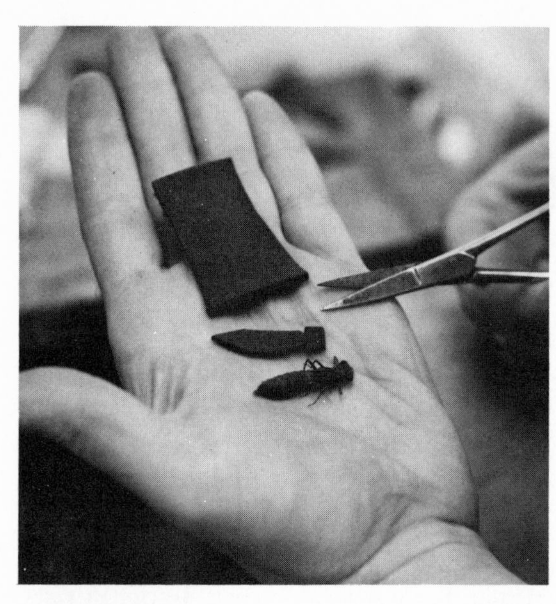

1. Cut up a Brooks Brothers' fedora and then trim a piece to shape as shown here. Note the live dragonfly nymph alongside for comparison.

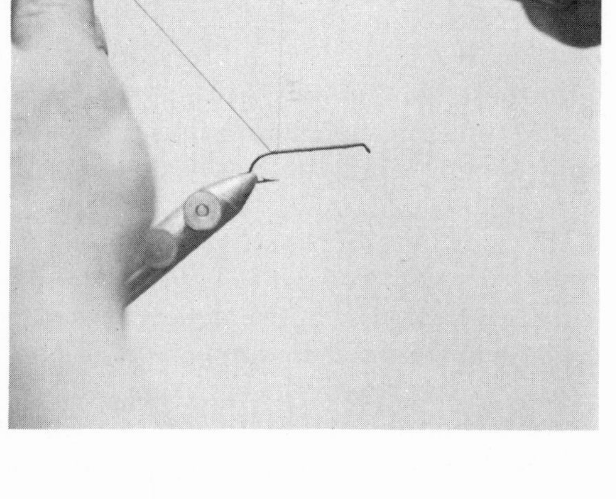

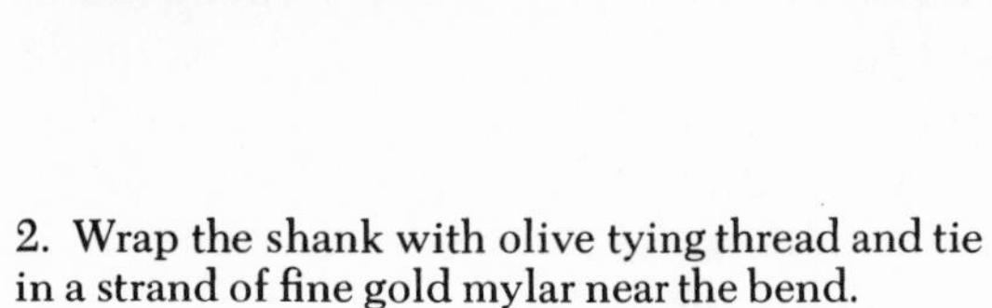

2. Wrap the shank with olive tying thread and tie in a strand of fine gold mylar near the bend.

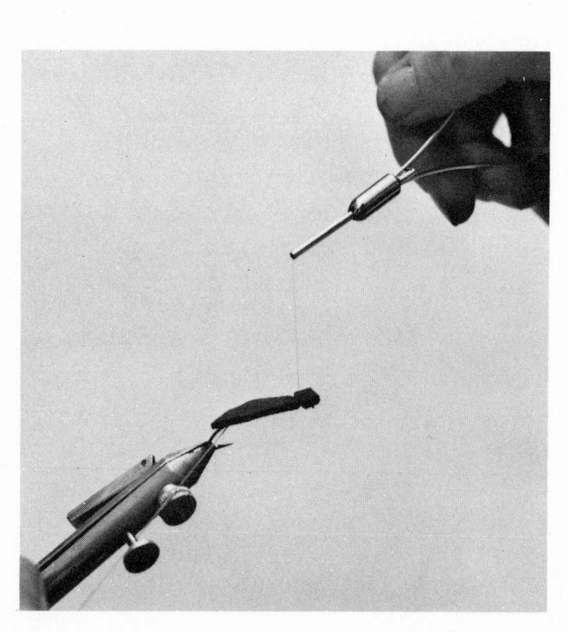

3. Coat the shank with fingernail polish, lay the felt nymph atop the shank, and start tying in the "neck" as shown. Work the tying thread up and down the nymph body until it is securely attached to the shank.

4. Spiral the strand of mylar forward ten times to mark the abdominal segments. Tie off the mylar at the top where the wing pads will go.

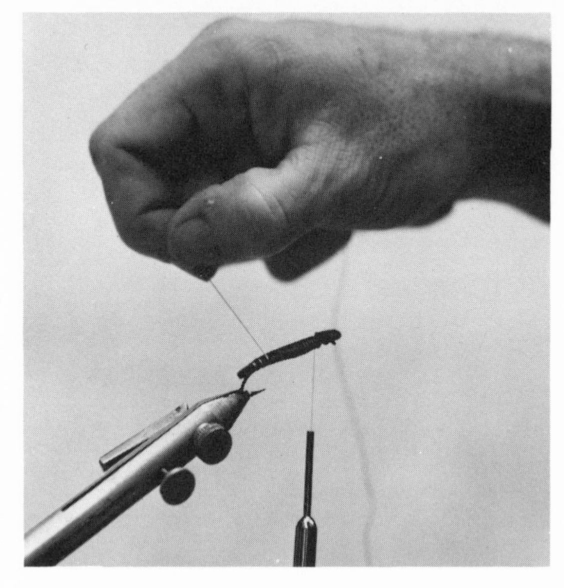

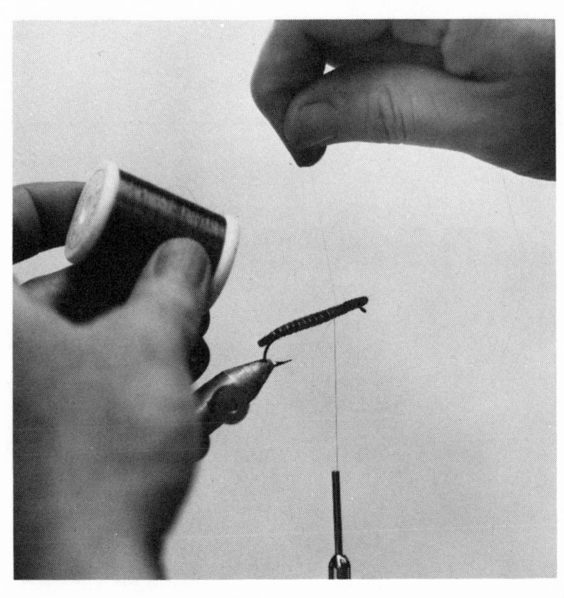

5. Tie in the transparent, dark Dyno thread and cover the body with it. The Dyno thread gives the artificial the serrated, chitinous appearance of the live nymph.

6. Tie in the wing pads. My preference is quill sheathing, dyed olive, stripped from the stalk of a large peacock, or a Canada goose, feather.

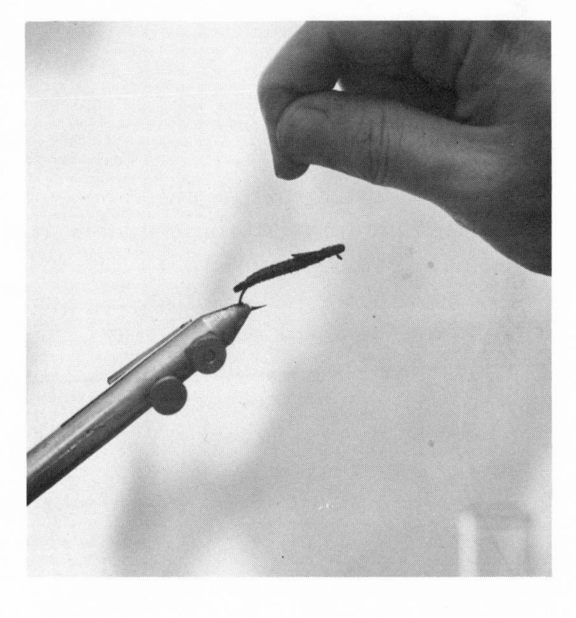

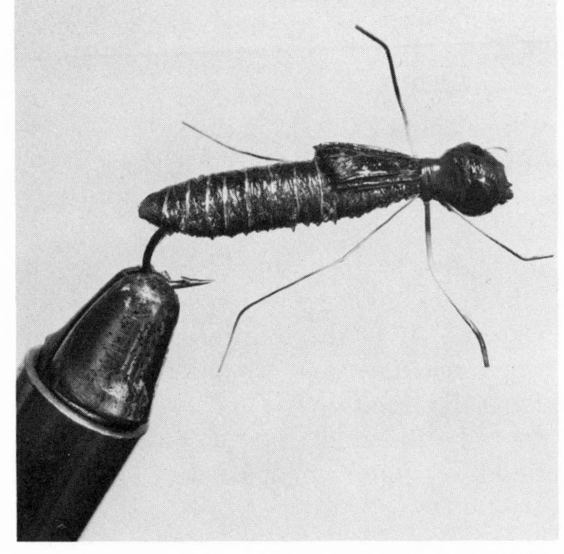

7. Build up the head with lacquer, let dry, then tie in the legs (in this case javelina) as shown in the photograph of the finished nymph. Coat the entire body with fingernail polish. *Photos by R. Hoebermann, Doran S. Moll.*

I have not fished Montana waters, but I suspect that felt-hat nymph bodies would serve admirably to duplicate the large stoneflies of the genus *Pteronarcys.*

7

The Damselfly Adult

by Russ Thomas

A westerly wind rolled tufts of mist across the pond. Scores of damselfly adults flitted about the surface while trout bolted to bring them down. I had witnessed this scene the previous weekend, when I found myself unprepared with a suitable imitation. Now, in the early morning hours on this southern California pond, I felt well equipped to deal with the situation. The pattern was a brightly colored, long-shank dry fly of my own design.

The trout fed for almost an hour while I cast my imitation damsel. Then all activity abruptly ceased, and there I was with nothing to show for my time other than the practice in casting. The fly I had devised was a total failure.

Not long afterward, my interest in damselflies and a fish-taking imitation was rekindled when my wanderings took me to one of Idaho's most treasured streams. It is a meandering, leisurely spring creek of storybook beauty, celebrated for its population of spirited rainbows.

Hatches on this stream are predictable and fecund to the point of being occasionally overwhelming. In the summer, the damsels appear in the morning at the tail end of a simultaneous emergence and spinner fall of at least three different species of mayflies.The damsels thrive here. Suitable water temperatures, a moderate current, and abundant vegetation provide ideal conditions and habitat.

It would take a specialist in the Zygoptera to identify the exact species, but they were of the genus *Enallagma,* commonly called the "bluets" because they are bright blue with black spots and translucent wings.*

**Editor's Note:* The bluets are a genus of about seventy species, and are found on every continent except Australia. At least forty of these species live in North America. They are exceedingly common in early summer along quiet streams and ponds, so much so that they probably are the most familiar damselflies of all, even to the most casual fly-fisherman who knows nothing of the genus and its importance to fish.

For a few days, I fished with a wide assortment of dry flies, and met with unmentionable results. It was obvious that the trout wanted damselflies, but I would not insult them by trying the long-shank pattern that had proved a failure in California. On the slick and lingering waters of this crystalline stream, the fish can carefully inspect any offering, and they are very cautious because of the legions of anglers who cast over them.

After an appraisal of the situation, I tied a new pattern of damsel with an extended body. Hopefully I cast all one morning, but all my casts were as unproductive as they had been in California. That afternoon I humbly returned to my vise to make some adjustments in the pattern. Again it was rejected. I continued to make scores of revisions of the pattern until at last I was rewarded with determined attacks on my damsel imitation. Inasmuch as the successful pattern was fairly similar to my past failures on the stream, I am at a loss to explain the difference in results except that this pattern worked and the others did not.

During the next two weeks, I hooked and released an abundance of trout. The new pattern was also responsible for most of my largest fish. In some cases I brought trout to net that could not be taken by any other means. This assumption was based on my discovery that the stomach contents of a random selection of fish contained only damselflies. They had entirely ignored the principal food fly in the area, the tiny (size 24) mayfly *Tricorythodes.* Here is the tie that produced the trout.

Russ's Adult Damselfly

Hook: size 10, fine wire
Tying thread: unwaxed Nymo, size A, or any similar *flat* working thread
Eyes: stem base of a white hackle feather
Body: monofilament line, three inches long, approximately .019 inches in diameter
Thorax: mono built up with tying thread
Wings: two blue-dun hackle points
Hackle: light-blue grizzly

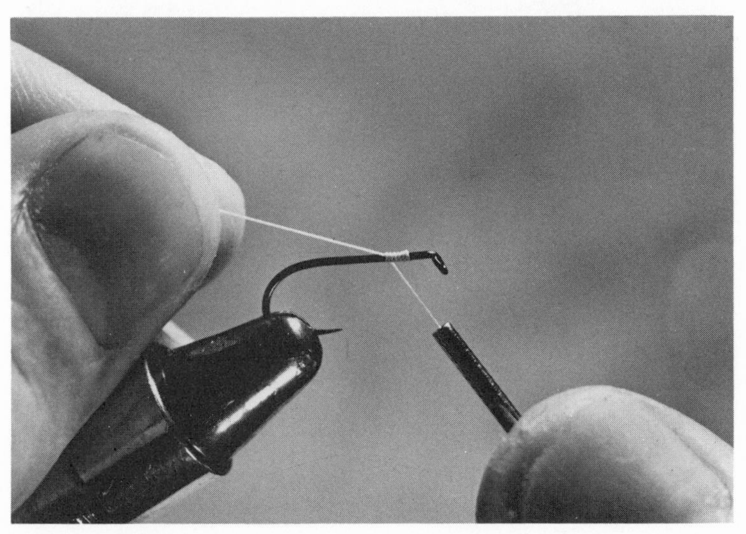

1. Wrap the shank of the hook with a foundation of thread.

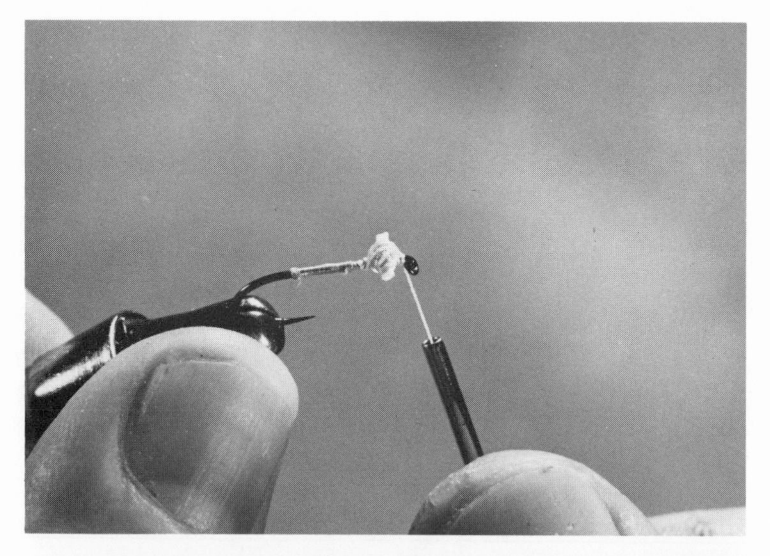

2. Cut off a piece of the stem of a white hackle feather approximately one-quarter of an inch long and lay crosswise across the shank in back of the hook eye. Secure with figure-eight wraps to build up a generous head. Now and then, apply a drop of clear lacquer while the head is being formed.

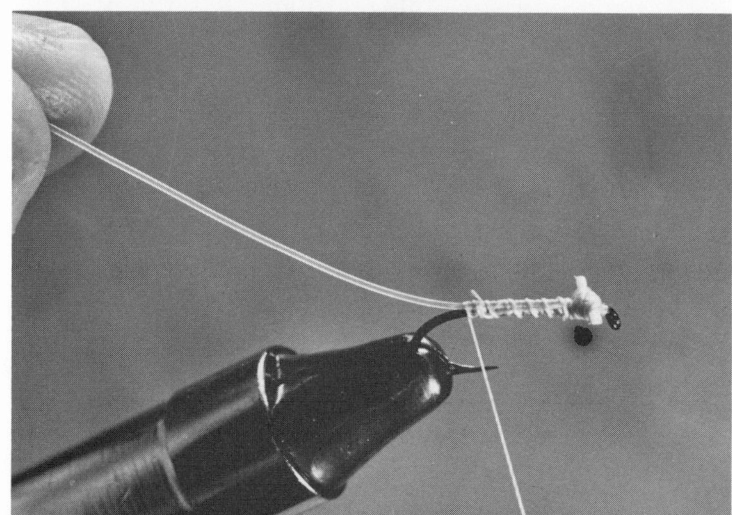

3. Cut off a three-inch segment of monofilament and tie down securely behind the head; apply lacquer.

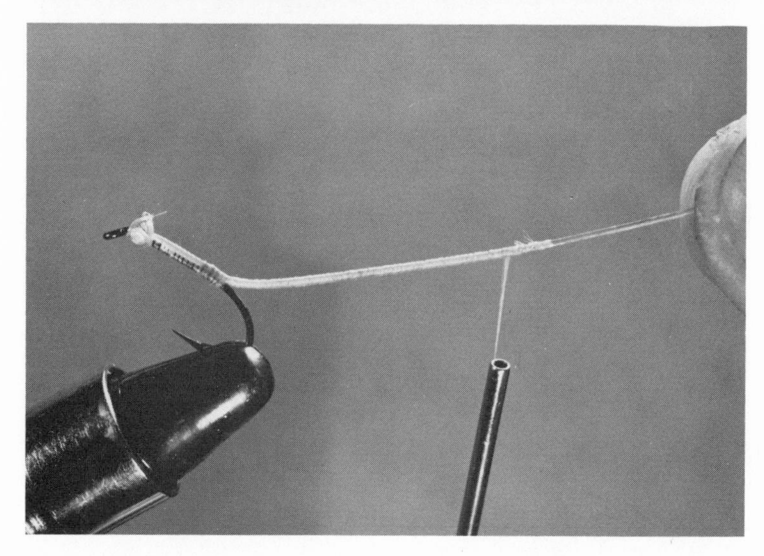

4. Wind thread to the bend and then cover the extended body of mono with closely wound thread to a point about one-and-a-half times the length of the hook. Then wind thread back to the bend and apply lacquer. Note that it is easy to cover the extended body if you remove the hook from the vise and clamp it at the eye.

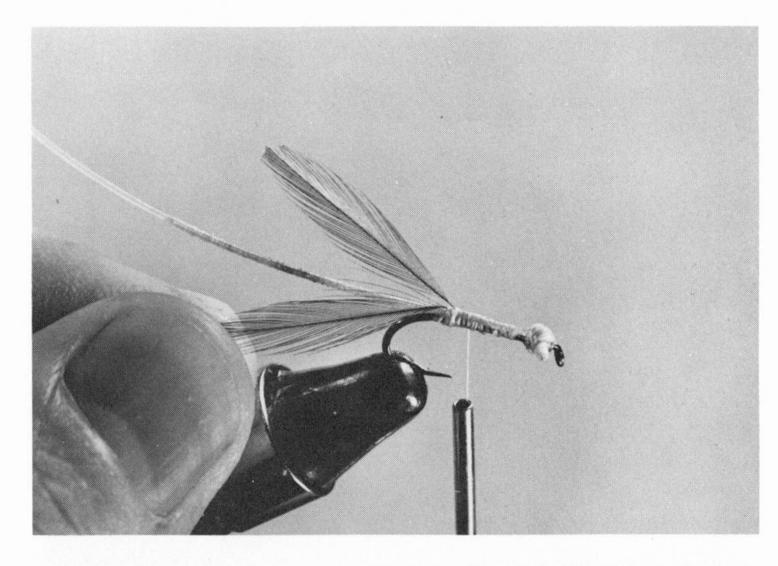

5. With the hook returned to the normal position in the vise, tie a blue-dun hackle point on each side of the body. The points (wings) should extend to a point approximately three-eighths of an inch short of the terminal end of the body wrappings.

6. Working forward from bend, build up oval thorax with working thread. Leave enough space for application of hackle between thorax and head. If broken water conditions are anticipated, white polypropylene dubbing can be substituted for thread wrapping.

7. Wind on light-blue dyed grizzly hackle. A permanent marking pen can be used in place of dyeing, if oils are carefully removed from hackle feather. Cut off tail excess.

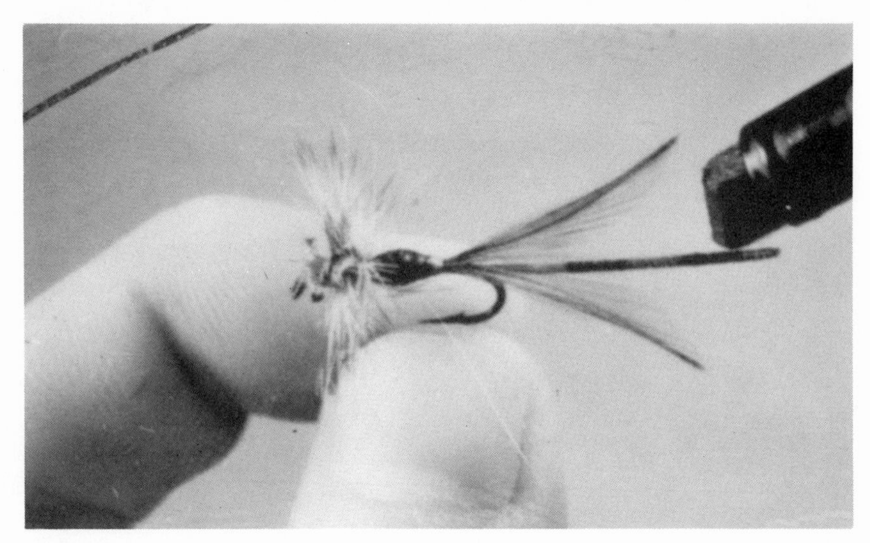

8. Using a permanent light-blue marking pen, preferably fluorescent, color the entire fly. Sparingly apply spots with black permanent marker. Be certain that spotting is in alignment from top to bottom. Also, take care that spots are comparatively less vivid on underside of fly.

A few details regarding damselfly presentation: As a rule, upstream presentations should be avoided on slick waters. For best results, the fly must precede the line and leader in its passage downstream. Whenever possible, I try to present the damsel with its slender abdomen or "tail" downstream. This can usually be accomplished with a slight twitch of the rod tip after the fly has begun its drift. Because the abdomen is so distinctive and true to life, it probably is of some advantage to have the fly enter the trout's window tail first. The extended hook-free abdomen probably is the trigger that sets off a no-holds-barred rush to the surface.

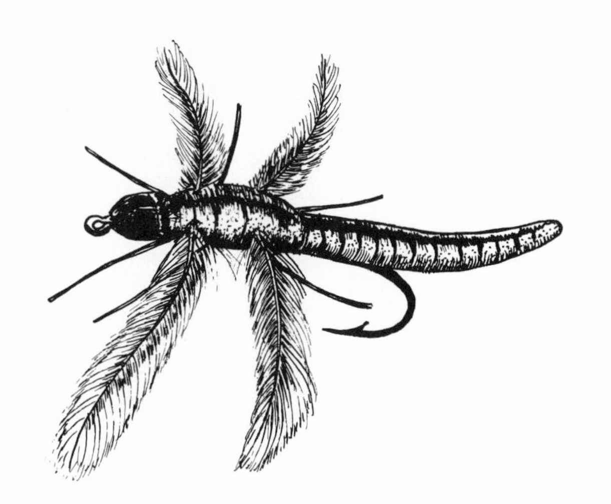

8

The Adult Dragonfly Bass Bug

by Robert H. Boyle

This dragonfly species, *Erythemis simplicicollis,* is of moderate size, the adult male measuring about forty-four millimeters in length, almost two inches. The head is black, dark brown, or green, the thorax green or bluish, and the abdomen bluish. The species is widely distributed, having been reported from Montana, California, Florida, New York, Maine, Ontario, Washington, and Arizona, among many other locations.

Dragonfly Bass Bug

Hook:	size 6 streamer
Tying thread:	Herb Howard's prewaxed black
Head:	shaped cork, rounded portion forward, painted black
Abdomen:	dyed-blue quill stub, segments drawn with India ink, balsa wood insert
Thorax:	green polypropylene yarn
Wings:	four long neck hackles
Legs:	strands of fine gray rubber

Although the point of the hook is forward of the tail of the dragonfly, I have had no trouble setting the hook when a largemouth strikes. The dragonfly bug will not become waterlogged like a deer-hair bass bug and will float all day. The dragonfly bass bug also has much less wind resistance than the deer-hair bug and casts that much easier.

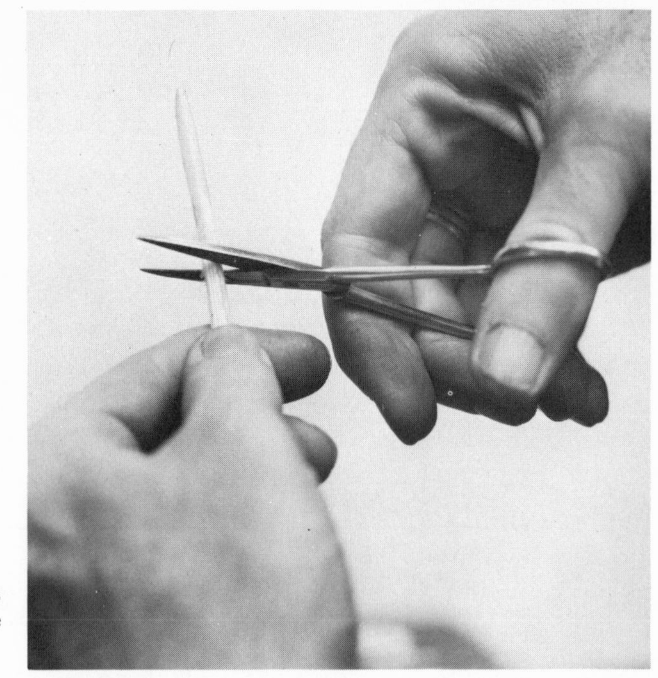

1. Clip the clear stub ends from a dozen quill shafts of a peacock, goose, or any other large bird. Dye them the color desired—in this case, blue.

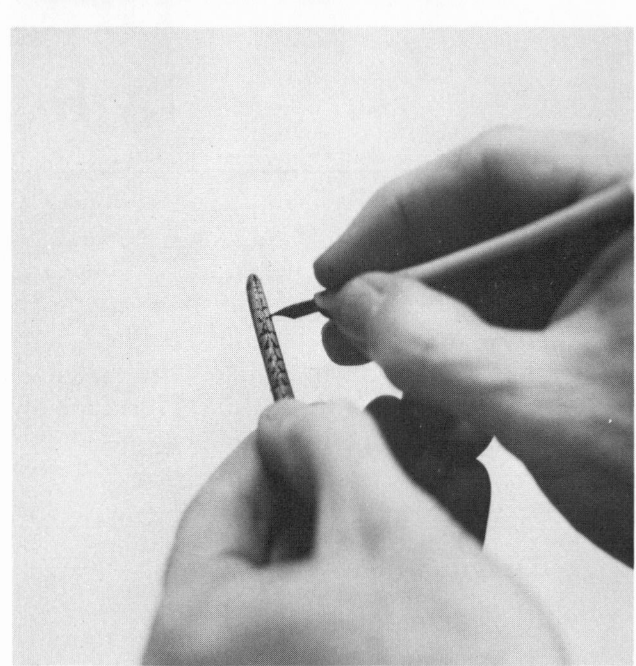

2. Draw the abdominal segments on the blue quill stub with a fine pen and black India ink. When dry, coat with nail polish or clear Krylon to fix.

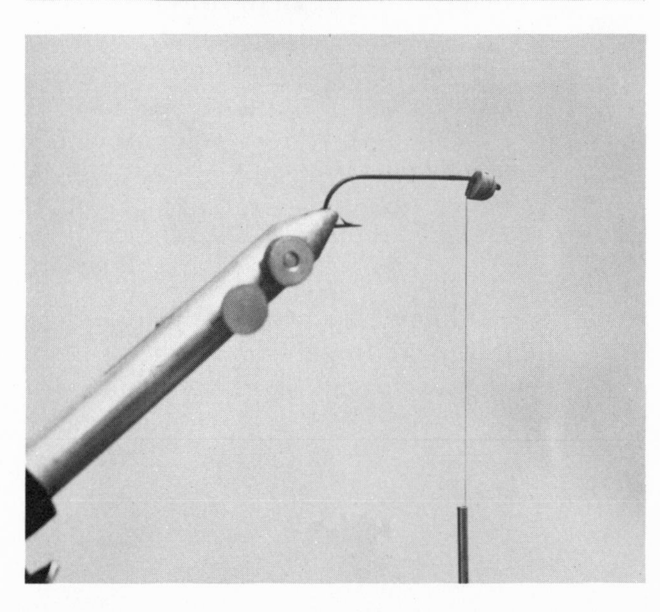

3. Attach a piece of shaped cork, notched through the top, to serve as the head. For minimum work, simply cut up round-ended cork bodies used for bluegill bugs. Secure the head with figure-eight lashings of the tying thread and lacquer with finger-nail polish.

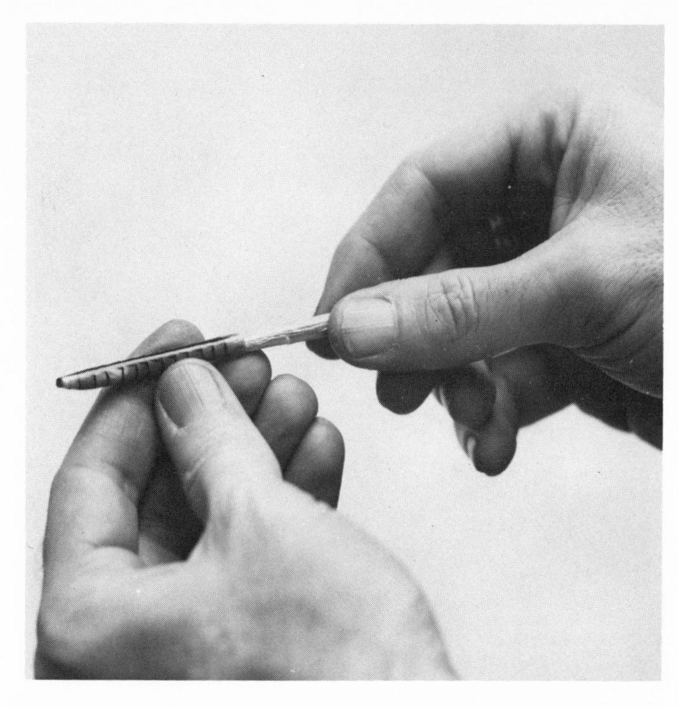

4. Insert a length of balsa wood snugly inside the quill stub. Before you insert it, be sure to lacquer it so that it stays in place inside.

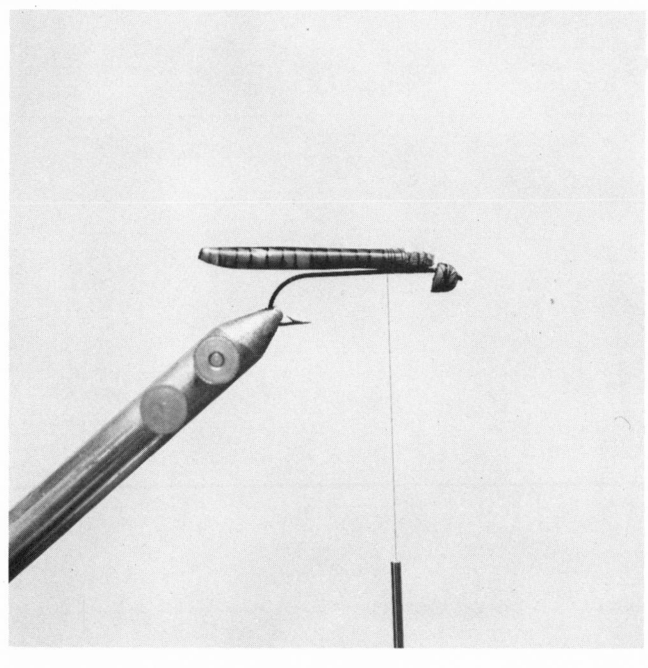

5. Lay the quill stub, with a piece of the balsa wood projecting, on top of the shank as shown and tie into place. The projecting balsa wood not only helps to secure the quill to the shank but also adds to the floating qualities of the finished dragonfly.

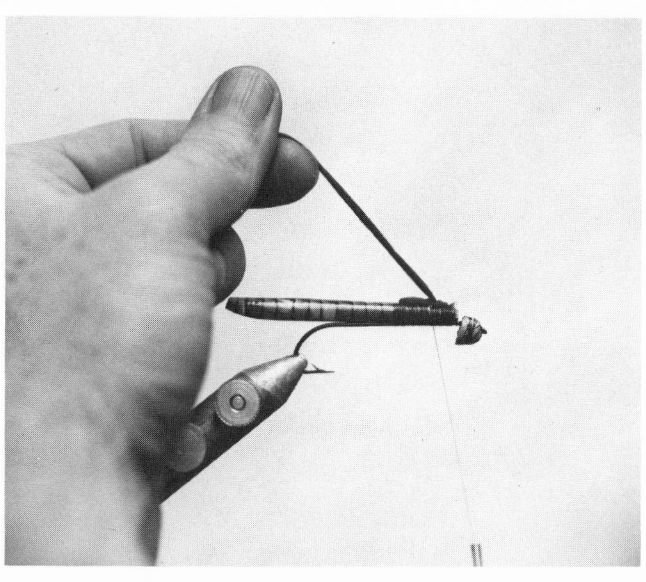

6. Tie on green polypropylene yarn as the thorax. Begin by laying it back and forth on top so that the finished thorax assumes the characteristic dragonfly profile with humplike shoulders.

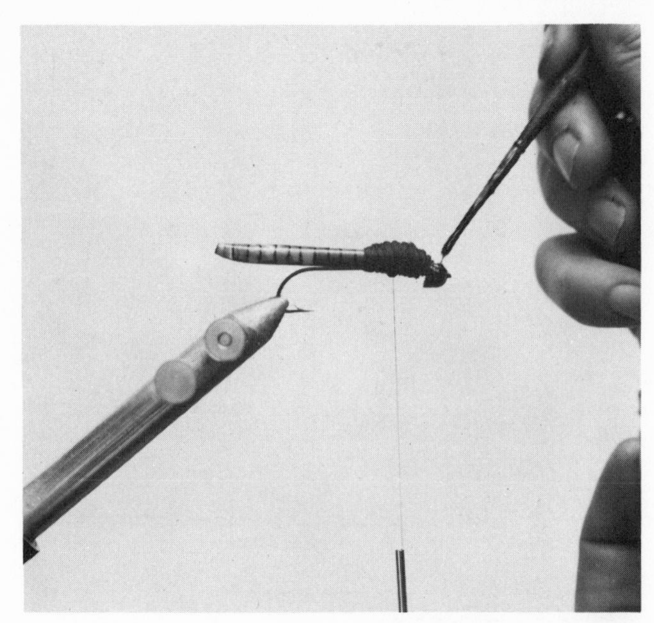

7. Paint the cork head with black Pla enamel or black lacquer and let dry.

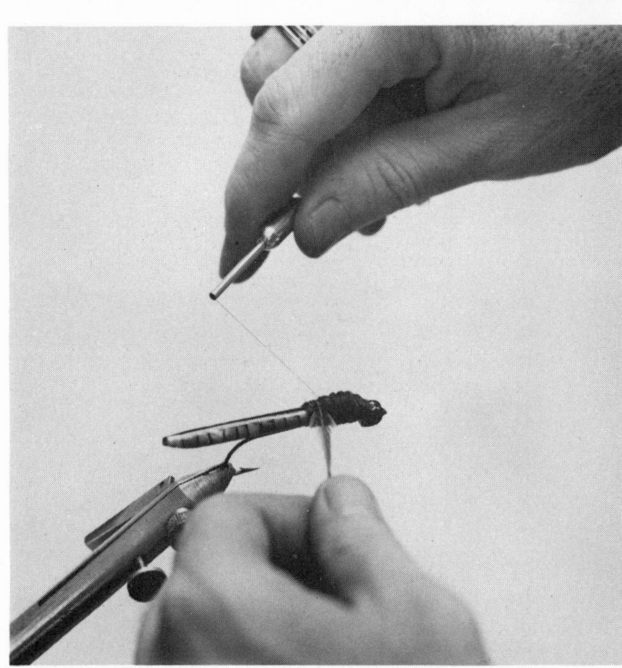

8. Tie in four long neck feathers for the wings. Tie them in individually, starting with the rear pair as shown. The rear pair should stand out at right angles from the thorax, whereas the forward pair should point forward slightly as shown. Apply fingernail polish to the windings.

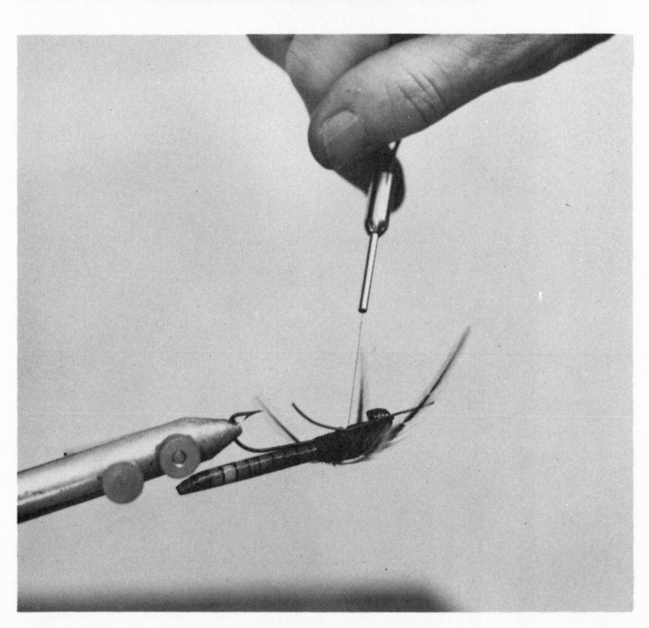

9. Turn the dragonfly upside down and tie in three pairs of fine, gray, rubber strands as the six legs.

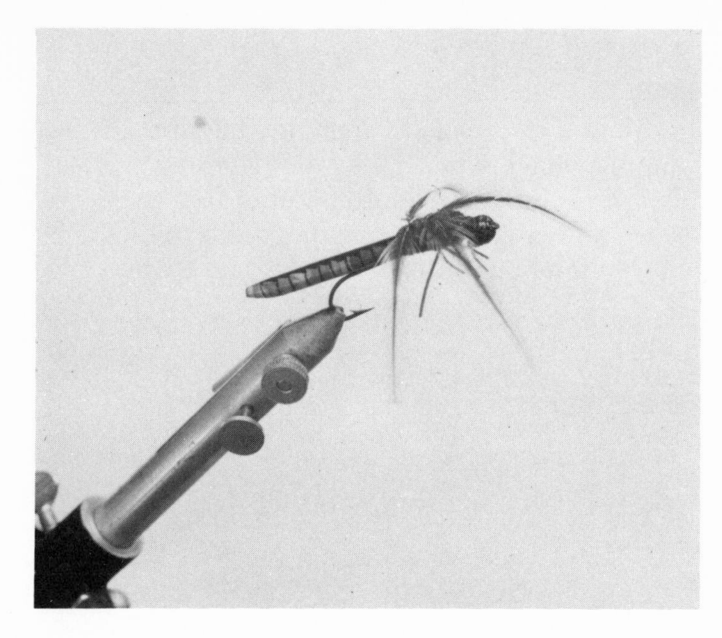

10. The dragonfly is now ready, except for some minor clipping of hackle. If you wish, you can dress it further by applying peacock or ostrich herl to the thorax. A more realistic and involved tie of the large *Anax junius* is shown in the color section. The wings are looped horsehair rather than feathers, and the thorax and head are pressed deer-body-hair painted with lacquer and then marked with India ink. The legs are javelina. *Photo by R. Hoebermann*

Here are brief descriptions of five more species of common dragonflies that an angler or a fish might encounter. All are easy for the flytyer to imitate.

Libellula pulchella is a brownish dragonfly nicknamed the Ten Spot because of the conspicuous spots on its wings. It belongs to a family called the "skimmers" because it flies a few feet above the water on bright summer days, pausing occasionally to rest on a twig or stem on the shoreline. The males appear to occupy a specific territory or beat, say twenty to thirty feet of shoreline, and given this predictable behavior and flight pattern are fairly easy to capture in an insect net for close-up examination. *L. pulchella* has a body length of approximately two inches (fifty-two to fifty-seven millimeters for those who want exact measurements) and a hind-wing span of slightly less (forty-two to forty-six millimeters). The species is found in most of the United States and southern Canada.

Plathemis lydia is closely related and is often found in the same habitat. This species has a chalky-white body and black-barred wings. Length is forty-two to forty-eight millimeters, while the hind-wings' span is thirty to thirty-five millimeters. This species is also found in most of the United States and southern Canada.

Anax junius is ordinarily the largest dragonfly to be found soaring around a pond or lake throughout the United States. Fittingly, the scientific name means "king of June." It has a green thorax and a blue abdomen. Exceedingly difficult to capture, *Anax* reaches a length of eighty millimeters and the hind wings measure as much as fifty-six millimeters from tip to tip.

Perithemis tenera by contrast is small, with a maximum length of twenty-four millimeters and a hind-wing span of nineteen millimeters. Very easy to recognize and very easy to capture. It has a robust reddish body and amber wings. A weak flyer, it flits only a few inches above the water and rests often on emergent vegetation, sticks, and logs. Quite widely distributed.

Sympetrum rubicundulum is a slender, red dragonfly, instantly recognizable in the northern states because it appears in the fall and is often the only species of dragonfly to be found flying in colder weather. Total length is thirty-four millimeters, with a hind-wing span of thirty millimeters.

Anglers should not underestimate the value of the realistic dragonfly bass bug, especially on those drowsy drone-filled summer days when largemouths are supposedly sulking in holes waiting for the cool of evening to feed. In point of fact, the really good artificial dragonfly bug can prove so realistic that live dragonflies will zoom in to attack or attempt to mate with it. No finer compliment can be paid to the flytyer's artifice.

IV

Saltwater and Steelhead Flies

Dave's Wiggle Damsel Nymph (Dave Whitlock)

The Quill-bodied Mylar Minnow (Whygin Argus)

Dave's Four-Phase Polymidge. *Bottom:* larva, pupa; *Top:* adult, flying adult (Dave Whitlock)

Dave's Matuka Streamer (Dave Whitlock)

The Leech (Thom Green)

The Glass or Grass Shrimp (Bob Boyle)

Dave's Wiggle-legs Frog (Dave Whitlock)

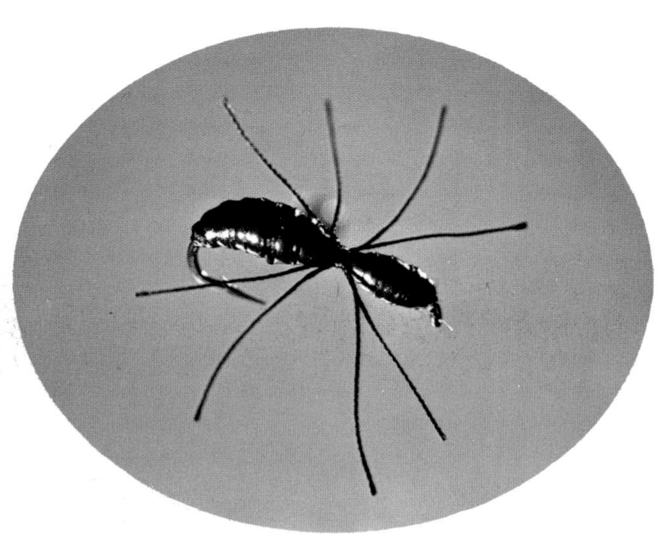

The Mold-Tex Ant (Bill Charles)

Charles's Stonefly Nymph (Bill Charles)

Dave's Hair Gerbubble Bug (Dave Whitlock)

Dave's Eelworm Streamer. *Above:* Palmer head; *Below:* trimmed head (Dave Whitlock)

9

Saltwater Flies

by Dan Blanton

In the early days of saltwater fly-fishing, the flies used to take marine game fish were rather simple. By and large it is still the same today. A sophisticated dressing will sometimes bring smiles from salty veterans of marine fly-rodding. "That's a pretty thing you have there," they might say, "but you don't need that fancy feather, the fish will hit most anything if they're feeding. Just get the thing in front of a hungry critter and get set."

I must agree that much of the time this line of reasoning is true. Some old-timers will remember, in years past, taking tarpon on popping bugs all along the Florida Keys. Today a large, noisy bug will scare the hell out of most tarpon in the same water.

As more and more anglers turn to the salt for their fly-rodding fun, fish, in turn, are getting wiser and harder to take. Some saltwater game fish seem to be more particular about what they ingest than others. Since many saltwater species are highly selective about their food, frustration has taken its toll on many saltwater flycasters.

I agree that simple dressings often produce tremendous saltwater fly catches, that they have a place in your selection of marine flies, and that they may make up the majority of the total volume. Today, however, you had better include a few patterns that are more realistic in their simulations of marine fodder, to entice the reluctant ones into striking.

Superior baitfish simulations and lifelike animation is what I am referring to when I speak of sophisticated saltwater flies. For example, the time-proven Joe Brooks's Blonds have taken hundreds of fish of infinite variety, yet they will fail miserably at times with certain species. A more carefully thoughtout fly such as the Lefty's Deceiver simulates a baitfish considerably better, and has taken fish the Blond could not.

One of the first great flytyers to think in terms of realistic simulation and exact imitation with saltwater dressing was Bill Catherwood, master flytyer from Tewksbury, Massachusetts. The Catherwood Originals were specialized patterns. Some were floaters, others sinkers; all were phenomenal creations! Using hair and feathers bound to steel, Catherwood fabricated exact lifelike imitations of marine baitfish and squid.

Over the years, I have aligned myself with Catherwood's thinking to some degree and have tried to coin saltwater flies that in fact simulate—through silhouette, color, and animation—marine baitfish in the most realistic manner possible, without having to imitate exactly, individual species of baitfish, crustaceans, and squid. Realistic simulation is, in my opinion, the key to a more productive saltwater fly.

I have contributed two patterns to this publication; both are proven simulator flies that have accounted for some remarkable catches of marine game fish.

The Sar-Mul-Mac

The Sar-Mul-Mac derives its name from three different saltwater baitfishes: the sardine, the mullet, and the mackerel. These are common baitfishes found in most oceans and seas around the globe. By varying the color of the dressing and length of the hooks used, many other species of bait can generally be simulated with this fly, such as the ballyhoo, half beak, needle fish, anchovy, herring, jack smelt, and many others. The Sar-Mul-Mac is a general baitfish simulator. It is a more complex pattern than those commonly used and does a superlative job of turning refusals into solid strikes.

Using hair, hackles, fluff, and chenille along with glass optics, a fly is created that possesses a proper baitfish silhouette, action, and appearance—in short, lifelike animation.

I developed the Sar-Mul-Mac in the spring of 1971. Since that time it has taken an infinite variety of marine game fish such as striped bass, bonito, oceanic skipjack, grouper, cabrillo, snapper, dolphin, halibut, pompano, rooster fish, and several others.

The pattern has been tested in the waters of the Pacific off the coast of California and in San Francisco Bay, the Sea of Cortés, and waters of the Central American Caribbean. The Sar-Mul-Mac proved in many cases more productive than many of the old standards, particularly when it came to finicky feeders.

The Sar-Mul-Mac is an oceanic fly in that it can be used successfully in any ocean or sea. It will be a productive addition to your saltwater fly box.

The Sar-Mul-Mac

Hook: Mustad 34007, sizes 2/0–4/0, stainless steel
Tying thread: white
Tail: white bucktail, medium bunch, length optional
Hackle: six white saddle hackles
five silver mylar strips, 1/64 or 1/32 wide; length, half that of saddle hackles

Underwing: medium bunch of white bucktail
Overwing or Topping: two long grizzly saddle hackles, natural color or blue, green, or yellow, as long or longer than white saddle hackles
Throat: red or maroon marabou fluff
Shoulder: gray marabou fluff
Cheeks: teal flank feather
Head Topping: loop of gray chenille
Optics: 8mm amber glass eyes obtainable from Herter's or a taxidermy supply house
Head: white chenille

1. The entire fly will be tied using the forward half of the hook shank. Start by tying on a medium-sized bunch of white bucktail. The length of the hair will determine the overall length of the fly. Wrap the hair stubs down to the eye of the hook.

2. The six white saddle hackles will form an overtail. Tie three white saddle hackles on each side of the bucktail. Splay the hackles for more pronounced action. Wrap hackle quill stubs down to eye of hook. Build a foundation with the various material stubs, and form a tapered head. Add the five silver mylar strips to each side of saddle hackles.

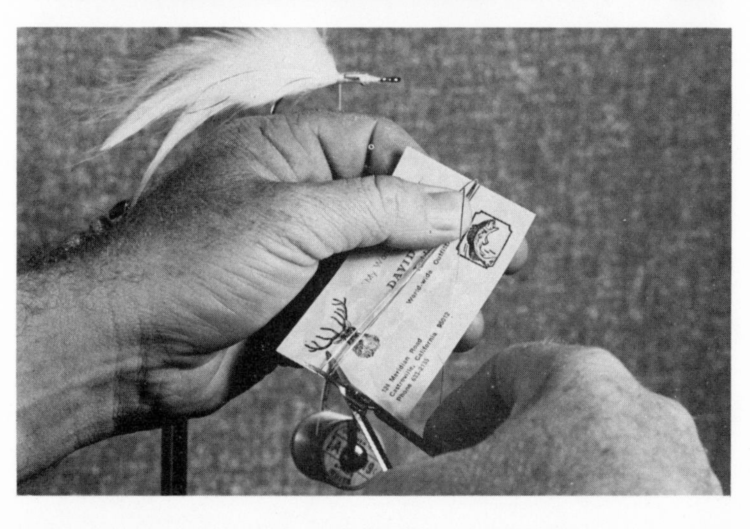

3. This step offers a tip on how to prepare the mylar strips for easy handling. Wrap the mylar around a business card five times. Cut the strips at each end; you have two equal bunches of mylar, exactly the same length.

4. Turn the fly over in the vise and tie on a medium bunch of white bucktail, forming the underwing of the fly. The hair will be three-quarters the length of the saddle hackles. Be sure to split the hair so that equal amounts are on both sides of the hook point. Wrap hair stubs to eye of hook.

5. The underwing step completed.

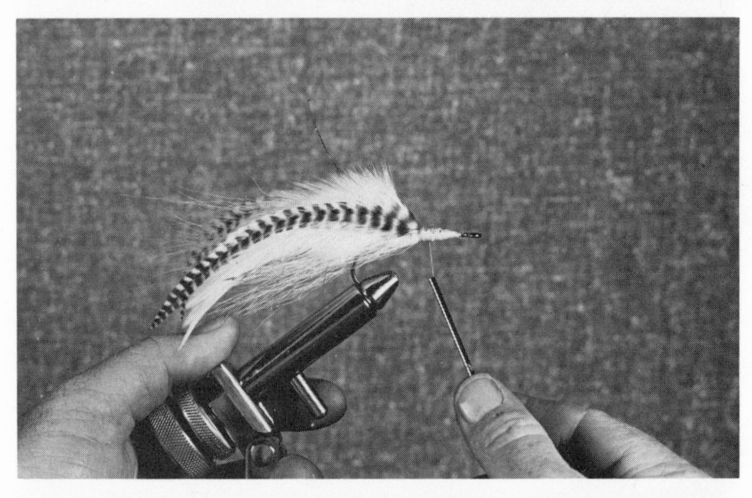

6. Tie two long grizzly saddle hackles tent-style over white saddles. This will form the overwing and give the fly the herringbone effect found on many baitfishes.

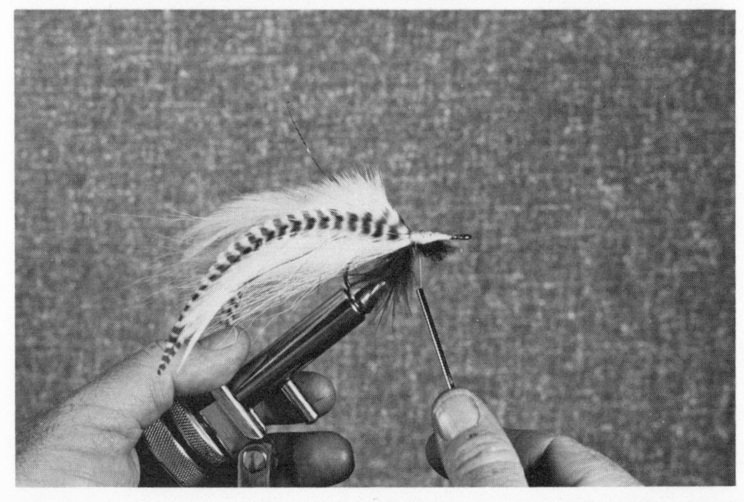

7. Tie on a red or maroon marabou fluff throat, fairly long.

8. Now tie on a shoulder of gray marabou fluff. Use a good amount.

9. Tie one teal flank feather on each side of the hook as shown. Coat the base of the feather with head cement to help keep the fibers married.

10. To form a topping for the head of the fly, tie on a long loop of gray chenille by the ends, just in front of the gray marabou. Fold the loop back out of the way—it will be used later.

11. The glass eyes come attached to a length of wire approximately four inches long. Bend the wire at a 90° angle to the eye as shown. Keep the bend close to the eye to avoid too large a gap between the eyes.

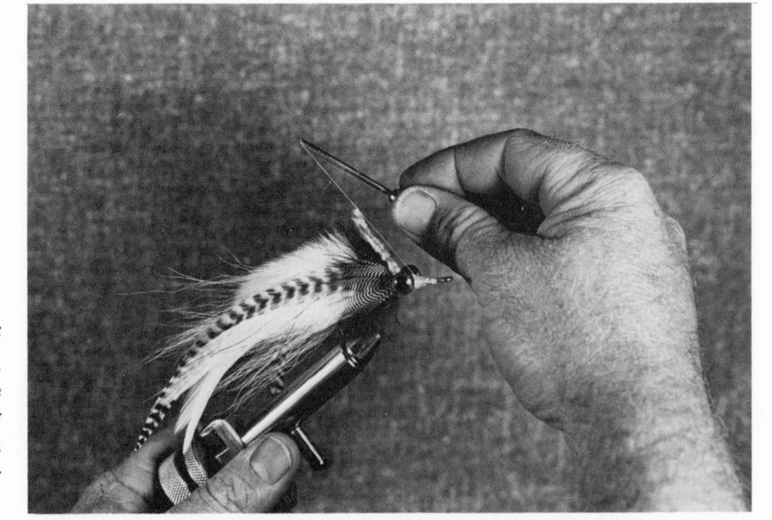

12. The glass eye should be centered on the side of the hook, halfway on the remainder of the shank. Cut the wire just long enough to clear the eye of the hook. Bind one eye at a time to the hook shank by the wire. Figure-eight between the eyes after both have been attached. Coat liberally with head cement.

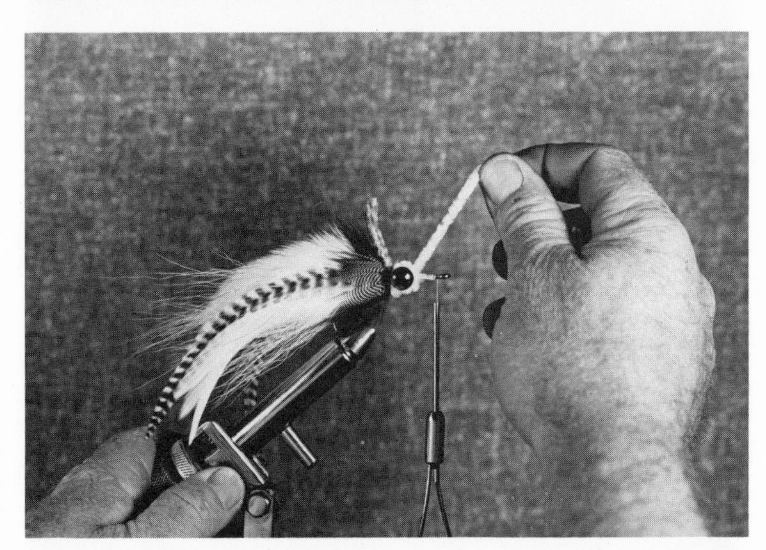

13. Tie on medium-white chenille behind the eyes. Then wrap it forward, crisscrossing between the eyes several times to build a full, neatly tapered head. Wrap the chenille to the eye of the hook and tie off.

14. To complete the head topping, bring the previously tied loop of gray chenille forward over the top of the head as shown, and tie off. This step completes the fly.

15. The completed Sar-Mul-Mac

16. A needlefish variation of the Sar-Mul-Mac

The Bay-Delta Eelet

I developed this variation of an eel simulator in 1972 and named it the Bay-Delta Eelet because it was tested in the waters of San Francisco Bay, the Sacramento-San Joaquin delta, and their river regions, with great success. It took many striped bass frequently in the twenty- to twenty-five-pound class.

It is common knowledge that stripers find the various species of eels highly palatable. Every year, striped bass of enormous proportions are taken by anglers using live, rigged, or artificial eels. Hundreds of smaller bass are taken on the same bait. It is reasonable, then, to assume that an artificial fly which properly simulates an eel will also take its share of striped bass.

The Bay-Delta Eelet does an admirable job of simulating a general variety of eels with extreme lifelike realism. At the same time, it remains basically simple, relying on its silhouette and undulating motion to mock a live eel and deceive stripers into striking.

Its feathers and hair stream back when wet, forming an outline shaping what is easily recognizable as an eel. As the fly is retrieved, it undulates over sand or mud bottoms, dipping and bobbing, looking extremely natural.

By casting to the many pilings planted in the bottom of San Francisco Bay, working the fly along rocky shorelines, or over grass-covered bottoms, I have taken many striped bass weighing more than twenty pounds with the Bay-Delta Eelet. Dark colors such as black seem to produce best, though brown, gray, or olive take their share of fish at times.

Striped bass spawn from early spring on through the first warm days of summer. Starting their migration in the fall of the year, they swarm into the Sacramento-San Joaquin delta, a vast system of interconnected sloughs, rivers, and backwater lakes called tracks. The Sacramento and San Joaquin rivers and their tributaries supply the lifeblood of this enormous delta region.

Many bass hold over for the entire winter in the lower delta, feeding on whatever is available. As they move farther upriver in the spring they become more active, and when not thinking of reproduction feed well.

Lamprey eels use this same system to propagate their species, and since they are in the rivers at the same time as the bass, they are fed upon by large stripers. The Bay-Delta Eelet is a good simulation of a small lamprey and has accounted for many good fly-rod bass.

My best river striper came from the American River, a tributary of the Sacramento. I took the potbellied bass, weighing a handsome twenty-five pounds eight ounces, on a Bay-Delta Eelet within the shadow of the California state capitol building. It was April, a beautiful time of year on the American. A stomach check of the fish revealed several salmon fry, and three eels, averaging eight inches in length.

Wherever saltwater game fish feed on eels, a smart fly-rodder will have in his box an effective eel-simulator fly. The Bay-Delta Eelet has performed well for my associates and I. I'm sure it will do the same for you.

The Bay-Delta Eelet

Hook:	Mustad 34007, 2/0–4/0, stainless steel
Tying thread:	black, size A Nymo
Optics:	⅛-inch silver chain-beads
Materials:	1) long black horse mane or dyed nylon hair (optional), length four to five inches, 2) twelve long black saddle hackles, two grizzly saddle hackles, 3) medium-black chenille

---

1. The first step is actually two steps in one. First tie on the 1/8-inch chain-bead optics. Leave 3/8 inch space between optics and eye of hook. Next, secure a medium amount of black horse mane to the bend of the hook, for a tail.

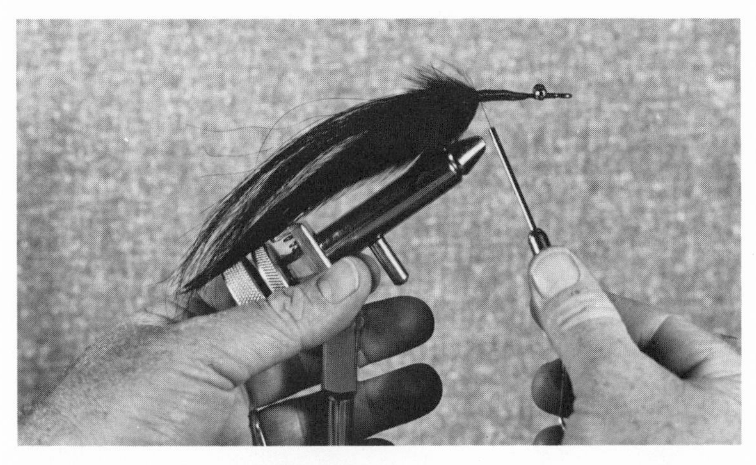

2. Undertail: Tie on six black saddle hackles to the underside of the hook at the bend. Three hackles (curved sides together) will be placed on each side. This will simulate an eel's belly fin and part of its tail.

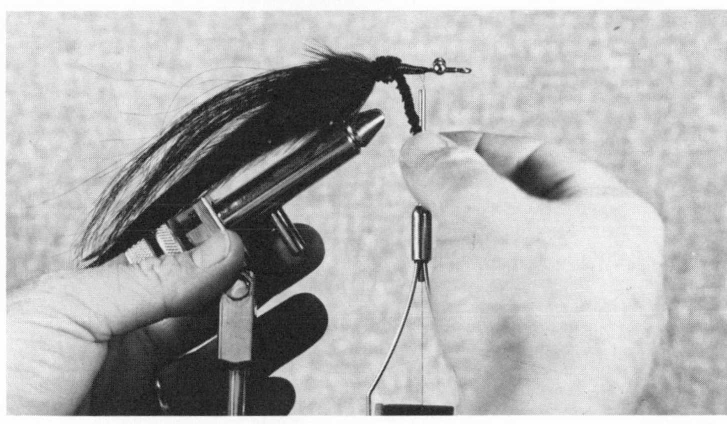

3. For the body, tie on a length of medium-black chenille at the bend of the hook, just in front of the horse mane and hackles. Now wrap the chenille forward half the distance to the chain-bead optics. Secure in place with hackle pliers or a material clip—do not cut the chenille.

4. For the wing, tie six black saddle hackles on edge, at the point where the chenille was stopped on top of the hook shank. Tie three on each side, curved sides together. This wing simulates the eel's long dorsal fin and the remainder of its tail.

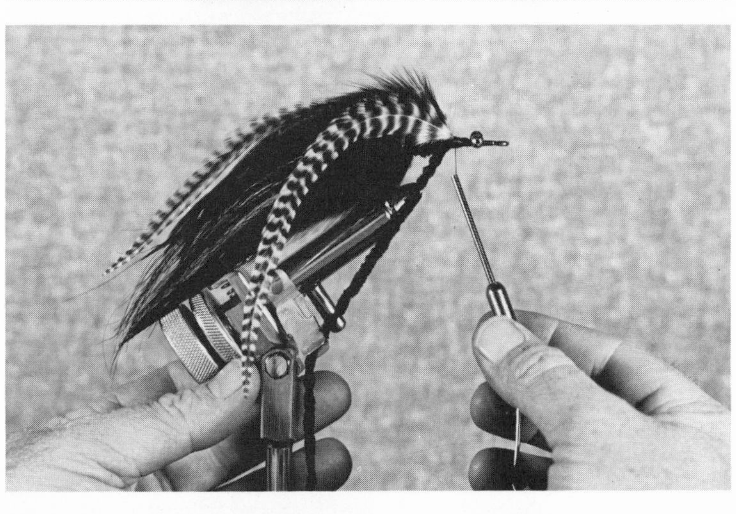

5. Many eels have blotchy markings on their backs. For the topping, tie one long grizzly hackle on each side of wing to simulate these markings. These will be tied in at the same spot as the wing.

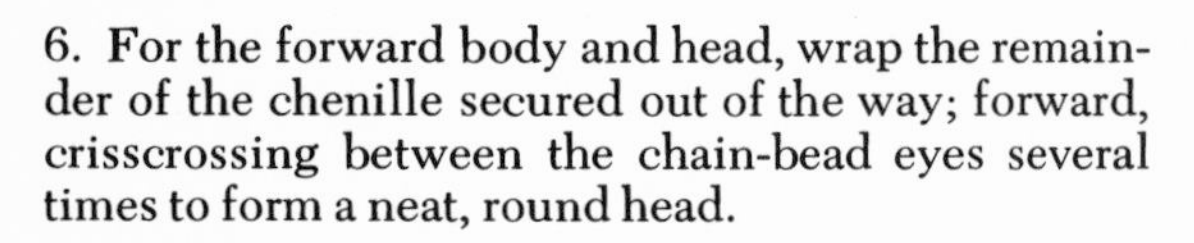

6. For the forward body and head, wrap the remainder of the chenille secured out of the way; forward, crisscrossing between the chain-bead eyes several times to form a neat, round head.

7. Cut off the remaining chenille close to the eye of the hook.

8. Take several wraps of thread to secure the chenille. Whip-finish and apply head cement.

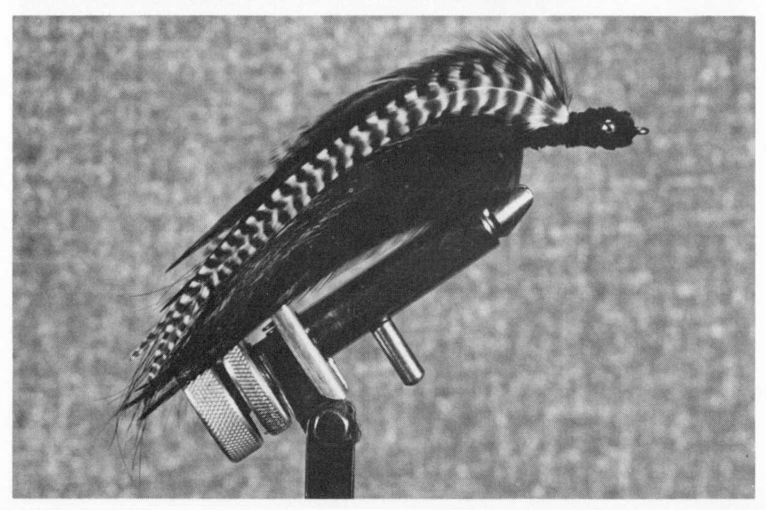

9. This is the completed Bay-Delta Eelet.

10

Steelhead Flies

by Darwin R. Atkin

In the course of my avocation as a flytyer I have tied several thousand steelhead flies. Most of these were of traditional feather and hair-wing construction. Steelhead flies are a beautiful and varied lot, ranging from the insectlike Brindle Bugs and Silver Hiltons of northern California, and the Dark Gordons and Skunks of Oregon's North Umpqua River, to the brightly dressed Painted Ladies and Skykomish Sunrises so successful in Washington and British Columbia waters.

Seldom included in lists of commonly used steelhead patterns are those that incorporate marabou into the fly. The effectiveness of marabou-winged flies for bass, panfish, and trout is beyond denial. Can there be any doubt that the marabou wings of a large streamer so effective for bruising brown trout in the Madison, Yellowstone, or Missouri rivers would not also be equally effective for steelhead in the Klamath, the Rogue, or the North Fork of the Stillaguamish? Perhaps the same streamer pattern would not be effective, but the problem might lie in the form or coloration of the fly rather than in the wing material.

Though the marabou does not have extreme durability of hair, its other qualities—lively action, proven fish-taking ability, and its sinking motion when thoroughly wet—recommend that it be represented in any steelheader's fly box. The material is common, inexpensive, and available from all fly-material suppliers as turkey marabou, though formerly it was imported stork marabou.

Without question, more types of fly action can be brought into play during one drift of a marabou-winged fly than with other materials. In steelhead wet-fly fishing, successful fishing equates with depth. The fly should be right down along the bottom rubble during its drift. Either added fly weight or one of the fast-sinking fly lines and presoaking of the marabou fly will get it down quickly. Once in a deep drift, marabou is capable of responding to the stream's currents far better than any other material.

The result is a most lively "dead drift." By extending line into the drift as the fly passes, the angler can prolong the fly's deep drift and continue its pulsating action as it searches its way along the bottom. The marabou wing is so sensitive that any change in its drift or the current's direction causes an immediate response not unlike a nymph or winged insect all askew, helplessly drifting and tumbling at the river's mercy. In short, it suggests life, but more importantly, life not in control of itself and therefore easy prey to be taken. As the fly reaches the end of its drift and begins its cross-current swing to the surface it takes on a new character, now perhaps as a hatching caddis or even a minnow. Whatever it might be taken for, it's definitely alive. Directly below the angler, the marabou wing slims to its sleekest form and conforms to the fly body contours, becoming a full-fledged minnow in form and action. Still influenced by the currents and now strongly by the angler's rod, the marabou-winged fly never ceases its action.

With the marabou's drift action in mind and the fact that few listings of marabou-dressed steelhead flies could be found, I was challenged to design one. Several criteria came to mind. First, the fly would be of a basic, simple-to-tie design. Second, marabou would be incorporated into the tail, wing, and hackle. Third, the pattern would be weighted. Fourth, if possible the colors would be used in regular and fluorescent shades as well.

In keeping with the desire for a simple design, I decided to use a weighting material that would itself serve as the body. Soft brass and copper wires were used many years ago by Peter Schwab in his Princess and Brass Hat bucktails for use in California's Eel River. The method I used in the new marabou fly differs somewhat from Schwab's and is explained below in the tying description.

I experimented with black and white marabou, and fluorescent yellow, orange, and red marabou for both the wings and tails. To complete the fly I added hackles, utilizing the maraboulike butts of saddle or neck hackles. Most tyers discard this material without realizing its possible uses. The last step in developing the new fly was applying fluorescent marabou cheeks of a contrasting color to provide a focal point on the fly just as jungle-cock eyes were formerly used.

The eventual result was not the one pattern hoped for but a whole series of eight new patterns called collectively the Mari-Boos. Each of these was given a name suggested by its color pattern. The Streaker was suggested because of its whiteness, with orange cheeks—an appearance not unlike that of the participants in a recent fad. The Pole Kat leaves little doubt about the origin of its name or colors. The Daisy is a white-winged, yellow-hackled fly of a generally light color but darker than the Streaker. The Dark Ember is the darker of the two Ember flies; it is a fluorescent orange-and-black fly with a copper wire body. The Bright Ember Mari-Boo is a bright version of the pattern. It features a fluorescent-orange-over-fluorescent-yellow wing with a black overwing and a copper wire body. The Chiquita is a bright yellow, brass-bodied fly with orange cheeks. The Bloody Mari-Boo is the steelheader's early-morning tomato juice. The Sun Burst is orange and yellow colored, bright enough to make an early-rising drinker wish for the real cocktail. The eight patterns are shown in the color plate and the complete dressings in the chart.

Here are the steps in dressing a typical Mari-Boo pattern, the Dark Ember in size 4.

Dark Ember Mari-Boo

Hook:	1XL–2XL long strong, gold, sizes 2 through 8
Thread:	fluorescent red Fly Master. I use this thread on all Mari-Boos
Tail:	medium bunch of fluorescent orange marabou
Body:	lacquered copper wire
Wing:	medium bunch of black marabou over medium bunch of fluorescent orange marabou
Hackle:	black hackle marabou
Overwing:	small bunch of black marabou
Cheeks:	fluorescent orange marabou tied short
Head:	fluorescent red lacquer. I use this on all Mari-Boos

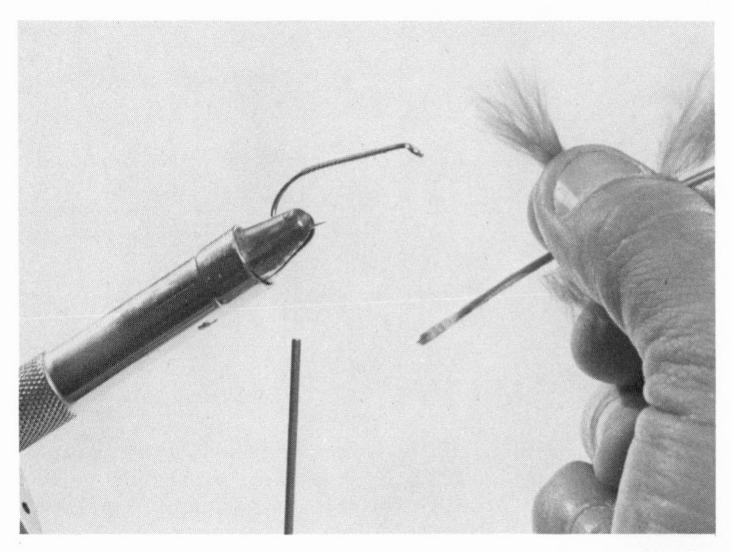

1. Wrap the shank solidly with tying thread. Cement the windings, since a strong base will prevent slippage later. Cut the tail of orange marabou, using the thickest fibers from near the base of the plume as shown.

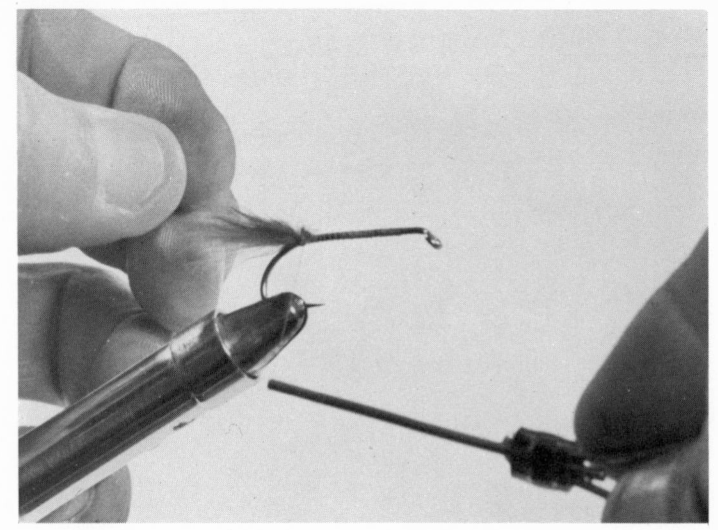

2. The tail material should be stripped or cut from the plume and tied in at the end of the hook. Allow a tail length of one and one-half to two times the hook gape. Wind down the tail butts as shown and return the thread to within ¼ inch of the eye. Cement all these windings well. I prefer a clear, fast-drying cement that is slightly thickened so it has some body to it.

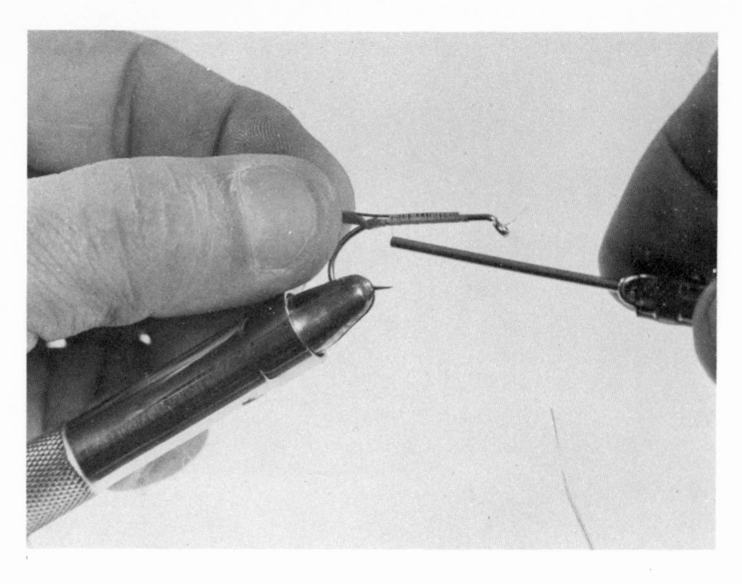

3. Cut off an 8- or 9-inch piece of 22 to 24 gauge soft copper wire. For any hook, try to choose a wire that has approximately the same diameter as the hook wire. Burnish the entire length of the wire with a pad of steel wool to remove the surface oxidation. Tie the wire to the top of the shank ¼ inch back of the eye with very close turns of thread. Wind the thread all the way back to the bend where the tail was tied in, as in the photograph.

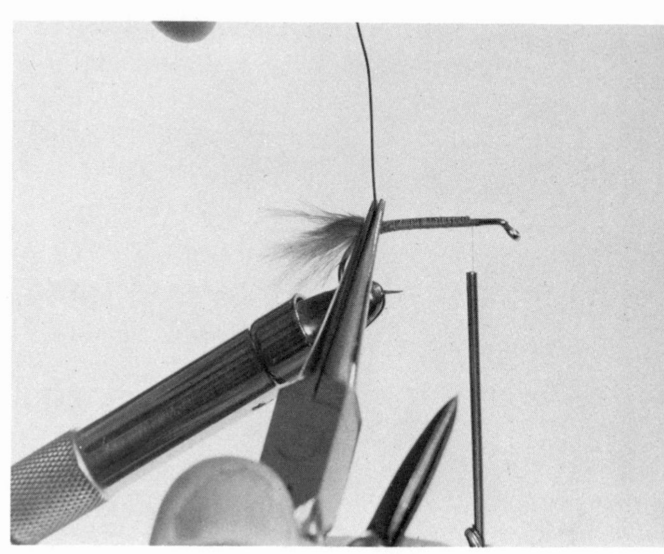

4. With needle-nose pliers, bend the wire to a right angle away from the shank and the tyer as seen here. This makes the start of the body turns much easier. Liberally cover the wire base and the windings with cement once more. When completing the first wrap of the wire, make certain the wire starts around the back side of the shank in front of the first turn. Each turn must lie tightly next to its predecessor to avoid any body gaps. This also pushes the excess cement ahead of the wire wraps, ensuring an even coating of cement.

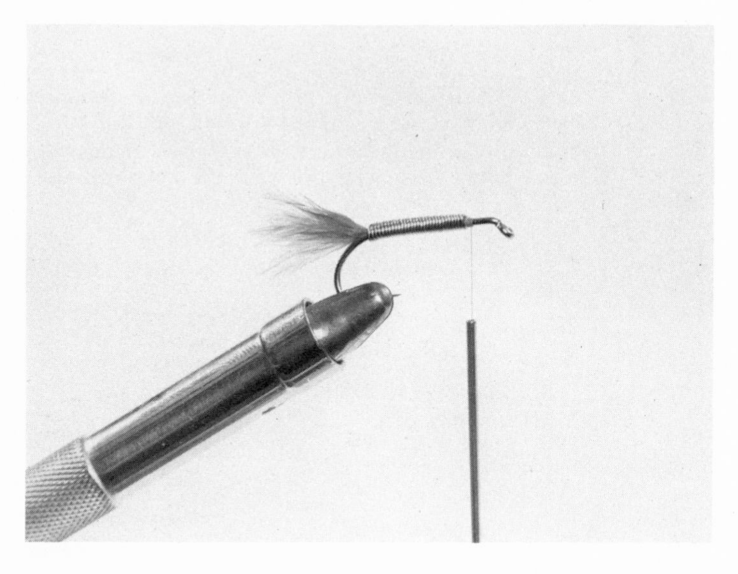

5. Continue the body forward to include one full turn of wire ahead of its original tie-in location on the shank. Cross the wire with six to eight turns of thread to tie off the wire. Clip off the excess wire and press down the cut end smoothly with the pliers. Build a small tapered wedge of thread, as in the photograph, and whip-finish. Next completely submerge the wire body (not including the tail) in thinned cement. Air bubbles will reveal the filling of small cavities with cement. When the bubbles stop, drain the excess cement and dry thoroughly. Usually two additional coats of cement are applied to cement the body firmly and preserve its brightness. These coats can be applied as new bodies are being tied.

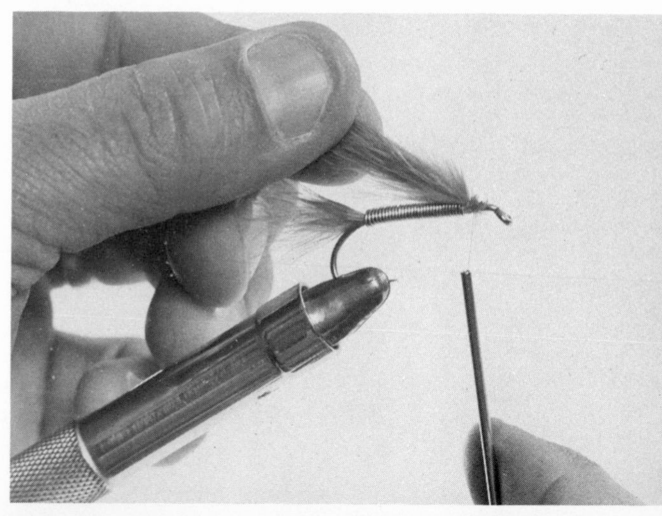

6. After reattaching the tying thread, wind a thread base nearly to the eye and return to the end of the body. Cement well. Strip off a medium bunch of fluorescent orange marabou fibers. When tied in, the length of this first wing section should reach nearly to the end of the tail, as shown. Trim off the excess material and wind the butt down after applying cement.

7. Apply the same-sized bunch of black marabou to the wing over the orange with as little color mixing as possible. Again wind the butt into a small drop of cement. Select a black saddle or neck hackle with a good length of soft, webby maraboulike fibers along its base. It is helpful if the center quill is not too thick. Size the hackle to the hook by the length of these fibers, about twice the hook gape. About 1 inch of these fibers will be needed. To ready the hackle for use, hold it shiny-side-up and prepare it as shown. Cut off the tip ⅛ inch above the marabou fibers. Save the tip section for other fly-tying uses.

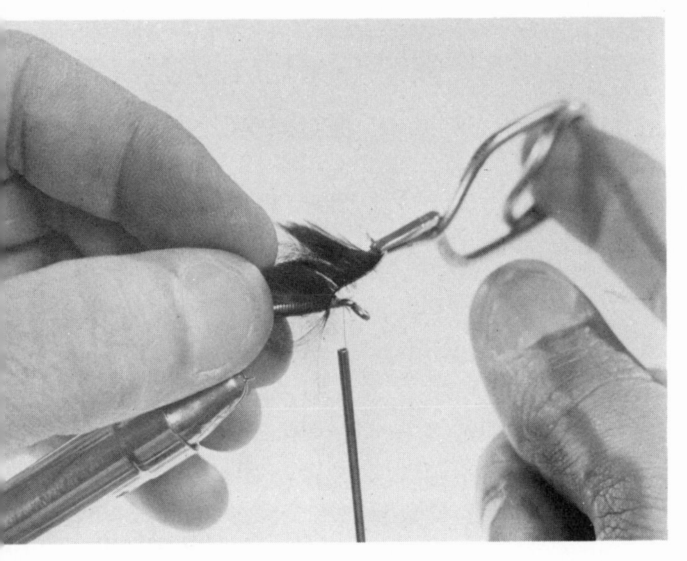

8. Tie in the prepared hackle by the tip end of the quill, as in the photograph, and make no more than three turns before tying off. Turn the hackle back in wet-fly fashion as it is being wound. Usually it is best to apply cement first and wind the hackle into it. In this way you can be sure it is embedded into cement. Cement the tie-off wraps and trim the excess hackle.

9. The final wing section is a small bunch of black marabou. Use about one-half the amount of the previous black wing section. Marabou wings are tied quite full, more so than would seem necessary, as shown. Despite being quite fluffy when dry, marabou greatly reduces in bulk when thoroughly soaked.

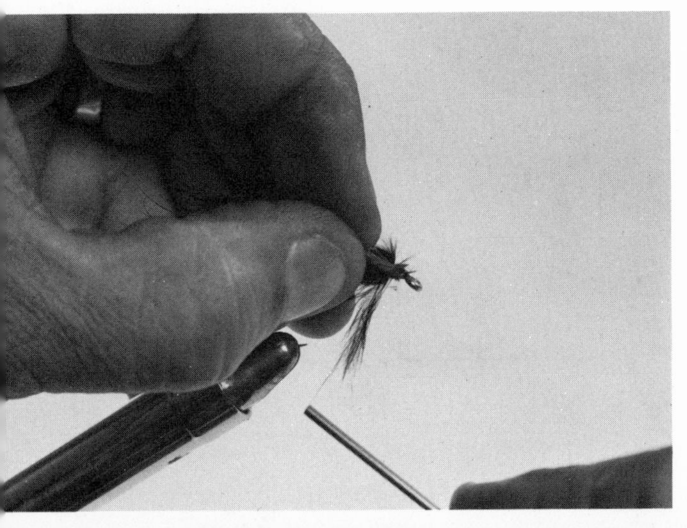

10. The fly is now ready to receive the cheeks. These are short, thick tufts of fluorescent orange marabou from the base of a plume or hackle feather. The length should be about ¼ inch. They are tied in at the sides of the wing. Trim the excess material very closely. Moisten the short fibers projecting from the head area and press them down. They can then be easily covered by the thread wraps as the head is finished. Fill out the head to a small, tapered wedge, and whip-finish. Usually I coat the head first with thinned clear cement, then one coat of fluorescent red cement, then one final coat of clear cement to enhance the gloss.

11. A head-and-cheek view of the finished **Dark Ember**.

12. A profile view. *Photos by R. S. Kilburn*

The Mari-Boo Dressings

PATTERN	HOOK	TAIL
Streaker	1XL–2XL Gold Nos. 2–8	Small bunch fluorescent yellow over white marabou
Pole Kat	1XL–2XL Nickeled Nos. 2–8	Medium bunch white marabou
Daisy	1XL–2XL Gold Nos. 2–8	Small bunch fluorescent yellow over white marabou
Bright Ember	1XL–2XL Gold Nos. 2–8	Small bunch fluorescent yellow over small bunch fluorescent orange marabou
Chiquita	1XL–2XL Gold Nos. 2–8	Small bunch fluorescent yellow over white marabou
Bloody	1XL–2XL Gold Nos. 2–8	Small bunch fluorescent yellow over small bunch fluorescent orange marabou
Sun Burst	1XL–2XL Gold Nos. 2–8	Mixed medium bunch fluorescent orange and yellow marabou

Body	Wing	Hackle	Overwing	Cheeks	Head
Gold mylar over lead wire rib	Large bunch white marabou	White hackle marabou	Small bunch white marabou	Fluorescent orange marabou tied short	Fluorescent red lacquer
Silver mylar over lead wire rib	Large bunch black marabou	Black hackle marabou	Small bunch white marabou	Fluorescent orange marabou tied short	Fluorescent red lacquer
Gold mylar over lead wire rib	Large bunch white marabou	Fluorescent yellow hackle marabou	Small bunch fluorescent yellow marabou	Fluorescent orange marabou tied short	Fluorescent red lacquer
Lacquered copper wire	Medium bunch fluorescent orange over small bunch fluorescent yellow marabou	Black hackle marabou	Small bunch black marabou	Fluorescent orange marabou tied short	Fluorescent red lacquer
Lacquered brass wire	Large bunch fluorescent yellow marabou	Fluorescent yellow hackle marabou	Small bunch fluorescent yellow marabou	Fluorescent orange marabou tied short	Fluorescent red lacquer
Lacquered copper wire	Large bunch fluorescent orange marabou	Fluorescent red hackle marabou	Small bunch fluorescent red marabou	Fluorescent yellow marabou tied short	Fluorescent red lacquer
Lacquered brass wire	Large bunch mixed fluorescent orange and yellow marabou	Fluorescent orange and yellow hackle marabou. One turn each, wound together	Small bunch fluorescent orange marabou	Fluorescent yellow marabou tied short	Fluorescent red lacquer

The reader will note that the dressings for three of the patterns (Streaker, Pole Kat, and Daisy) call for a body of either gold or silver mylar over a rib of lead wire. This makes for a lightly weighted and very bright fly. After much experimenting, I devised this style of body, which should also prove of use for trout streamers and wet flies.

Tying is easy, especially since mylar has a certain amount of stretch. Here is what you do. First, cover the hook shank with a solid thread base and cement well. Attach the tail fibers and tie in two strips of mylar tinsel. Sheet mylar works best. The strips must be cut slightly wider than the expected width between the turns of the ribbing. Start the ribbing on top of the hook slightly ahead of the rearmost tail windings. It will be easier to hold the wire end if pliers are used to start the ribbing's forward spiral. On a size 4 hook, leave about one-eighth inch between the turns. About five turns should bring the wire to the tie-off point one-quarter inch behind the eye. Clip both ends of the rib to a taper and tie down first at the rear with two or three turns of thread. Advance the tying thread by closely following the rib without crossing it. Tie off the front of the rib.

The next steps are most important and must be followed very closely. Take up the first strip of mylar, pull it tightly so that it stretches, center it on the rib, and follow the exact spiral of the rib forward. Tie off one full turn beyond the end of the rib. The second strip must also be pulled tightly so it will stretch. Make one full turn over the base of the tail behind the rib, and spiral the strip forward, following the ribbing but lying between the turns of ribbing. This strip fills in the body gaps and binds down the edges of the first strip. Take one full turn ahead of the rib end and tie off to complete this style of body.

V

A Boxful of Unique Flies

Midges, Leeches, Minnows, Shrimp, and Special Bass Flies

11

The Four-Phase Polymidge

by Dave Whitlock

Sooner or later if you fly-fish for trout or grayling in lakes or streams you will meet the midges. Usually you will be properly introduced to them by the most selective and rude large trout you've ever seen. Such an introduction creates instant frustration, since these trout all but ignore your company as their attention turns totally to the midges. Most of the truly outstanding trout fishermen I've known are reduced to playing a poor midge-rise game.

For a number of years I avoided midge-fishing, or did so only as a last resort. This was not because I didn't realize how seriously trout take them but because I could not seem to find the right technique to fish these situations. Then two things happened: I read *Selective Trout* and became acquainted with its authors, Carl Richards and Doug Swisher. As a result I became much more serious about aquatic insects and general aquatic entomology. To add to this new awareness I met a brilliant young flytyer and protégé of the No-Hackle Twins. His name is Bill Monoham, and he specializes in very small flies. Bill ties most of the Swisher-Richards patterns and has helped Carl and Doug make a lot of improvements on their patterns—second and third generations.

Bill sent me my first polypropylene-bodied midges. Before this I had tied most of my midge patterns with hard quill bodies or beaver belly underfur. I tested Bill's samples on Armstrong Spring Creek a year ago last August when a few big midging browns made my life miserable. The pattern was a green-and-brown size 24 pupa, that worked like magic on the very largest fish I saw (a 19¾-inch brown). After that I began using the Orvis Poly II developed by Dave McMann and Doug Swisher on all my midge bodies, with excellent results. (I asked Bill Monoham to do a midge section for this book but he was too busy with college and a full-time job. I hope to include him in our next issue.)

Midges, the common name for the family Chironomidae of the order Diptera, have a complete metamorphosis—larva, pupa, and adult. Since all three are extremely important to imitate, I've designed a polymidge pattern that can be tied to imitate these three stages. Simplicity, suggestiveness, and size are the three major factors in tying good midge imitations such as the Four-Phase fly. It is easy to add additional parts to the base larva pattern.

Since the midge adult rests on the water and commonly hovers above it, I've expanded the adult phase into two flies to fit both situations. However, based on observation and stomach-pumped contents, trout usually concentrate on the larva and pupa stages for most of their midge feeding. Even when trout are making showy rises or leaping clear of the water to snap buzzing midges, they are probably taking ten subsurface midges to one on or above the surface.

Body color seems to be secondary to size and method fished, but color selectivity does occur. The most common body colors I've seen are grayish dun, tan, olive, and black. Others are brown, red, green, cream, whitish, yellow, and orange. Occasionally I've seen a few bicolored midges such as one with a medium-olive abdomen and a dark-reddish-brown thorax, or a honey abdomen and brown thorax. Also, the pupa and adult have a somewhat darker thorax than abdomen. I've not witnessed this variation of shades so much in the larvae.

The wings are usually shorter than the body and tend to be light shades of gray, tan, or white. I prefer hen-hackle tips of dun, grizzly, and white. For the buzzing midge I use a shade of grizzly hackle that suggests a light or darker wing. Also, I use an oversize hackle similar to that used in the variant style of dry fly to create more flutter and hold the midge body off the water. I have not found it necessary to tail these adult forms to achieve flotation or realistic illusion.

For most situations I fish midges only when I can observe heavy feeding activity to them—that is, when I see the flies on the water and trout visibly working on them—or when the contents of a jump-caught trout reveal fresh or live larvae or pupae. Yes, I said live. Most of the time, if trout are feeding on subsurface life their throats and stomachs will contain these insects not yet killed by the digestive juices.

Since these active midges usually have some sort of countercurrent movement even if they do not totally overcome it or a surface wind, I fish most midge forms by casting downstream to the fish, using some sort of appropriate slack-line cast or mending. The least bit of drag will create this realistic countercurrent movement that is suggestive of active midges. The fluttering or buzzing midge pattern can also be pulled off the surface and skipped upstream similar to skating a caddis adult, but with less speed and distance.

I have chosen the Mustad 94843, 4x short, turned-up eye, 3x fine hook, so that a much smaller fly can be tied on a larger-gaped hook. This eliminates the loss of fine fish and makes it easier to tie smaller body sizes. If you do not care to use this style of hook my second choice would be a more standard Mustad 94842.

Dave's Four-Phase Polymidge

Hook: Mustad 94843, sizes 12 to 24
Thread: prewaxed 6/0 nylon, Danville's or Herb Howard's (color to match body)
Tail: none

Body Weight:	(larva only) small lead wire
Body:	Orvis Poly II dubbing or Fly Rite
Thorax:	Orvis Poly II dubbing or Fly Rite
Wings:	hen-hackle tips
Hackle:	grizzly or dun shades
Special Tools:	If available, use a tying vise that has pointed, thin jaws. Use an illuminating magnifying lamp or headpiece for easier tying of these tiny flies.

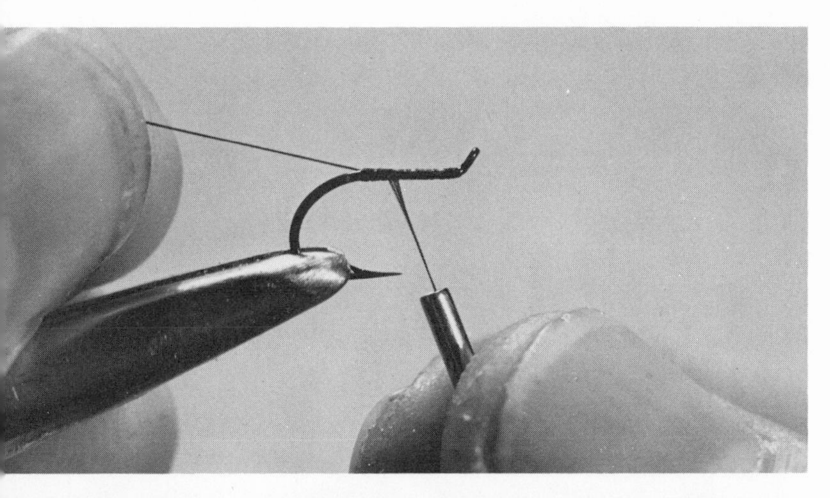

1. Hook and thread: Place hook in vise with maximum amount of bend exposed above the jaws, but do not clamp hook point and barb in vise jaws. Hook at this step can be tilted forward a bit to make forming the abdomen easier. Attach thread just behind hook eye and wrap entire shank and approximately one-half of hook's bend. (If you're doing the larva and it is to be fished deep, the shank should be weighted with a few turns of fine wire before the abdomen and thorax dubbing is applied.)

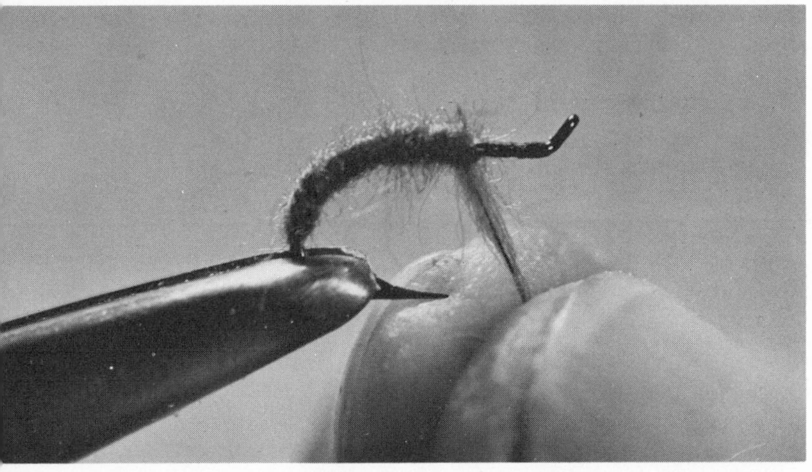

2. Abdomen (larva, pupa, and adult): Pull a pinch of Poly II dubbing from the Poly II sheet and tease its filaments into a dubbing mat. Spin on the tying thread. Begin dubbing the abdomen at the middle of the hook's bend, advancing forward while slightly increasing the thickness of the body dubbing as you move toward mid-shank. Stop dubbing at mid-shank. This forms the abdomen of all three stages of the midge. Be sure to keep abdomen rather skinny.

3. Larva thorax: Continue dubbing the same color Poly II toward hook eye without increasing the thickness of the thorax. Taper thorax down near the hook's eye. Stop dubbing just behind the hook eye, and with thread form a small, neat head.

4. Whip-finish the head, and the Polymidge larva is complete.

5. Pupa thorax: Mix an equal amount of the abdomen-color Poly II with a darker color Poly II. With this blend of Poly II spin on the thread and build the pupa thorax. Make this approximately twice the thickness of the abdomen. It should also be a little more roughly dubbed. Complete thorax directly behind hook eye, then with the tying thread finish off head, and whip-finish. Remove from vise.

6. With scissors, trim the top portion of the thorax to approximately the same size as the abdomen. With dubbing needle or bodkin pick a few fibers of the Poly II loose on underside and front of thorax. (This simulates the antennae, wing case, and legs of an emerging midge.) Pupa is complete.

7. Adult thorax and wings: Using the same light-and-dark Poly II blends as in step 5, dub a slightly enlarged thorax area, stopping approximately one-half the distance between the abdomen and hook eye. Select two hen hackles and cut tips of each one-half to two-thirds the length of the total length of midge body. Tie each wing, spent style, to right and left side of hook so that wings point slightly more toward abdomen than perpendicular to shank.

8. Adult thorax: With more of the two-color blend on thread, dub another small amount just in front of the wings. Dub this more roughly than first half of the thorax directly behind wings. Build a small head directly behind hook's eye with thread, and whip-finish. Pick out a few fibers to the front and sides of the wings to simulate legs and antennae.

9. Flying midge adult: Starting with step 7, select a cock hackle that is slightly larger than the size hackle called for in a given length of body, and attach to hook shank with tying thread, directly in front of the wings. With hackle pliers wrap hackle three or four turns, forming a collar of hackle fibers directly in front of the wings. Tie down hackle tips and trim excess. Finish fly by forming a small head behind hook eye. Whip-finish and coat head wraps of each type of midge with liquid vinyl cement or head cement.

12

My Friend the Leech

by Thom Green

Selecting a name for a new fly is exciting, for the name could well determine the fly's future and popularity. Tradition dictates that trout flies be given such glamorous names as Royal Coachman, Queen of the Waters, Parmachene Belle. If regal names do not adequately describe the fly or nymph, waggish names such as the Rat-Faced MacDougall or Mickey Finn may help propel the fly to fame. Attempting to attach either a glamorous or a clever name to a fly tied to imitate the slimy and unpleasant Hirudinea (leeches, to my philistine colleagues) is nearly impossible. "The Leech" is so unglamorous a name that it will probably not become a popular fly—but will be condemned to be fished by a few foolish, unlearned anglers who seek and catch *huge trout.*

Recognition that the leech was a staple in the diet of large trout in the alkaline waters of western lakes was for me a slow and prolonged process. Curiously, I have not found leeches among the contents of trout stomachs, even from fish caught on leech flies. This absence cannot logically be explained. For the most part, the stomachs of these trout contain the ever-present "freshwater shrimp," snails, and seasonal hatches of nymphs such as that of the wiggly damselfly. That these trout which grow up to more than twenty pounds feed on "shrimp" is further attested by their brilliant red-orange flesh. Numerous postmortems suggested that I concentrate my fly-tying efforts in duplicating "shrimp." Tie "shrimp" flies I did. Catch trout I did!

Despite the cocktail quality of my flies, the trophy fish invariably was caught by an uncouth individual fishing an elongated and dark monstrosity of a fly, usually a woolyworm. I now know that the absurd and ugly flies which were snagging the biggest fish from the waters of such highly productive lakes as Henry's and Duck probably looked like a leech to the fish.

At many waters famous for big trout the "hot" fly is probably a leech counterfeit recognized as such by the trout if not by the angler. A number of years ago, king-size rainbows were being taken from Wyoming's Lake De Smet on a streamer tied with black and red hackle for wings. The long brown Cary Special continues to be the fly for big rainbows in the lakes of interior British Columbia. For years, the top fly at Henry's Lake in Idaho has been an elongated hair-fly appropriately named the Thunder Bug. Far to the west, in the lee of the rugged Sierra Nevada, fishermen have extracted big cutthroat and rainbows from the overly alkaline waters of Pyramid Lake—the fly, a big black woolyworm. In Montana, Georgetown Lake has been dredged nearly weedfree with large dark woolyworms, and during the mid-fifties, Duck Lake, snuggled close against the Canadian border, yielded unbelievably large rainbows to anglers heaving large woolyworms tied on No. 2 4X long hooks. At Duck Lake I first gleaned an inkling of what the "long darkies" were trying to tell me.

John Walker of Great Falls routinely won the annual fly-fishing contests with monsters yanked from Duck Lake on a fly reported as the "Walker Leech." I wrote to Walker asking, in effect, "What in hell's name is a Walker Leech?" By return mail I received two big brown flies and a letter of instruction on how to fish them. Walker's letter was very complete, both as to the natural history of the leech and the fishing techniques for leech imitations. Ten years of study and observation have added little to the knowledge presented in that letter. Unfortunately, the Walker Leech casts poorly; I caught fish on it, but the knots in my leader caused me to discard the fly.

Shortly after my Walker Leech experience, E. N. Pearson of Provo, Utah, came up with a brown woolyworm with a tail of red marabou; he also called it a leech. Pearson usually tied his leech on a No. 6 3X long hook. His fly was, and still is, very popular at Henry's Lake. For several years, I fished Henry's with what I consider to be an improvement on the Pearson version. I trimmed the palmer-tied hackle and substituted a brown marabou tail for the red, leaving the tail a little longer and cutting it square. The modification performed well for me and a number of fishing friends who used the fly regularly. During this phase of my "leeching," I noticed that a group of fishermen from Nampa, Idaho, were catching more than their fair share of big fish with a leech formed by wrapping a long shank hook with brown mohair. Clearly, the mohair is superior to the chenille body. I combined the mohair body and the marabou tail and have found the result excellent. I have fished this pattern in Idaho, Wyoming, and Colorado with marked success. Friends report excellent catches with the fly from waters throughout the West.

Fly-fishermen tend to try a new pattern only when the old reliables do not interest the fish. In this regard, I have an amusing tale to tell on my good friend Nick Lyons. Nick had been using the chenille-bodied leech and had caught fish. So when I gave him one of the new, improved leech patterns, he was noticeably reluctant to give it a try. Following the morning's fishing, I dropped by Nick's cabin for a cup of coffee and a report on the fly. Nick told of catching several fish on the old leech pattern, tied with chenille, but reportedly could not get a strike on the new version. I chided him on not giving the fly a fair trial. Nick told me he had to leave at noon the next day, but for me he would fish only the new leech. I was out on the lake that morning and didn't return until after he had left. Several days later I received a postcard reporting that he had done very well on the new leech. The phrase "very well" appears to be modest. My wife sat on the cabin porch and through binoculars counted twenty-seven fish that Nick caught and released during that mid-morning hour of fishing. At Henry's Lake, twenty-seven fish come to about eighty-one pounds of trout! The episode probably motivated the request for this chapter.

Besides catching fish, the leech has an added attribute which places it high on my list—it is simple and easy to tie.

The Leech

Hook:	sizes 2 through 10, 3X long. At Henry Lake, I use size 6/3XL
Thread:	Herb Howard's prewaxed black, brown, tan, or olive green to match the color of the leech
Body:	mohair dyed with one part olive and one part dark brown obtained by mixing equal parts of Rit dye. Other leech colors that work well are black, olive, brown, dark brown mixed with gold dye, and magenta
Tail:	marabou, same color as mohair
Hackle:	soft, same color as above

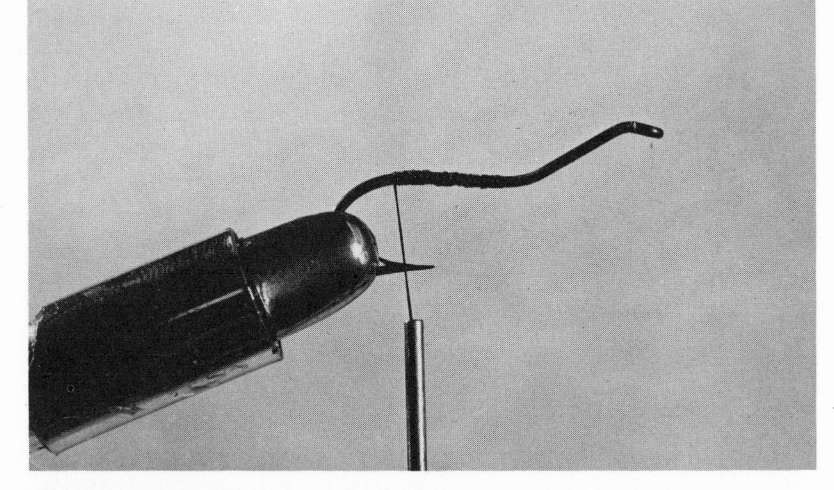

1. Place hook in vise and bend the shank as shown so that the eye of the hook is horizontal. This step is optional; in my opinion, the bend adds to the appearance of the fly.

2. Tie in the marabou tail as illustrated. Be sure to use enough marabou, since it decreases in bulk when wet.

3. Tie in mohair and let hang. Wrap rear third of hook with lead wire approximately .025 inches in diameter, as shown.

4. Wrap the mohair heavily at the rear and taper it toward the eye as in the photograph. Leeches have broad, flat tails and small, narrow heads. (Come to think about it, this describes many fly-fishermen.)

5. Tie in the soft-fibered hackle just behind the head. Go easy on the hackle, as a little is too much.

6. Cut the tail straight. It should measure about two-thirds the length of the body, as shown. Tie off and fish it.

I can add little to John Walker's fishing instructions, so will relay them in my own words. The leech is a lazy fellow who undulates very slowly through his environment. To imitate him we must fish slowly. Walker uses a floating line, but I prefer a slow-sinking one. The leech must be fished more slowly than a medium- or fast-sinking line will permit. The retrieve is about right if pulled slightly slower than you feel is too slow. The slow pull causes the marabou tail to straighten behind the fly. The separating pause permits the rear-weighted leech to sink slowly, letting the marabou tail trail upward. Thus, the slow pull-and-pause reasonably duplicates the slowly oscillating, monotonous progress of the leech.

It may be well to describe the mechanics of the slow retrieve. Keep in mind that large trout more often than not take a fly with the gusto of an aged sucker with pyorrhea. In deference to this easy take, it is imperative that the rod be aligned exactly with the line. (These instructions are for a right-handed angler; if left-handed, reverse the procedure.) The right index finger acts as a line-hold or brake clamping the line against the rod handle. The left or pulling hand must be in line with the rod and the fly line. The straight pull of the left must be along the extended line of the rod axis. The right index finger releases the line with the straight pull of the left hand and clamps the line against the cork in the pause that separates the pull. Inexperienced anglers tend to pull downward and to the left from the right index finger. This angle, no matter how slight, makes the soft strike more difficult to detect and delays the setting of the hook. Again, keep the pull along the line of extension of the fly line and rod. Fish being creatures of nature often resort to such perverse tactics as striking between pulls. If the angler carefully observes the few inches of fly line from rod tip to water while retrieving, he can detect the imperceptible twitch caused by a trout taking between pulls. Make certain that your leader tippet is strong enough to withstand the attrition of continued casting of the big weighted fly and the yanking slash of a big fish.

The witching hours for fishing the leech are the last hour of darkness through the first hour after sunup in the morning, and again in the evening from sunset through the first hours of darkness. I cannot remember not catching fish while fishing the leech during these periods.

The leech is sometimes effective during daylight hours, as Nick's experience shows. Occasionally, during midday the leech is more effective when fished relatively fast. But by and large, fish the witching hours—and slowly.

Leech fishing can be expensive. Tackle, travel, lodging, food, and beverage costs are about the same as for using other fly patterns—but the leech might well cost you brutal taxidermy bills as well.

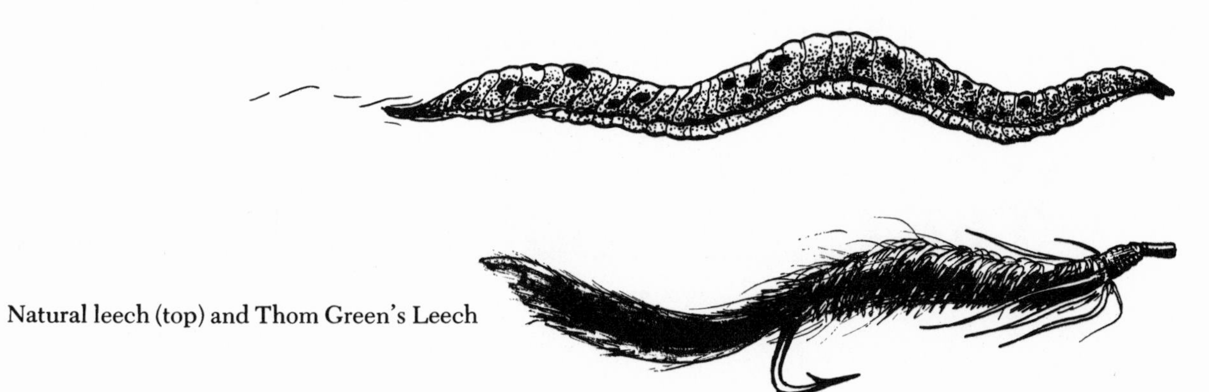

Natural leech (top) and Thom Green's Leech

13

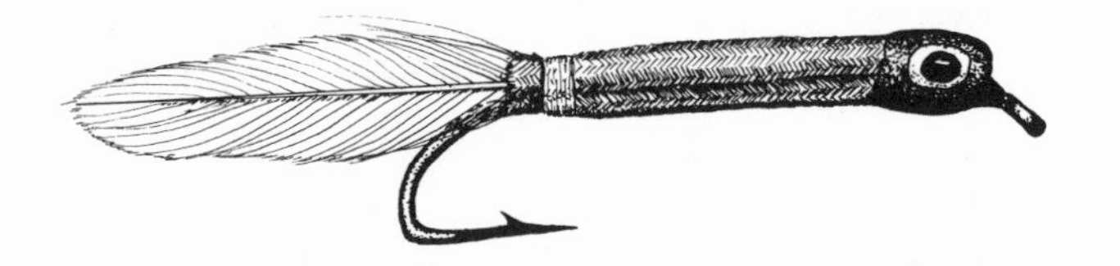

The Quill-bodied Mylar Minnow

by Whygin Argus

A very simple minnow for largemouth bass and other surface-feeding fishes can be made from a segment cut from a quill shaft. If you think sleeve-mylar streamers are effective, try this pattern imitating a topwater baitfish. Since it also casts very easily and will float forever, it is a lethal miniature plug for the fly-rodder.

Hook:	size 8 streamer
Thread:	Herb Howard's prewaxed red or black, then Dyno transparent thread as shown (optional)
Tail:	white saddle hackles or bucktail. Also tie in some fine strands of silver or gold mylar (optional).
Body:	length of quill shaft from peacock, goose, or other large bird
Outer Body:	sleeve of silver or gold mylar tubing
Head (optional):	painted eyes
Shoulder dressing (optional):	hair or hackle

By elaborating on the basic steps shown above, any flytyer can imitate the topwater baitfish of fresh- and salt water, such as silversides, killies, and spottail shiners. The basic body can also be used as a permanently floating base for a sinkproof mudler, grasshopper, and other patterns.

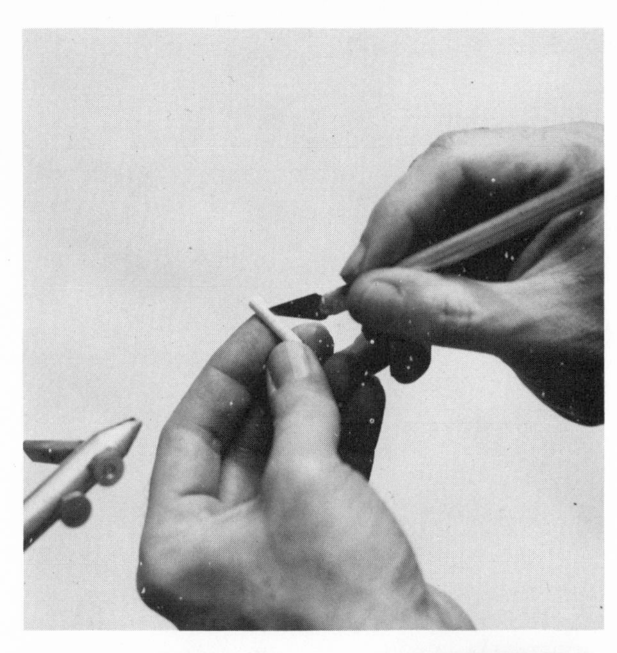

1. Cut off a segment of quill from the shaft. The segment should be slightly shorter than the length of the shank of the hook. Cut a slit halfway through the length of the rough "underside" side of quill.

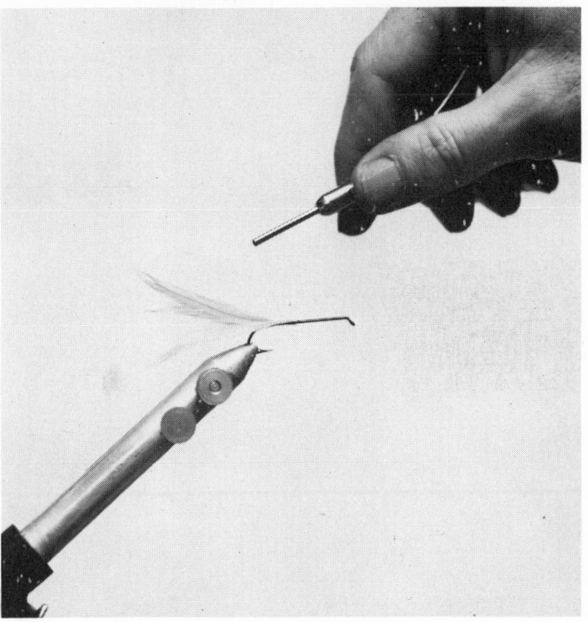

2. Tie in saddle hackle tails, then spiral the tying thread forward, up and down the shank. Coat windings with fingernail polish or clear lacquer.

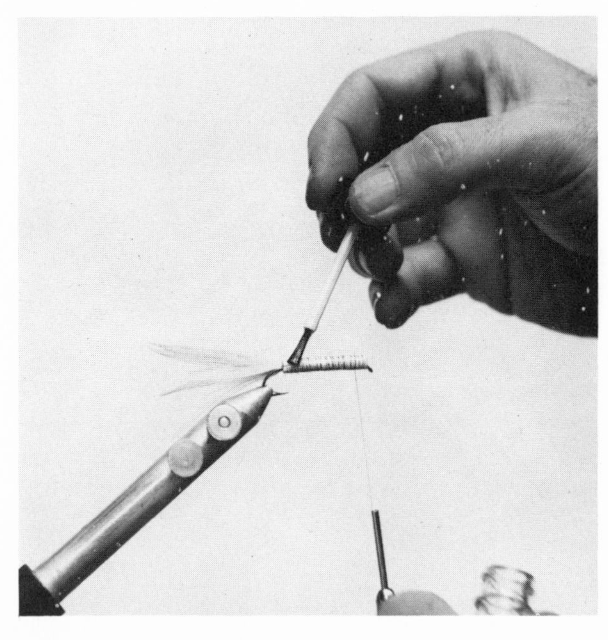

3. Place quill segment on top of shank and gently press down before securing with wraps of the tying thread. Coat wraps with fingernail polish. Tie off the Herb Howard thread.

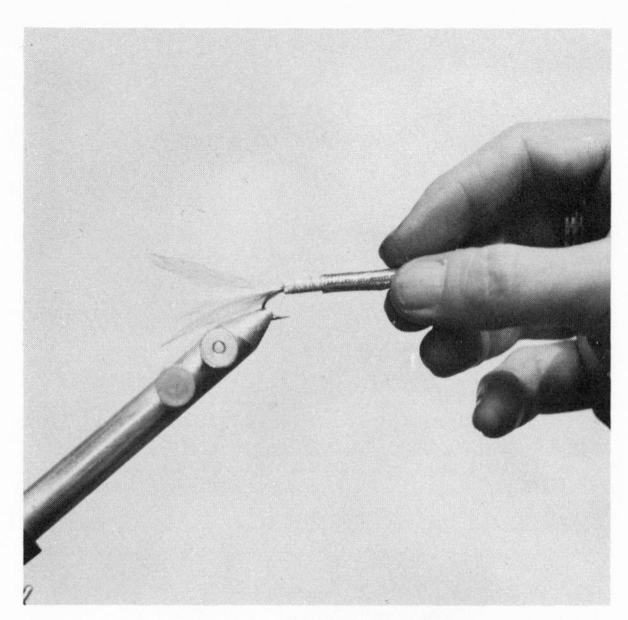

4. Tie in Dyno transparent thread just to rear of quill segment, then slide a length of mylar tubing over quill.

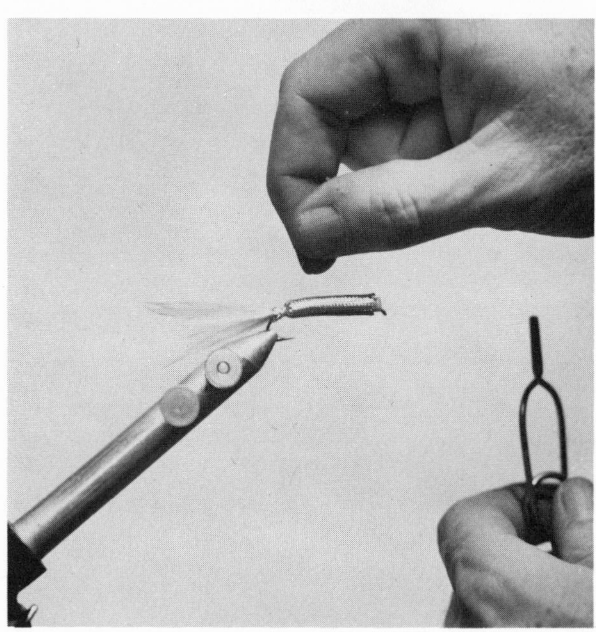

5. Secure mylar at tail with transparent thread. Tie off separately at tail and head, or spiral forward to head, as shown here, before tying off.

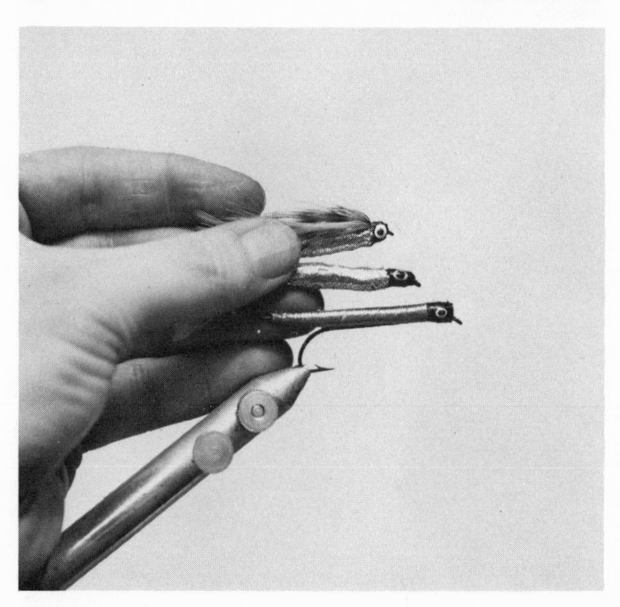

6. Eyes and shoulder dressings (optional): Upper two shown here have inner bodies of pressed deer-body hair. I tied them to compare with the quill-bodied minnows. They are not nearly as good—they take more time to tie, weigh more, and absorb water with heavy use. *Photos by R. Hoebermann*

14

The Matuka Streamer

by Dave Whitlock

Let me introduce or reintroduce you to a unique and effective type of streamer fly—the Matuka, a version of which Harry Darbee ties for salmon. This fly is one of the most dynamic styles of streamers ever conceived but has too long waxed and waned between obscurity and popularity.

I first learned of the style from a wonderful friend and great flytyer, Leo Michl of Decatur, Illinois. Leo sent me a Xerox copy of the streamer as it appeared in print at least six or eight years ago. I was not taken by its look then, and perhaps others as unimaginative as myself felt the same way; so the style didn't catch on in American flytying the way the bucktail, marabou, or standard hackle-wing streamer have. Then I was reintroduced to it, first by Dave Inks of Creative Sports Enterprises, then a few months later by Doug Swisher. This time it stuck, and I began to learn its tying requirements and many virtues. Today it is my favorite feather-wing streamer style, not to mention my first choice of streamer style, in my fly boxes.

Why? It comes closer to giving me a perfect minnow imitation than any other style I've ever used, tied, or observed under water—and the fish totally agree, if my catches are any true reflection of their tastes.

The Matuka is a style, not necessarily a pattern. To the best of my knowledge, it was originated and popularized in New Zealand, though the style is also used often in England and Australia. It is the unique method of marrying the hackle wing to the body that creates this fly and makes it one of a kind among the best streamer styles.

The winging method creates the illusion of very realistic form true to the actual shape, form, and action of a small fish. Most streamer styles feature a wing and body joined only at the head, and as these are fished, separation occurs between these two major parts of the streamer. This splitting is apparent when viewed under water as the fly is paused or dead-drifted. The Matuka does not do this, and thus holds its true form. Another fine characteristic, especially for us herky-jerky casters, is the almost foulproofed feather-wing. When I fish standard bucktail or hackle-wing streamers I sometimes average less than 50 percent of my retrieves without the wing being wrapped doglegged aroud the hook's bend. The Matuka eliminates all but a small percentage of such problems.

Tying the Matuka wing requires a little practice to master, but it is well worth the effort. Today I tie all my spine feather-wings Matuka style, including such unusual patterns as the Spuddler and Sculpin. I've even been experimenting with marabou wings with a Matuka twist.

The pattern of Matuka I've included here is basic; it will introduce you to its wing-forming method but not necessarily "the" Matuka pattern. I suggest that after you master Matuka winging you apply it to all your favorite streamer patterns. I'm particularly fond of using badger, furnace, grizzly, or cree hackles. It also seems that streamers tied with thickly dubbed bodies are most effective. Besides being *the* streamer style for trout, I consider them even more effective for bass and saltwater species.

Matuka Streamer

Hook:	Mustad 79580 1/0 through 12, or any 4X long streamer hook
Weight:	lead wire
Thread:	Nymo Size A yellow (color should match body for other patterns)
Rib:	size 18 oval gold tinsel, or gold wire
Body:	light yellow Orlon wool dubbing
Throat:	red Orlon wool dubbing
Collar:	two soft, webby, dark, badger neck hackles
Wing:	four well-marked, dark, badger neck hackles

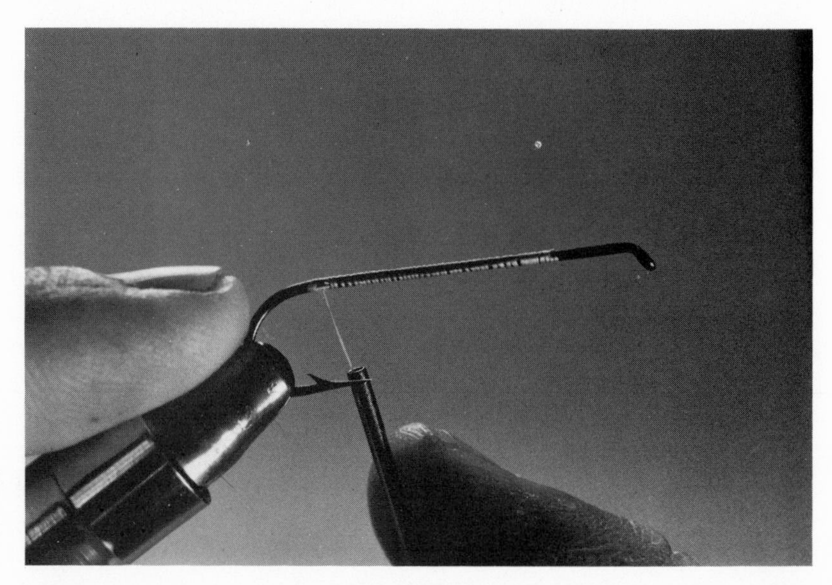

1. Place streamer hook securely in tying vise (size 4 is illustrated) so that point and barb are exposed. The shank should be parallel with tying table, or horizontal. Wrap rear three-fourths of hook shank with tying thread, working from front to bend of hook.

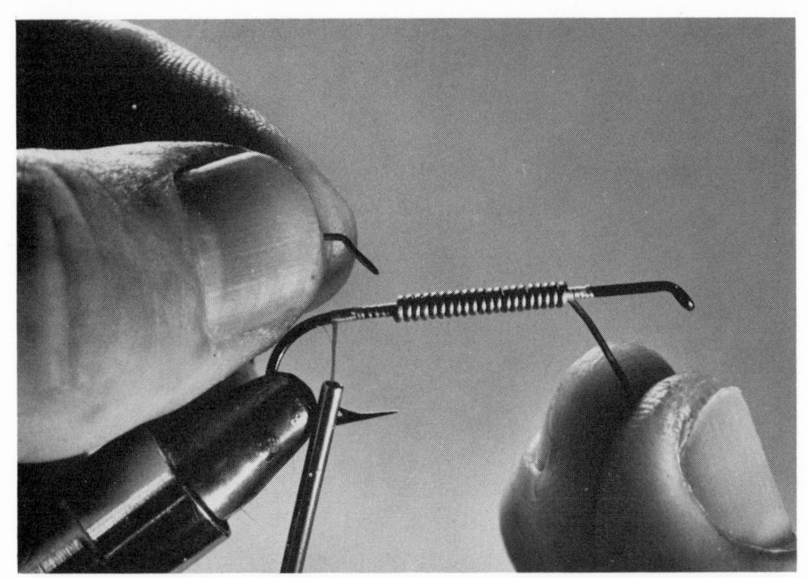

2. In center half of hook, wrap twelve to twenty turns of lead wire (optional, but recommended for good fly performance). Pull and stretch both free ends of lead to effect a taper on shank at the first and last lead turn.

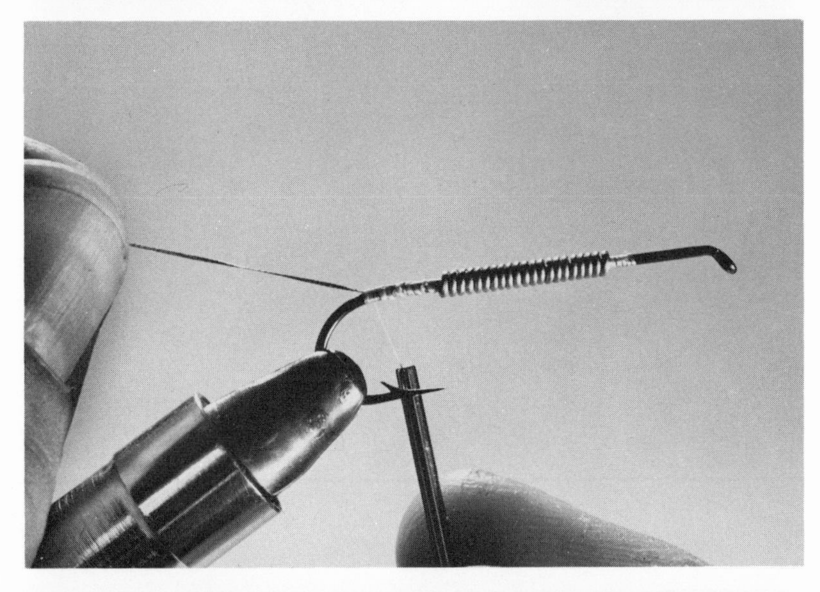

3. Cut a 3- to 5-inch piece of oval tinsel or light wire and tie it to rear portion of hook shank behind the lead wraps, with free end point to rear of hook. If vise is equipped with material clip, place rib material in it to avoid its becoming entangled during dubbing of body, etc.

4. With a small brush or bodkin, coat the wrapped shank with some sticky, slow-drying cement. I prefer Pliobond thinned with acetone for this step. It cements the lead to the hook, rustproofs the hook, and provides a receptive bond for the Orlon dubbing. Spin Orlon dubbing on thread and from rear forward wrap a tapering but rather thick body. Stop at a point one-quarter of the shank length from hook eye. Front taper should be more extreme than rear taper.

5. Spin onto tying thread a very small amount of red Orlon wool and wrap over a small area of the yellow body next to front part of hook shank. This red dubbing creates a realistic throat or gill effect on completed streamer, so commonly apparent in crippled or dying minnows.

6. Select two matched right and left pairs of very soft, wide, well-marked cock-neck hackles. These should be exactly twice the length of hook's shank, or just slightly shorter. With bright sides of each pair out, tie butt tips of each pair on top of hook shank immediately behind the hook eye; left side, then right side. Hackle pairs must match in length and overbody position to be right for Matuka wing—observe closely the accompanying photo. To butt tie-down area, put a small drop of fast-setting head cement.

7. When cement is set, with your left thumb and index finger pull wing hackles taut. With right index finger and thumb pull topside hackle fibers to a 90° angle to hackle stem along area of hook's bend forward to butts. This prepares feathers for forming the Matuka wing.

8. Still holding the wing taut, pull it directly down over the streamer body, taking care to keep hackle straight and sides vertical. Starting in front of hook's bend, begin to wrap the rib (oval tinsel at the end) with your right hand, over the wing and around the body. Great care should be taken to go between the upright hackle fibers rather than over them. With each spiraling rib wrap, pull rib down very tightly into body and hackle stem . . . and keep pulling the hackle tips with your left hand . . . until at least three wraps are accomplished. Continue until total body is ribbed and tie down rib material at butt area of wing. Trim excess wing.

9. Closely examine the wing (in or out of vise) to see it has remained on top of the hook, broadside, and is indeed bound tightly to the body.

10. Just ahead of wing base, tie one or two hackles on shank with convex or bright sides out. Wrap around shank directly and closely in front of wing. Tie down hackles and trim off excess hackle-tip points.

You can now see the need for keeping the hackle pulled taut, for positioning the fibers up, and ribbing very tightly so that the wing will be durable and tight on the body. Chenille, wool yarn, or mylar over curon also make excellent bodies for the Matuka-style streamer. The feathers used in the Matuka wings can also be other than cock hackle. Hen hackle, pheasant, turkey, duck, and similar materials all work well for certain patterns where a wider, more opaque outline is desired.

11. With tying thread build a small, tight, neat head, and apply whip finish. Cut away thread excess. Then, after step 12, finish head with varnish, epoxy paint, or head cement.

12. With your bodkin point or a needle, carefully pick out all hackle fibers that were accidentally bound down during the ribbing (Step 8). The object in forming a good Matuka wing is to effect a thick, even wing over body that is similar to a small fish's back and extended dorsal fin. Therefore, the more hackle fibers that can be freed, the better this streamer looks. I also make every attempt to free the bottom hackle fibers if possible.

15

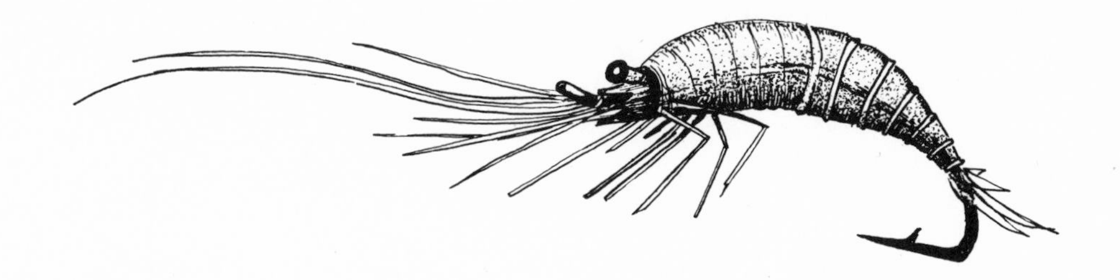

The Transparent Glass or Grass Shrimp

by Robert H. Boyle

Few species of invertebrates are more enticing to fishes in brackish and salt water than shrimp. This also holds true when shrimp are found in fresh water. There are a surprising number of freshwater species, such as *Macrobrachium ohione,* which occurs in the southeastern, southern, and central United States, and *Palaemonetes kadiakensis,* which ranges from lakes Ontario, Erie, and Michigan down into the Mississippi basin.

The realistic shrimp tie described here is modeled after the transparent glass or grass shrimp, *Palaemonetes pugio,* abundant in the brackish lower Hudson River and the tributary Croton River. *Pugio* attains a maximum length of two inches and so closely resembles several other members of this genus in fresh- and salt water that experts have become confused identifying the various species. Although this makes for bad biology, it simplifies fly-tying, because this pattern should then serve in almost any situation where members of the genus are to be found. Moreover, since some very young crayfish lack coloration, this transparent pattern can also serve to represent them.

Originally I devised this shrimp pattern for striped bass and white perch in the Croton River, but it has gone on to catch other species as well, including weakfish, smallmouth and largemouth bass, yellow perch, Atlantic mackerel, brown trout, rainbows, and some big bluefish, which would tear the hell out of it when they weren't hitting anything else. When I was up in Quebec last year on an Atlantic salmon story for *Sports Illustrated,* I gave a shrimp tie to Pete Dubé, a guide in Matapedia. Afterward, Pete wrote that he and Ted Caldwell, another guide, went fishing at the Four-Mile Pool of the Assemetquagan. "When we arrived, Ted fished the pool with a wet fly while I went down to the next pool. About two hours later, knowing that Ted had gone further downriver to try for a few trout, I decided to return to the Four-Mile Pool while waiting for him. I worked over the pool with some wet flies. No luck, except for a few trout following. I then tried a dry fly, Grey Wulff. On the fourth cast, a salmon came for it and missed. I tried over and over again but no results. At about 10:30 A.M., Ted returned, and as I was closing my tackle box for the day he noticed the shrimp and asked, 'What the hell is that?' So I explained. 'Did you ever try it?' he asked. 'No,' I said, 'but I will now.'

"On the first cast that covered the water above the salmon, he came up and took it wickedly. I played the fish for about thirty-five minutes and then landed it. A nice fresh twelve-and-a-half-pounder."

Since then other anglers have used the shrimp fly with success on Atlantic salmon in Norway and Iceland.

Several years before, I was in Los Angeles covering a track meet for the magazine. I was tying some shrimp in my hotel room (and early crude patterns at that) when George Long, who was to photograph the meet at the Forum, arrived. It turned out that George was an enthusiastic fly-fisherman, so I gave him one. I would have forgotten about the incident except that I later received this excited letter: "I was on a fishing story on the Colorado River just below Hoover Dam," George wrote. "We were photographing Virgil Ward, who has a fishing TV show and several fishing championships. They used everything, bombers, Flat Fish, spinners, poppers, and cheese—nothing would work. They were talking about the fish feeding on freshwater shrimp. I told them about your shrimp. Virgil tried the one I had and caught a couple of two-and-a-half to three-pound rainbows—before a rock caught the shrimp. It worked so well, I hoped we could get a few more from you . . ."

When I first started tying this pattern, I used successively lighter-test monofilament lines to build up the body. This was exhausting work, more of a construction job than tying, and I am grateful to Ralph Graves, an ardent and skilled Westchester flytyer, for putting me on to the clear plastic sheeting that winds quickly, easily, and effectively around the hook shank. This medium- or lightweight plastic sheeting, which I cut into two-foot-long strips about 1/32 of an inch wide with a pair of double cutters, is sold in hardware and notion stores under different brand names such as Clorpane and K-Clear. The sheets are ordinarily used to cover typewriters, lampshades, and other office or household articles against dust. It makes a marvelous transparent body, not just for shrimp but for streamers imitating minnow fry and some other patterns that I dream about, including a quick-sinking "see-through" muddler.

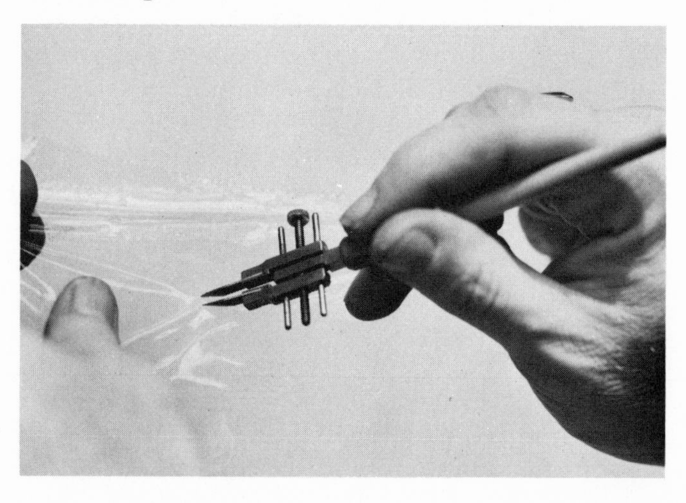

Using double cutters to get strips of clear plastic for transparent shrimp. *Photo by R. Hoebermann*

The Glass Shrimp

Hook:	Mustad Wide-Gap bait hook, turned-up ball-eye, bronzed, slightly reversed, sizes 2 through 12
Thread:	Dyno transparent sewing thread (masks beautifully into the pattern)
Tail:	clear quill cut from end stub of a goose, peacock, or herring-gull feather primary or tail, scissored to fan shape. (Quill is easy to cut and shape if first soaked in lukewarm water. Lately I have also been using scales from large shad netted in the Hudson, an idea I got from *How to Tie Flies for Trout,* by the gifted English flytyer Harry G. McClelland, who died in 1898 when only in his early twenties.)*
Body:	clear plastic strips wound round the shank and secured in place with Dyno transparent thread
Segmentation:	fine silver or gold mylar
Small Antenna:	five polar-bear hairs, tapered ends forward
Long Antenna:	two hog bristles, tapered ends forward
Lips, Plates, and Rostrum (Nose):	clear quill scissored to shape
Eyes:	two bulbous ends of a chicken or duck feather tipped with black Pla enamel or lacquer
Legs:	the butt ends of the small antenna
Pleopods (the small swimming legs between main legs and tail):	polar-bear hair tied in and splayed. (If I seem to go heavy on polar bear, it is because I laid in a modest stock several years ago when it was easily obtained. Imitation polar-bear hair, monofilament, or whisks of white hackle may be used instead.)

Incidentally, legs of shrimps or nymphs can be permanently crimped to shape by careful use of a heated needle. I lash a needle to a small paintbrush stick, heat it over the front burner on the stove, and then when the red glow has subsided, judiciously touch the tip of the needle to the part of the leg I want to bend. This technique works well with hog bristle, mono, javelina, and some hackle stems, but it takes practice to get the right touch. A final note: If the shrimp shown in color appears to have a greenish-yellowish glow, it is because I first tied in several spirals of DuPont's fluorescent gold Stren, fourteen-pound test, before winding on the clear plastic body. In fact, I have gone so far as to lay in a length of dyed-red mono so that the shrimp had a stomach and an intestinal tract.

Because of its weight, the larger-sized shrimp can be awkward to cast. However, its weight causes it to sink quickly. It is best fished with short, quick jerks on the retrieve.

*G.E.M. Skues, using the *nom de pêche* of "Val Conson," wrote that "in him the art of fly dressing has lost . . . probably the most prolific, ingenious, and inventive intellect of the century."

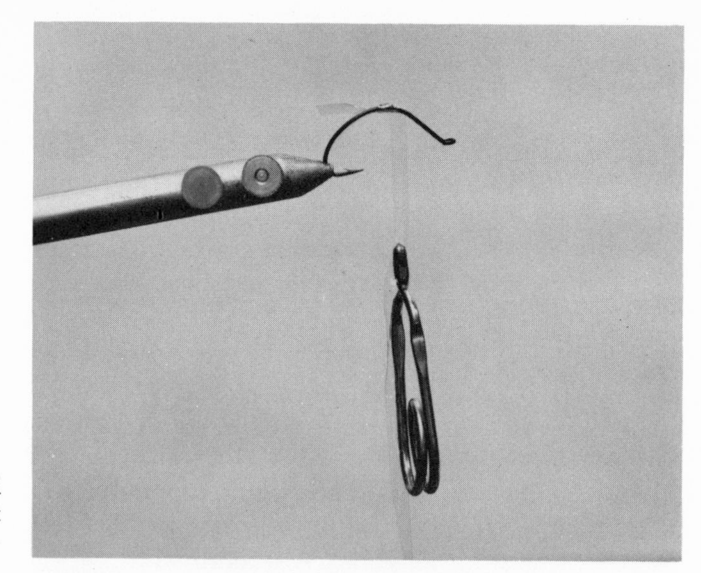

1. Lay a strip of clear plastic sheeting on the shank and secure it, just as you would tying thread, by giving it three or four wraps over itself.

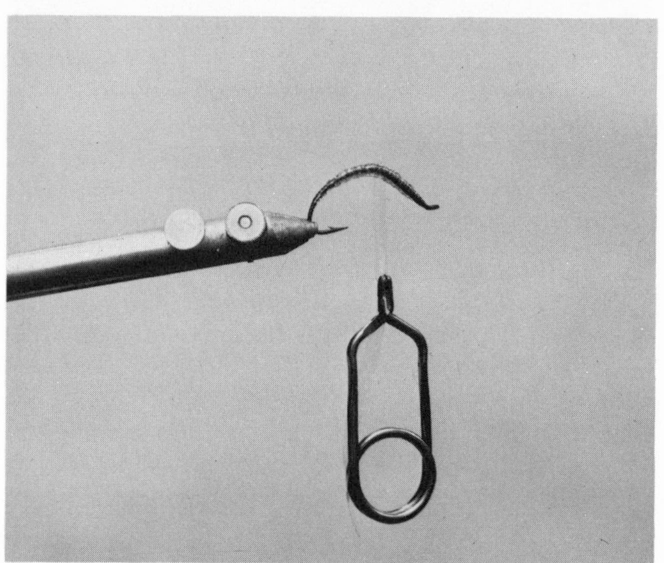

2. Spiral the remainder of the strip up and down the shank so that the body is less toward the tail than the head.

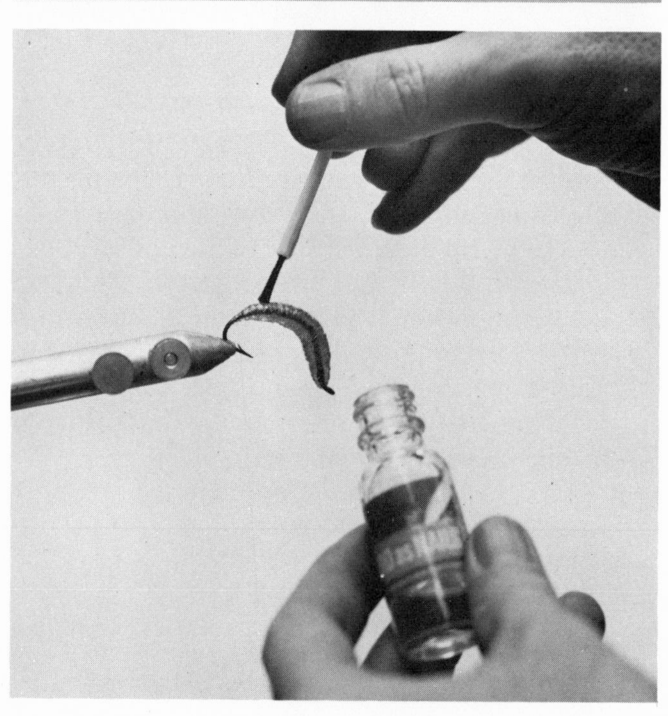

3. When the body is the right size and proportion, secure the last turn of plastic by tying on the transparent Dyno sewing thread, then use clear fingernail polish (I favor "Hard as Nails" brand) as an overall coating. This not only adds to the transparency and luster of the body but also gives the body a slightly tacky surface so that the mylar can be spiraled forward without slipping.

4. Tie in a fine strand of silver mylar at the tail and spiral forward two-thirds of the way toward the head seven to nine times with nice even spacings. Clip off mylar on the underside or belly after securing it in place with Dyno thread. By cutting off mylar here, the end of the segmentation will not show on finished shrimp because the legs and pleopods will hide it.

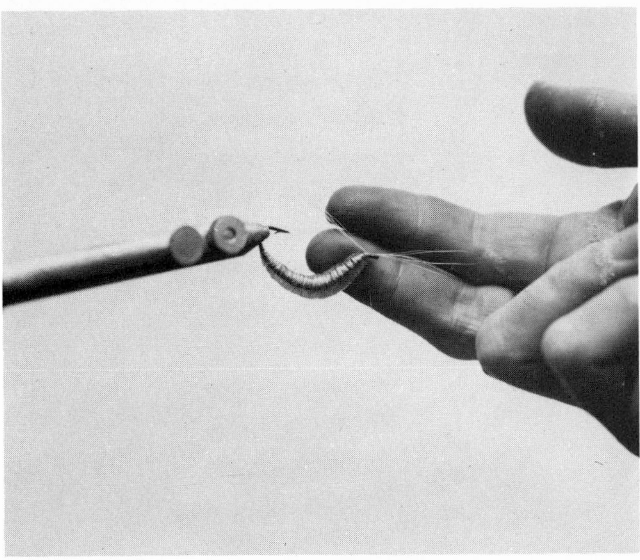

5. Turn shrimp upside down in vise. Bring tying thread forward to eye of hook and tie in five polar-bear hairs as shown. Do not cut off the butt ends; they will serve later as legs. Lacquer the thread with fingernail polish.

6. Tie in the lip plates so that the two plates extend forward from the eye of the hook. Lacquer them with fingernail polish.

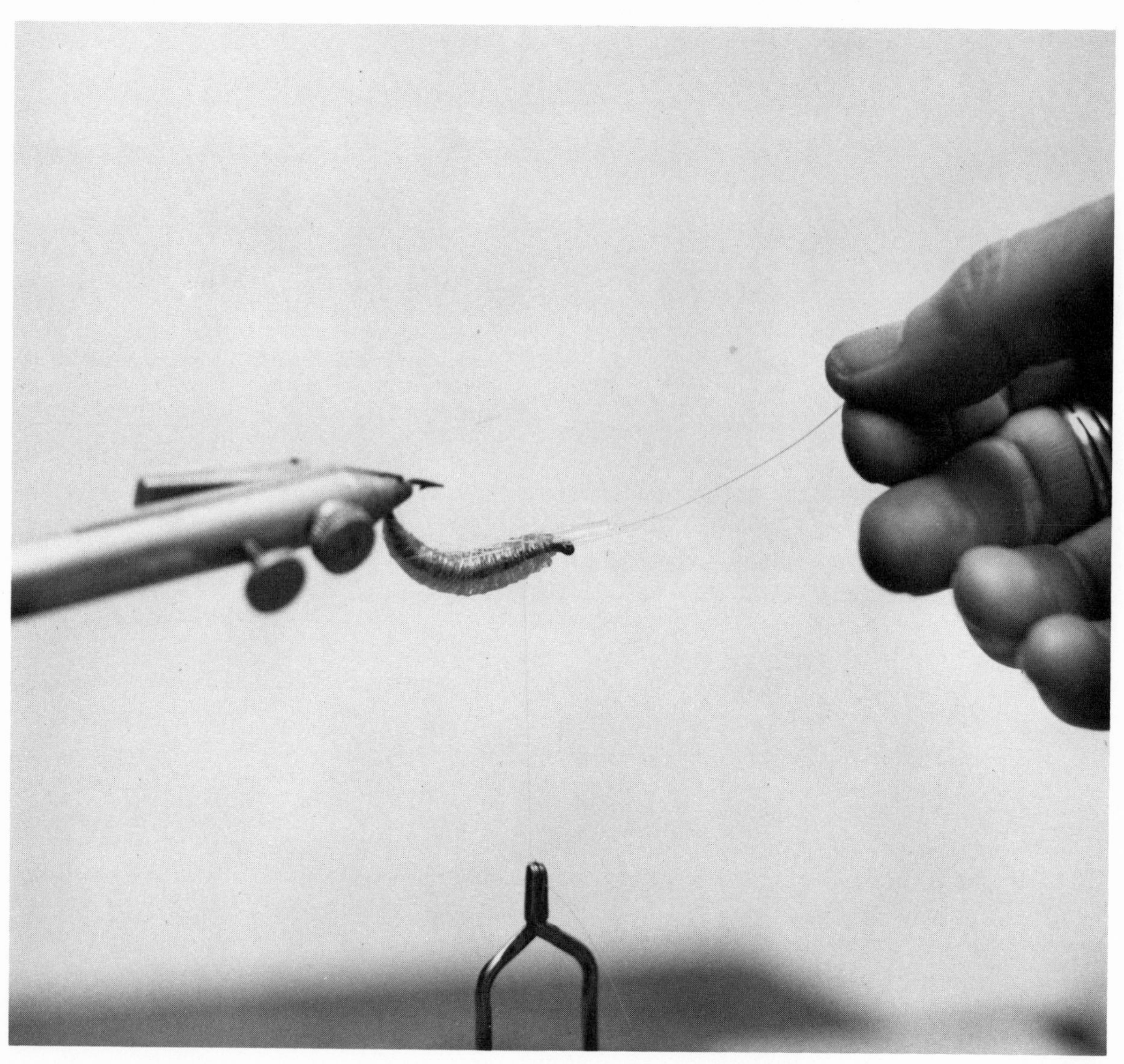

7. Tie in two hog bristles on top of lip plates so that tapered ends extend well forward of eye of hook. If you wish to flare or curl the bristles, draw them quickly between your thumbnail and forefinger.

8. Turn shrimp right side up and tie in the clear stub ends of two hackles on both sides of head. When secured, clip off excess stems and lacquer with fingernail polish.

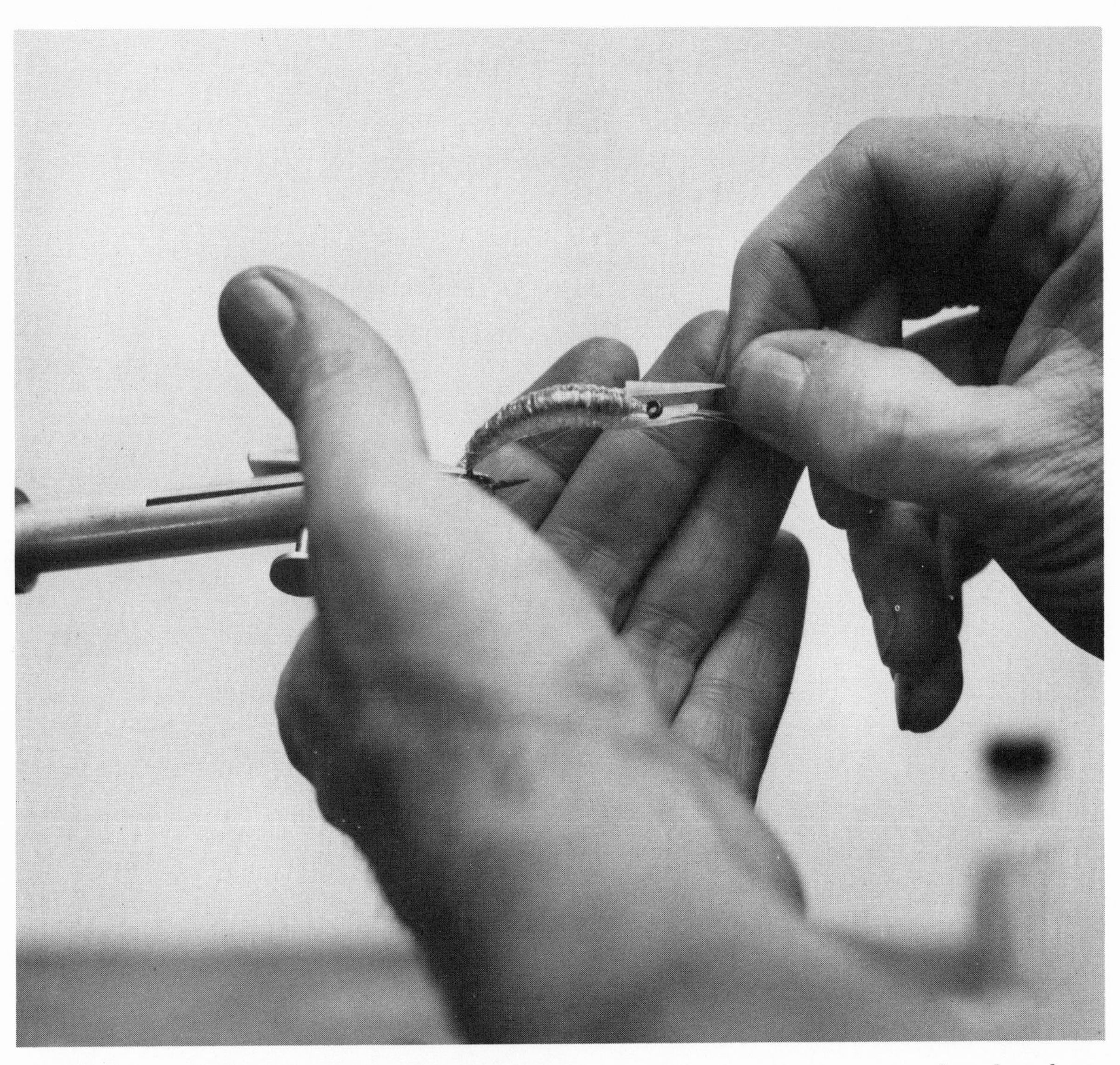

9. Tie in the rostrum or nose, shaped as shown, between eyes so that pointed tip of rostrum lies on gap between the two lip plates. Use fingernail polish to cover the wrappings of tying thread around the rostrum and eye.

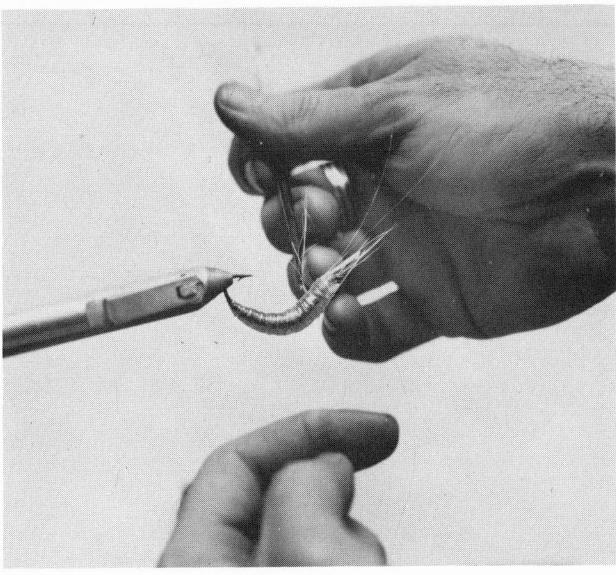

10. Turn shrimp upside down in vise and spiral the tying thread to make butt ends of polar-bear hairs stand erect as legs.

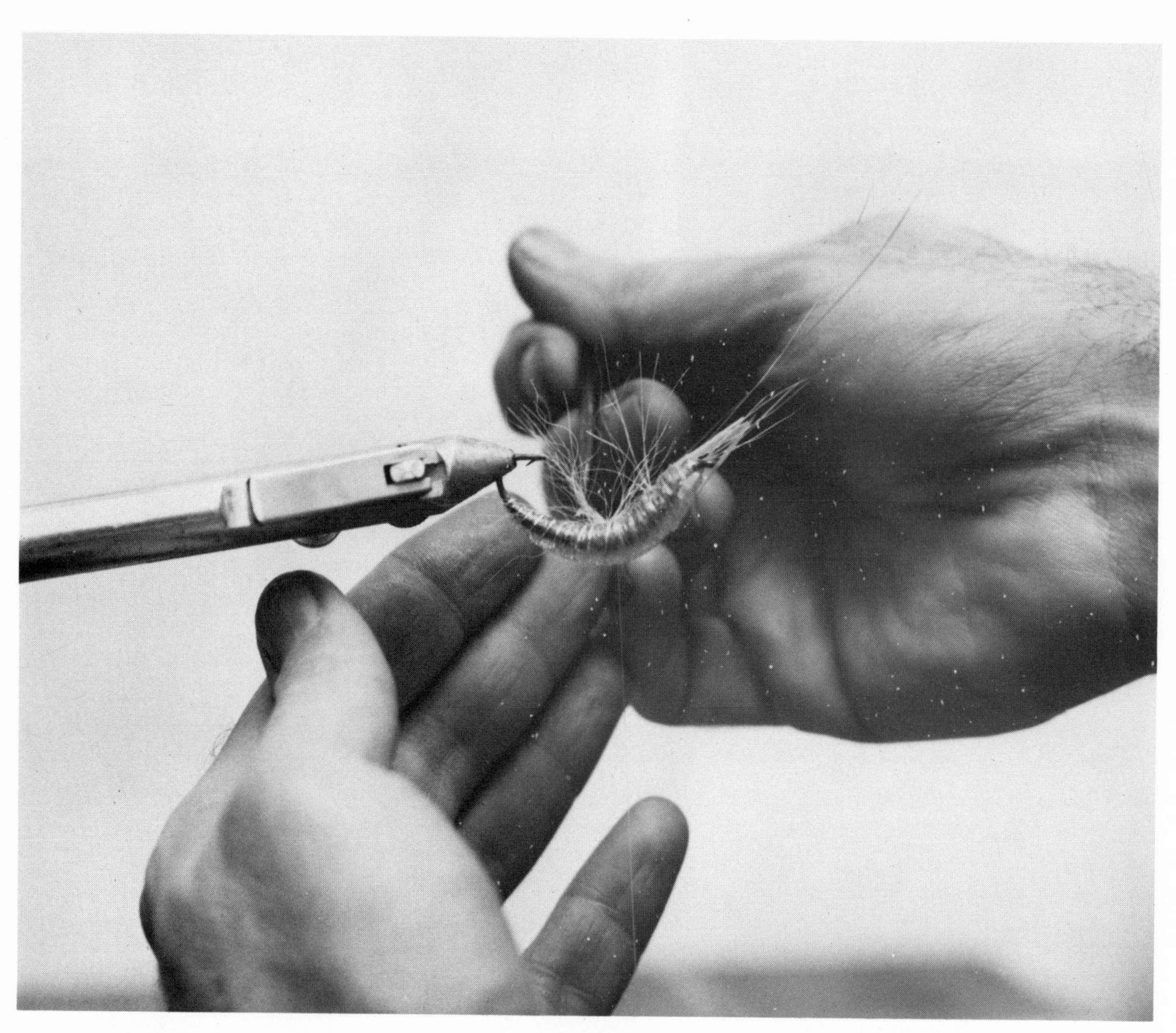

11. Tie in a small bunch of polar-bear hair as the pleopods in the midsection so that they flare upward between the legs and tail.

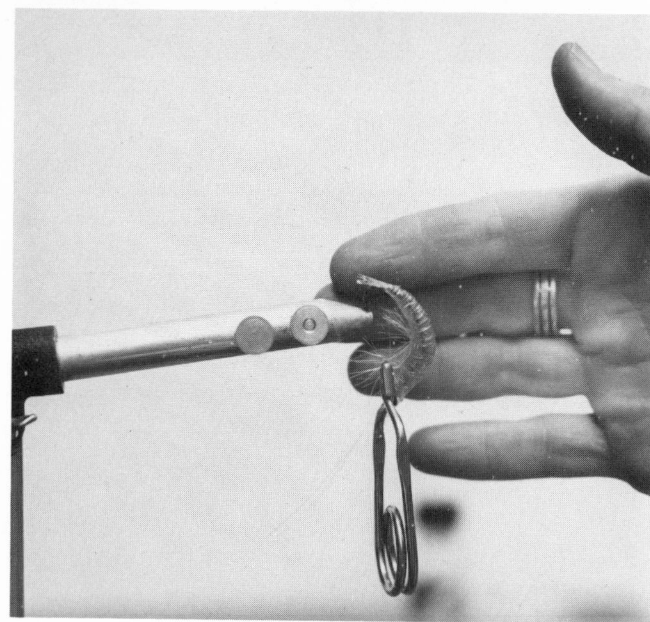

12. Turn shrimp right side up in vise, head down. The tying thread, spiraled toward the rear in separating the pleopods, now is used to tie in the fan-shaped tail. Coat entire body with fingernail polish so that the transparency and luster are enhanced.

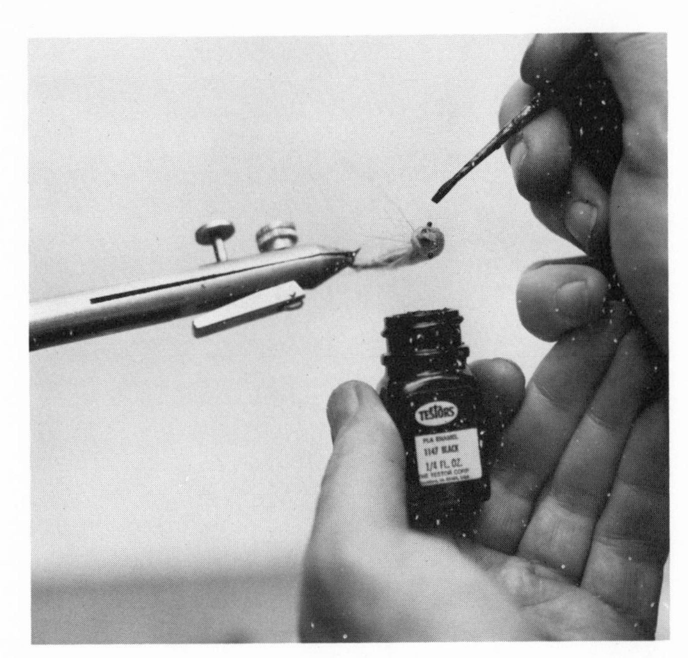

13. Touch black enamel or lacquer to tips of eyes.

14. Remove shrimp from vise and let dry. If finished shrimp body has dips or bulges, as shown here, apply additional coatings of fingernail polish and the body will become glassy smooth as shown in the color photograph of a slightly fancier tie, using crimped hog bristles as legs and a strip of white hackle laid in as the pleopods. *Photos by R. Hoebermann*

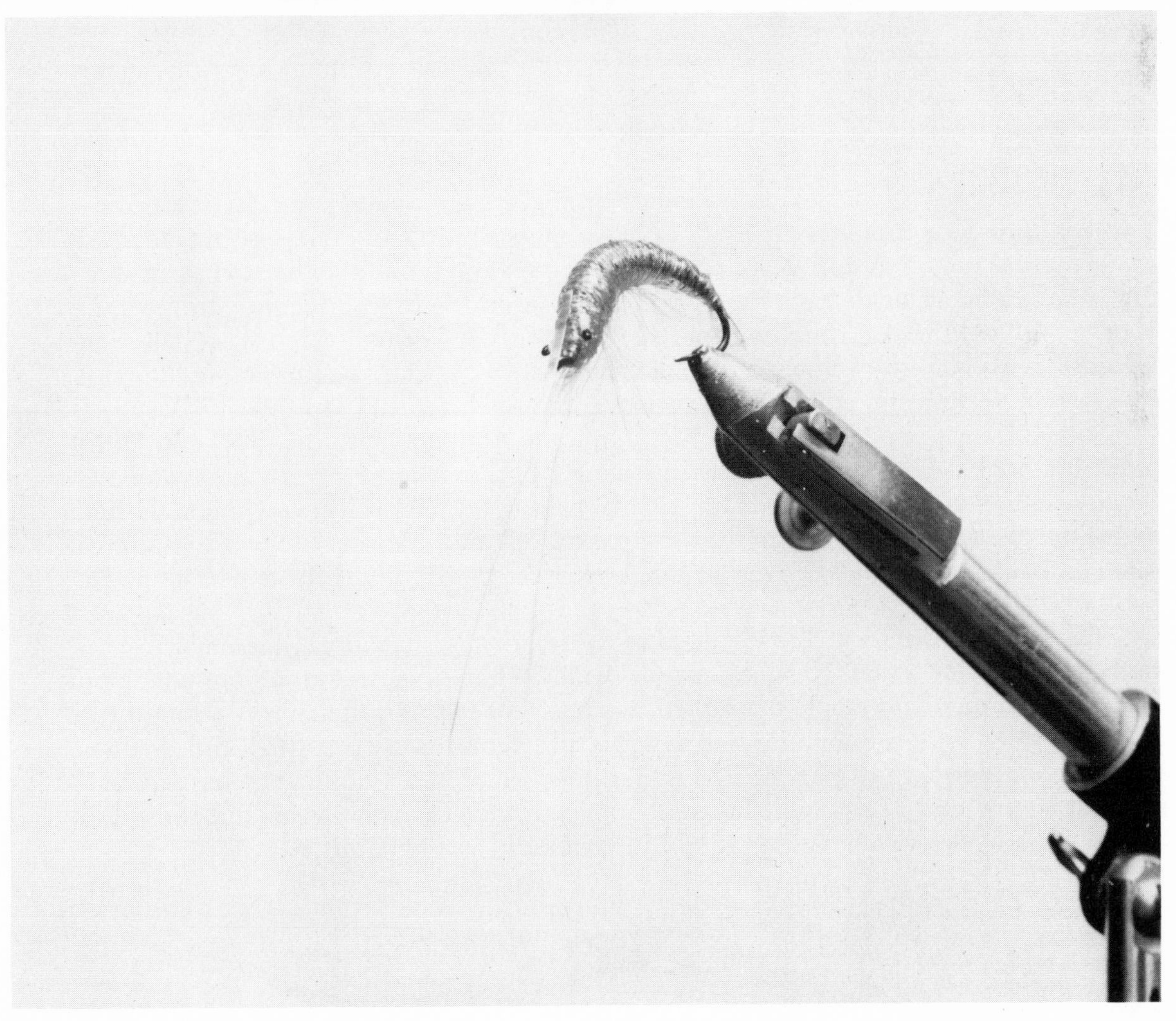

16

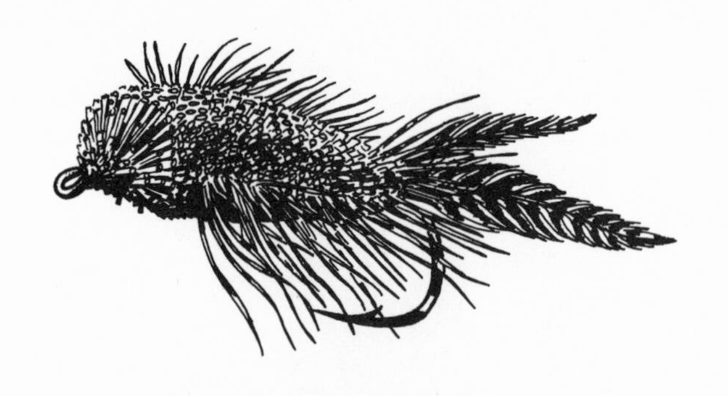

Special Bass Flies and Bugs

by Dave Whitlock

For the past nine years I've made it an almost absolute law each time I've gone bass-fishing, to leave my spinning and bait-casting tackle at home and use only a fly-rod. Most of us will take several types of tackle to bass waters and usually end up neglecting the fly-rod under anything but perfect bugging conditions. Wind, cold water, brush, deeper swift water, bass boats loaded with bait, and spincasters all help to discourage use of a fly-rod. My initial sacrifice brought about my most interesting and educating experience in fly-fishing.

Some of what I've learned is included in three *Almanac* patterns. But soon I will publish a book devoted entirely to the great art of fly-rodding for bass and associated species with modern methods and tackle. Fly-fishing for bass is a great sport and often excels the challenges and joys of fly-fishing for trout and salmon. Those who disagree have probably never really invested much time in fly-rodding for bass in its prime habitats.

The bass-fishing scene has changed more drastically than any other major American sport in recent years. New waters, old waters changing, and an all-out attack on bass by fishermen and tackle manufacturers has resulted in quite an evolution of the sport. Working with the premise that a bass is affected by these pressures and changes and by good new and old ideas, I have designed or altered a number of bass-fly patterns. It is obvious to those who have fished bass for ten to twenty years that these fish are undergoing drastic changes in their life-styles and eating habits.

The Hair Gerbubble Bug

The cork or balsa-bodied Gerbubble Bug was created in the late 1920s by Tom Loving of Baltimore. This great favorite of earlier-day buggers such as Joe Brooks has always interested me, but I was never particularly fond of it. Since I am a hairbug addict, I crossed its general physical shape with deer hair instead of wood-bodied originals. With this variation I feel the great bug is vastly improved as a bass bug. Tests over the country's bass waters have verified this almost without exception. The use of deer hair has lightened the bug, given it more durability, provided more fish appeal, and allowed the flytyer a big savings in tying time. For the bass bugger that has discovered that there is more to buggin' bass than a lot of fast casting and popping retrieves, this new variation is for you. Bass go nuts over it when it is used with a soft cast, wait–twitch–wait retrieve. The original's shape and winging make it effective, since it does not have all the fast moves and popping associated with general popping bugs of less eye appeal to bass. Also, it handles well on very light tackle—at least a size or two lighter rod and line per given hook size.

Hook size:	sizes 2/0 through 10
Thread:	size A Nymo thread
Tail:	four soft, wide, hen-neck hackles
Cement:	rod varnish or Pliobond
Tail skirt:	two soft, webby cock hackles
Body:	deer, elk, or antelope body hair (natural or dyed)
Whiskerwings:	four large, soft, cock-neck hackles (I prefer grizzly natural or dyed)
Snag Guard:	stiff nylon monofilament (approximately .018″ to .024″)

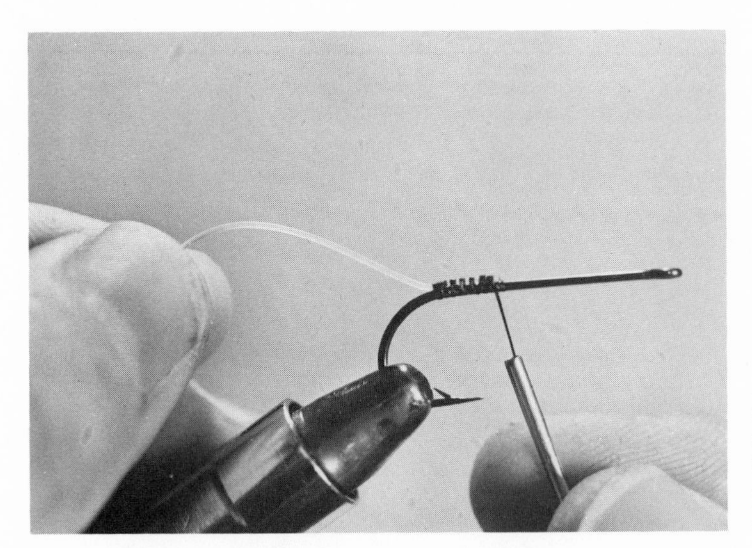

1. Hook and snag guard (Step 1): Place hook in vise, attach thread just in front of hook's bend. Tie on top of hook near bend a three-inch piece of stiff nylon that has had its end flattened a bit. Add a small amount of cement to the area as you tie down the nylon strand.

2. Tail: Take two pairs of hackles approximately one-half to three-quarters the length of hook shank and tie over the nylon strand, allowing each pair to flare to right and left of shank.

3. Tail skirt: Directly in front of these hackle tips, tie down butts of two neck hackles to wrap wet-fly style. Wrap each hackle around shank to form a hackle collar at tail of fly. Hackle should be one-and-a-half times the length of hook's gape. Trim excess tips when tiedown is accomplished.

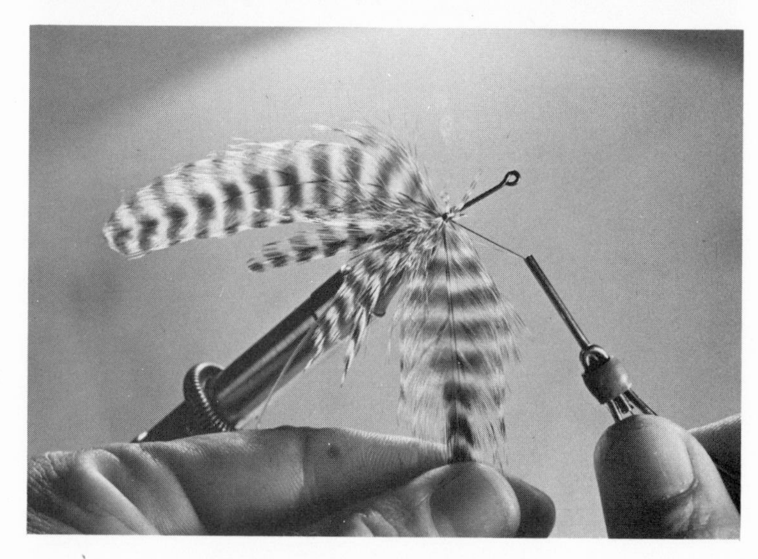

4. Gerbubble Whiskerwing (Step 1): Bring thread directly in front of collar. Now tie to each side of hook shank, at rear, two large neck hackles that have been sized one-and-a-half to two times the width of hook's gape and folded together. Hackle should point to tail and be at least two lengths of hook shank or more.

5. Body (Step 1): Three-quarters of hook shank should still be exposed in front of hackles that will form whiskerwings of the bug. Now using deer- or other similar body hair, tie in and flare several bunches.

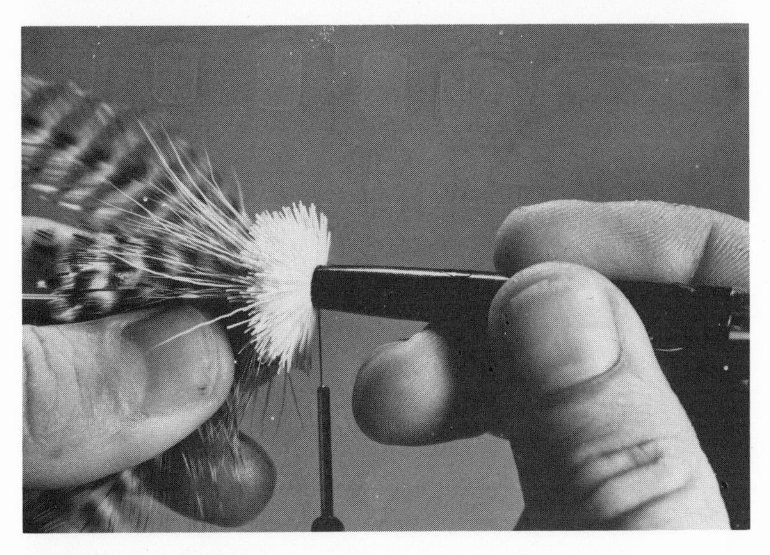

6. Pack each bunch tightly against the other. Use a packer or your thumb and index finger. I try to use as short–cut bunches as possible to avoid obstructing so much of the hook from view. Should you wish a banded effect, alternate two or three colors of hair. I usually tie this bug with only one color except for front of head. Stop deer hair approximately one-quarter shank length behind hook's eye.

Shaping body: Put two half-hitches in front of deer-hair body, then cut thread and remove unfinished bug from vise. With new razor blade or sharp scissors, trim body to shape. I leave the sides a bit flat to accommodate whiskerwings better.

7. Whiskerwing (Step 2): Return hook to vise and secure. Grasp each pair of whiskerwing hackles separately, holding fibers all to one outside position.

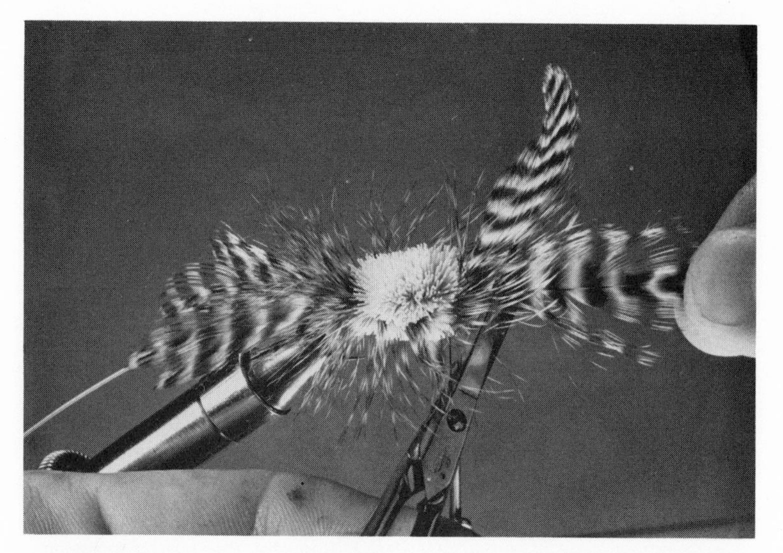

8. Pull pair forward, allowing hackle stems to embed into deer-hair body side almost to hook shank. Stems should be in line with shank. Now tie down hackle tips in front of trimmed body. Do same with right and left pair, forming characteristic gerbubble-bug look. Trim away hackle tips. Add a drop of cement to this area.

9. Body (Step 2): Add one or two more tightly flared, packed bunches of deer hair directly in front of these whiskerwings.

10. Head: Now add a bunch of white or lighter-colored matching deer hair to shank to effect a visible front on the bug. Add two half-hitches to hook eye area with tying thread. Remove bug from vise. Trim the head area to shape, leaving front rather wide and flat.

11. Snag guard (Step 2): Return the bug to vise with nylon strand between the jaws. Bend nylon strand from rear beneath the hook and pass it through hook's eye. Secure strand with tying thread. Adjust its length so that loop passes below and in front of hook's point approximately one-quarter to one-half hook's gape.

12. Bug finish: Tie down securely and whip-finish head off. Trim excess nylon strand away. Add varnish or Pliobond to head and along bug's belly, just in line with hook shank, to effect a good bonding and seal.

Wiggle-Legs Frog

Big bass love a soft little chewy live frog as much as I love to catch bass on a fly-rod bug! So with these two facts in mind I've worked several years on designing a good frog bug that suited the needs of buggin' bass where they are most likely to dine on select frogs.

A frog bug should do the following seven things:

1. Look and feel like a frog
2. Float like a frog
3. Act like a frog at rest or swimming
4. Fish where frogs live—on the shoreline or along weedy or lily-filled surfaces, without constant snagging on every obstruction

5. Not cast like a spastic helicopter on a fairly light rod and line
6. Hit the water softly enough to attract (without alarming) buster bass and friends
7. Hook a tough-mouthed bass but discourage smaller panfish from accidentally being hooked

My frog on most days does all these things if carefully applied to the right waters! However, because of its complexity I'd advise you to begin tying ole-wiggle-legs froggies early each fall after the water chills and you are sitting at home, so you will have one or two completed by the first warm days of late spring when frogs and bass are getting together again. A strong lock on your bug box and thirty-pound tippets might also provide the insurance you'll need to protect your froggies against fly-finaglers or brutish bass.

Hook:	sizes 6 through 1/0. Ringed-eye round bed. (Herter's 993R size 1 is used in illustrations.) For rear legs (two per fly), use any ringed-eye inexpensive hook. (Illustrations use Herter's 993R size 4.)
Tying Thread:	white or yellow size A Nymo
Snag Guard:	stiff nylon monofilament size .018″ to .026″
Rear Legs:	rump hair of deer—natural white, yellow, and dirty olive
Leg Hinges:	.006″ to .010″piano wire
Body:	body hair of northern whitetail deer. Natural white, yellow, and dark olive
Front Legs:	white rubber hackle, large or medium size
Eyeballs:	two fake plastic pearls—painted frog-eyeball colors
Cements:	vinyl liquid cement or rod varnish and 3M adhesive cement or Duco cement
Paints:	olive, black, and yellow enamel and black waterproof felt-tip marker

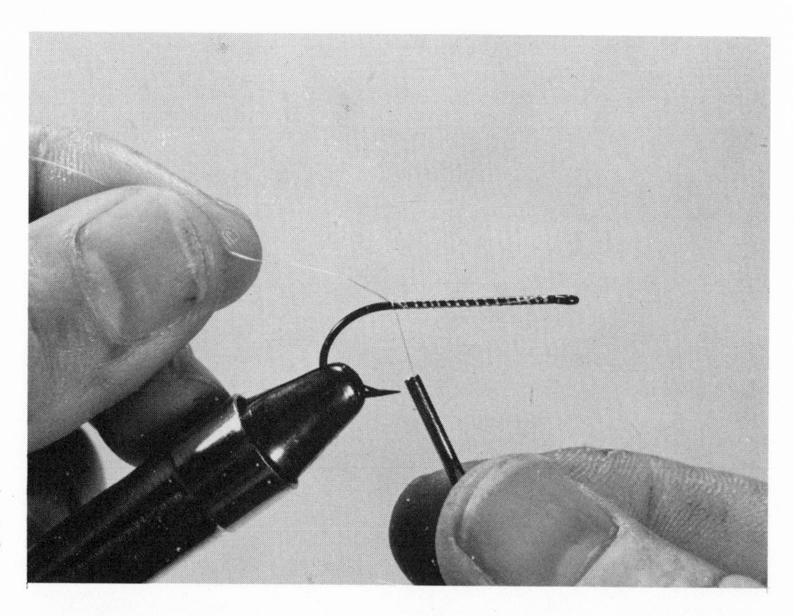

1. Rear frog legs: Place one of the two hooks selected to build legs on in vise in standard tying manner. Attach tying thread to shank near hook's eye. Wrap entire length of shank with thread.

2. Rear legs: Select three small equal bunches of white, yellow, and olive deer rump or bucktail hair. While doing so, also cut three additional bunches for second rear leg and set aside for repeat procedure. I usually cut larger bunches, clean out the underfur or shorts, then divide each bunch equally for both legs.

3. Rear legs: To just past mid-shank to the rear, tie butt tips of all three hair bunches with tips pointing forward. Tie white on lower shank, yellow in the middle, and olive directly over the yellow. Make sure each is very tightly tied to hook's shank. Firmly advance tying thread over the hair toward hook's eye. Just behind the eye, make six or eight very firm wraps to secure the hair tightly at this point. Apply small amount of cement over shank area.

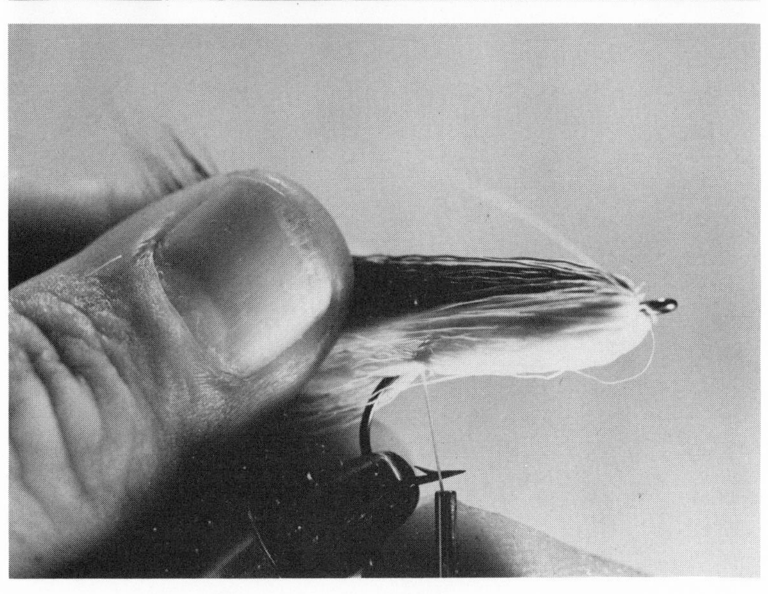

4. Rear legs: Wrap tying thread back to rear of shank to just in front of hook's bend, and hold there. With left thumb, index, and middle fingers, carefully fold all three colors separately backward, taking care not to allow them to twist together and mix. Olive should then be on top, yellow on sides, and white on bottom.

5. Rear legs: With tying thread, carefully encircle all three colors and wrap them tightly to hook's shank just in front of hook's bend. This forms main section of large rear leg. Wrap thread over a small section to form an anklelike area. Whip finish; remove thread. Put a coat of vinyl cement over these wraps.

Repeat these five steps to form second rear leg. I usually tie a dozen or so legs and match them in similar-sized pairs. It is quite a trick always to get any two consecutively tied to look alike in size and shape. You can also store extra pairs for future use.

6. Rear leg hinge: With a small pair of pliers, cut a one-inch length of piano wire (.010″–.014″) and make an open loop bend in its middle. Insert it through ringed eye of rear leg. With pliers twist the wire together but leave an open loop at the leg's ring eye. Trim the excess wire away, leaving twisted length of about one-quarter inch in length (not including the loop). This will be the hinge for wiggle legs, to be tied to main hook shank later.

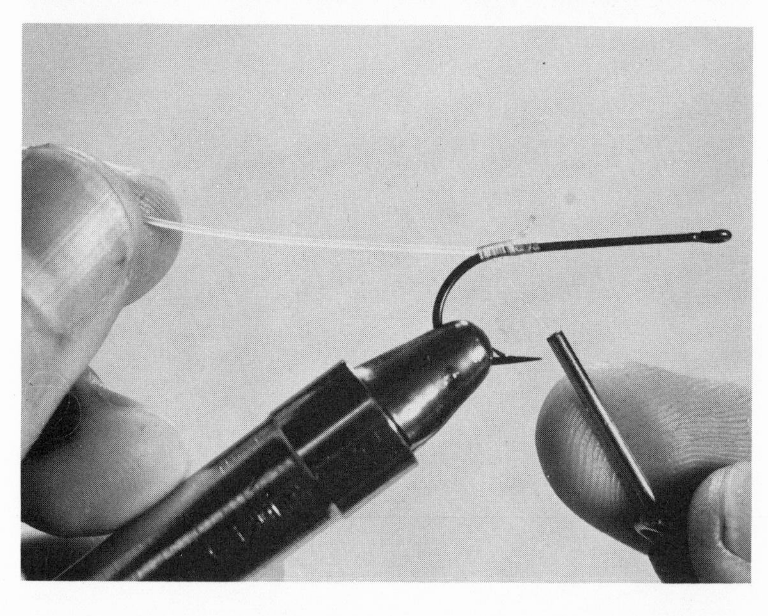

7. Snag guard: Cut a 3- to 4-inch piece of stiff nylon monofilament about the same diameter or slightly larger than the hook's wire. With pliers, flatten or roughen one-quarter inch of one end. Place body hook in tying vise and attach thread just in front of hook's bend. Lay flattened end of nylon monofilament on top of hook over thread wraps. Tie strand directly to hook shank, with length toward rear. Add a drop of cement to the area.

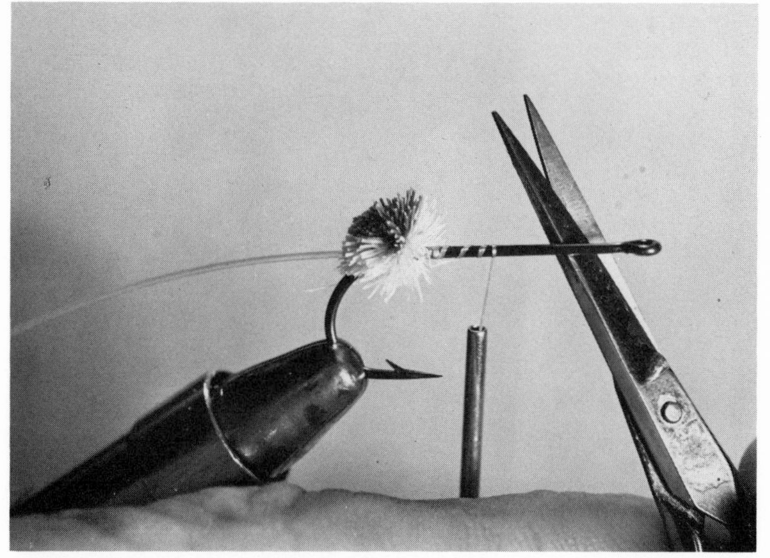

8. Frog body butt: Immediately over the snag guard tiedown, add a very small bunch of white deer hair. Wrap and flare it to shank, allowing it to roll *under the hook.* Add another small bunch of yellow directly over white, then olive bunch over yellow in the same manner. Result will be olive over yellow or white. I call this procedure "stacking" deer hair. It gives the tyer the method to have a layered color for deer-hair bodies. Trim with scissors down to a small rear, as shown.

9. Wiggle legs: Directly in front of this deer-hair butt, tie on very firmly the wire-hinge base of each rear leg to the right and left sides of the hook's shank so that the legs extend to each side and the rear. Coat this tie-down area with cement. Make sure the two are equally positioned on hook shank.

10. Main frog body: In the manner of stacking the three colors of deer hair described for the butt, begin to apply the three colors of deer hair to the hook's shank over and forward of leg hinges. After each of the three colors are applied, advance the thread forward and repeat procedure. Each tricolor bunch should be kept aligned and tightly butted up against the last bunch with packer or fingers to form a densely packed, durable body. I often add a small drop of vinyl cement or Pliobond to each bunch's base during this procedure. Build body up to one-quarter shank length behind hook eye.

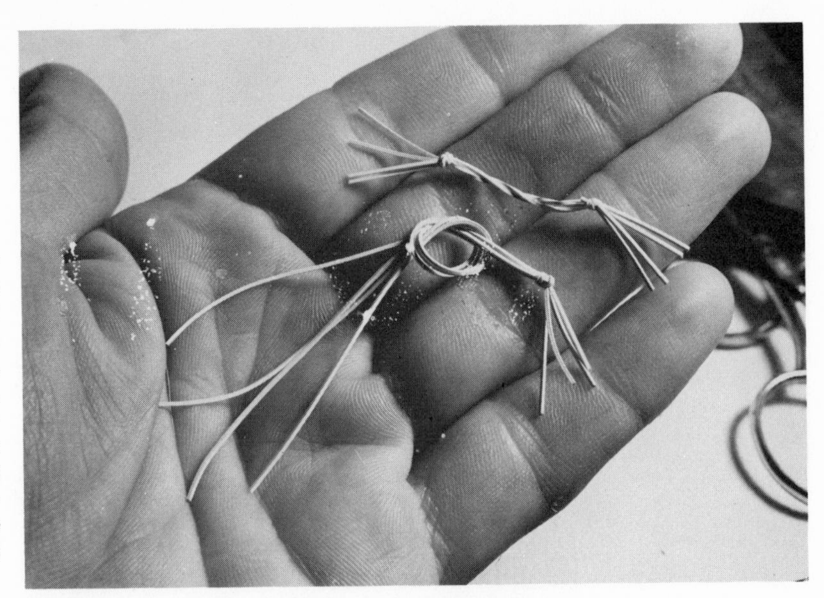

11. Front legs: Take four equal-length (3- or 4-inch) strands of medium or small-sized white rubber hackle and put an overhand knot in all four together near one of their common ends. Now carefully do the same with opposite ends, keeping them even. Draw overhand down, leaving about three-quarters to one inch between the two. A little practice and it is simple to do. Trim free ends to approximately toe length of frog front feet per hook size (see photo). (Again, I make six or eight pairs at one time, best done before actual body tying is done.)

12. Front legs: To the hook shank place the rubber legs at midpoint, stretching them slightly. With thread wraps, secure the pair to the hook's shank in a manner that has each leg sticking right and left and slightly downward on body as you would see in a real frog. You can easily set position after legs are secured to shank with thread.

13. Head: Directly in front and up against legs, tie on one or two more bunches of tricolor deer hair to form frog's head. Half-hitch twice just behind hook's eye, cut off tying thread, and remove fly from vise.

14. Shaping body: With curved or straight-blade scissors or a very sharp razor blade, give the frog's body a haircut, shaping it like a small frog's body. Make sure you trim most of the hair off under the fly to expose maximum hook bite. Take great care not to cut off front legs accidentally. Taper the head to a sloping point. Also trim rear area so that legs move or hinge freely. You can hardly cut too much off the body, as frog should float very low in water as naturals do. (Check photos for general body shape.)

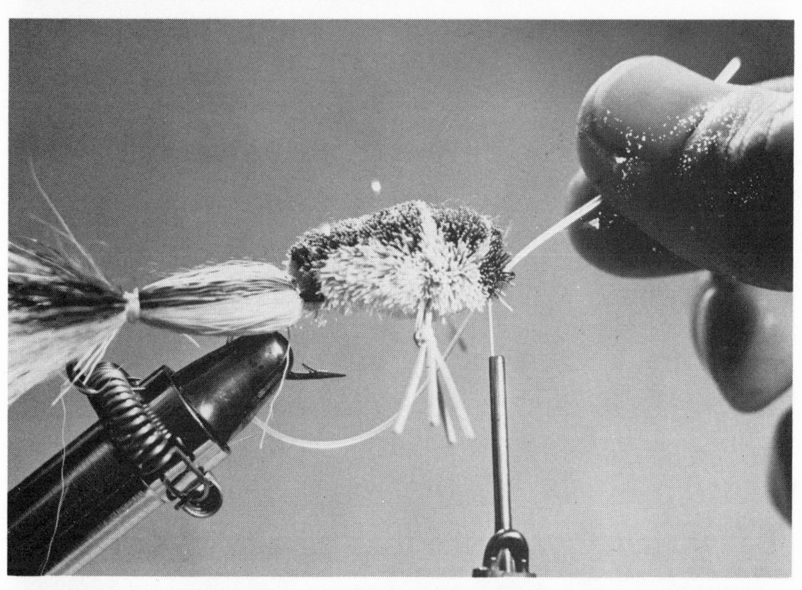

15. Snag guard (Step 2): Return hook to vise. Attach thread again behind hook's eye. Pull nylon strand beneath the body, forming loop as it is passed through hook's eye. Adjust loop so that it extends about one-half of hook's gape below the point. Wrap strand securely to hook shank and trim away excess. Whip-finish and cut away tying thread.

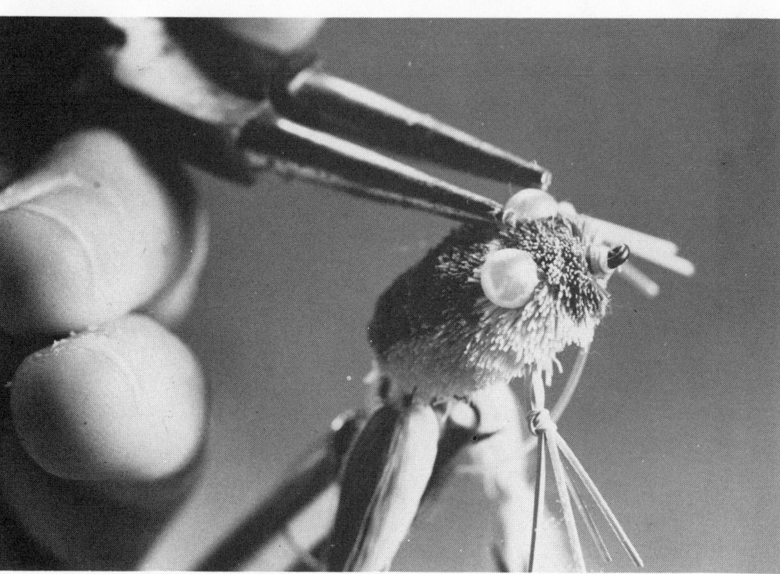

16. Eyeballs (optional): With scissors points cut two eye sockets in top of frog's head. Select two attached or separate plastic beads of appropriate size and set beads in top of head with cement. After cement has hardened, paint each bead to imitate frog's protruding eyeballs. Check a picture or real frog for this coloration design. I often apply either vinyl cement or rod varnish to the bottom of this frog if I have not bonded each bunch of hair during actual tying with cement. I also clip off rear leg hooks just at bend with dike pliers.

17. Marking trim: With a felt-tip marker, bar and spot the rear legs and back in a design appropriate to a spring or leopard frog.

If the frog tends to light on its back, you can use a heavier wire hook and/or take more care in trimming and balancing the body hair on your next frogs.

The hinge legs should fold backward easily, which makes castings easier by eliminating the major wind-resistance problem. They also will appear more lifelike in the water if they wiggle easily. This frog usually fishes best by spot-fishing, not using a lot of retrieving action. In any event, it is my most productive big-bass topwater lure. I do not recommend using any water repellent on this hair frog to enhance flotation. Frogs naturally float very low in the water, usually with just the tops of their head and eyes showing.

Body shape details for Dave's Wiggle-Legs Frog. The legs should move freely as you retrieve the frog.

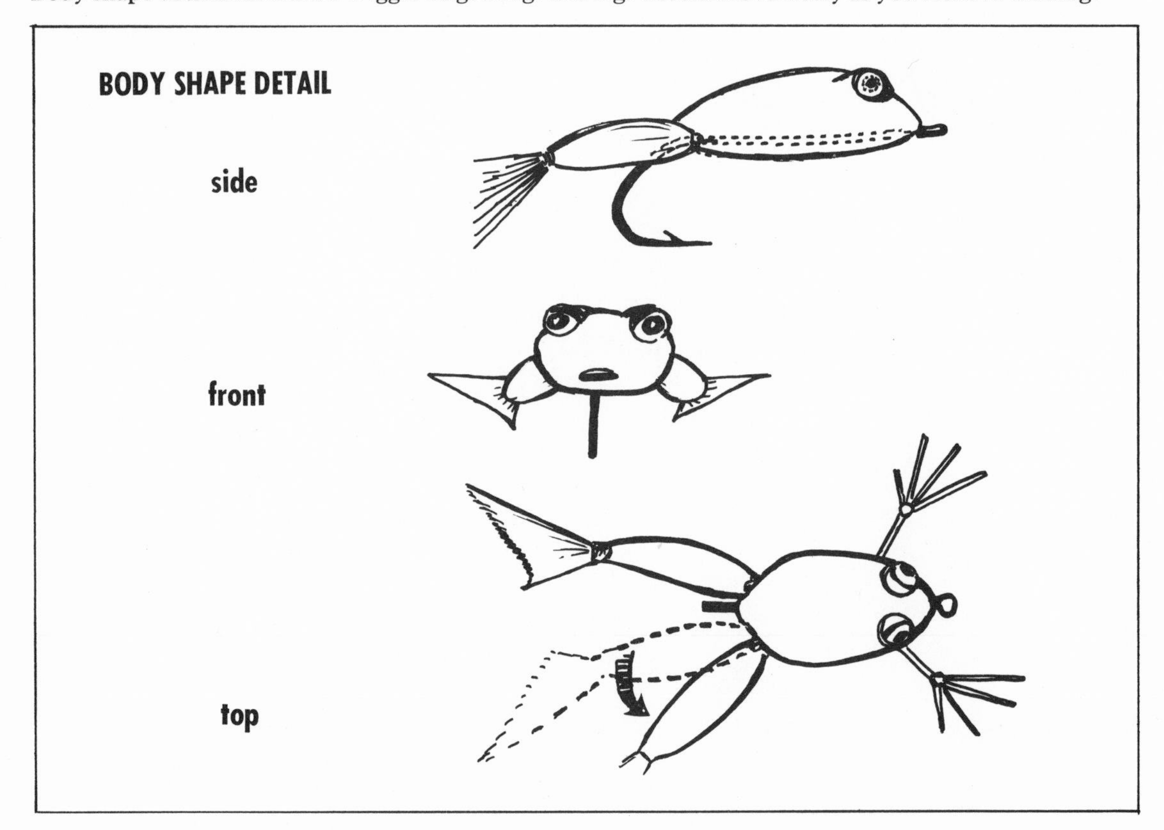

Eelworm Streamer

The Eelworm Streamer is a fly-rodder's answer to the plastic worm and/or the jig-and-eel bass lures that share two of the top three places with the Spinnerbait among bass fishermen across our country. Without a doubt this is the most effective large-mouth bass streamer I've ever used for bass living in reservoirs and natural lakes. You'll note that there is some similarity to Larry Green's Serpent Fly. In fact, when Larry published his first article on the Serpent Fly I used several of his ideas as well as those of local friend Bill Greenway to perfect further my Eelworm. However, now the pattern is about right and I consider it to be accomplishing exactly what it was created to do—cast for cast, it will compete with the jig-and-eel or plastic worm to entice big-bass strikes.

The Eelworm Streamer should be fished like the jig or plastic worm; that is, along the bottom very slowly and erratically. Usually a high-density sink-tip and a short leader are called for; occasionally I use a floating-bug taper or lead-head shooting line when the bass are in shallow or very deep areas.

Most important are the snag guard, the overbalance weight at the head, and very flexible, long saddle hackle. All three factors contribute greatly to fishing the fly properly. The snag guard allows you to fish where the bass live—right under the pads, in the brush, timber, or structures. I usually put the nylon loop inside the hook's bend for best performance.

The overbalanced head created by the bead-chain eyes and lead wraps sink the fly quickly and give it a head-up-and-down jigging action which sets the tails into action. But due to the length of this fly, the extra weight does not create casting problems. I'm not implying it will cast like a Number 14 Adams, but it does glide well and doesn't come in low from the backcast if your timing is good.

The thin stem long saddles (I call them floppy saddles) have fantastic action that pulsates with every twitch or fly contact with an obstruction or current eddy. Also, like a good floating pork eel or plastic worm, the hackle tends to tease upward because the head stays on the bottom during pauses.

I prefer to use grizzly saddle hackles and dye them various bassy shades. My favorites are brownish purple, black, blue, lavender, brown, and avocado (olive). But white and yellow are also supergood at times with grizzly or solid-color hackle.

I also know that this fly is a super pattern for big, big pike, muskie, ugly ole browns, stripers, and other saltwater thugs!

Dave's Eelworm Lure

Hook: Mustad 36890, sizes 6 through 3/0, or any good extralong heavy wire hook with straight or turned up eye

Loop Snag or Guard: stiff nylon monofilament, .018″ to .025″ (depending on hook size used)

Cement: Pliobond and fast-setting epoxy

Tying Thread: black Nymo size A and Herb Howard's fluorescent orange

Eyeballs: hardware store ball or bead chain, three sizes, for range of hooks

Weighting:	lead wire
Tailwings:	six narrow grizzly saddle hackles with very flexible stems, ideally paired right and left, dyed to desired color. Blue, black, purple, and brown usually best for bass
Rib:	one or two very soft grizzly saddle hackles dyed to match tailwings
Body:	dubbing blend of 50 percent Orlon wool and 50 percent rabbit or muskrat fur. Should be same color as dye used for tailwings

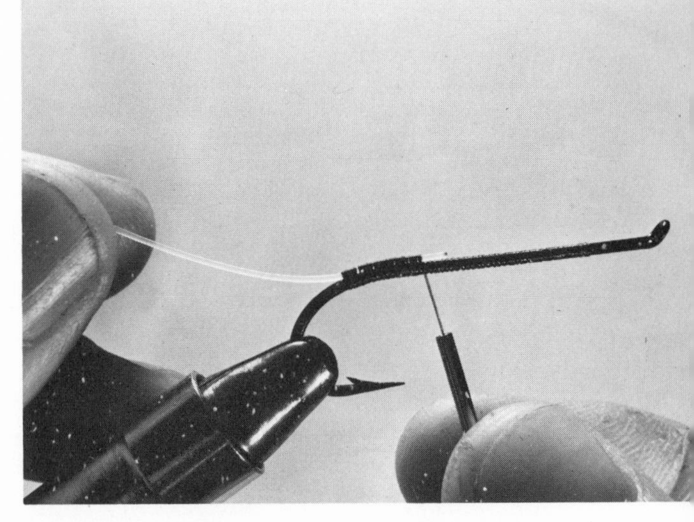

1. Place hook firmly in vise jaws with point and barb exposed. With black Nymo tying thread wrap entire hook shank, working from eye to bend. Select a stiff nylon strand approximately the same diameter or slightly larger than the hook's wire. Cut a portion about three or four inches in length. With a pair of pliers, flatten or roughen about one-quarter inch on end. Just at hook's bend, wrap roughened end of strand to top of hook. Stick strand into vise's material clip.

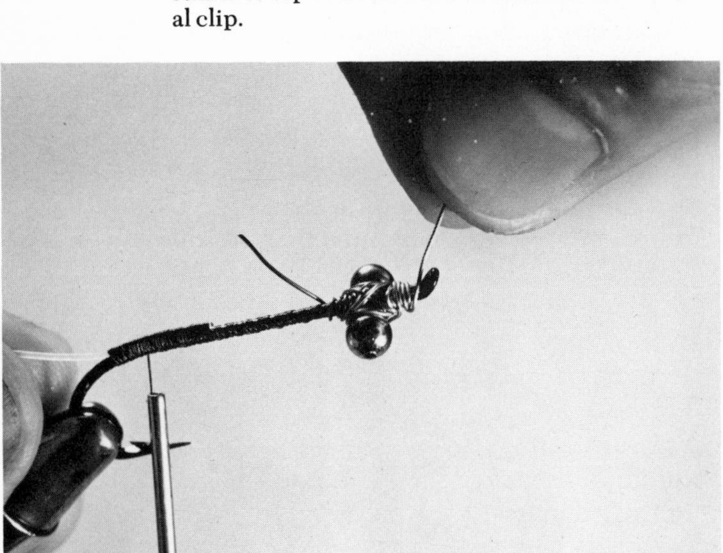

2. Eyeballs: Advance tying thread up to behind hook's eye. Wrap a pair of bead-chain eyes to lower side of hook's shank with figure-eight pattern. Eyes should be about one-quarter the shank distance behind eye of hook, never closer! Double-half-hitch thread, and cut from hook. With a length of small-diameter lead wire, wrap in front of, between, and just behind the bead-chain eyes. Bulk of lead should be about equal to that of eyes. This weighting is important not only in sinking the fly but also in providing a balance for proper action in the water. With quick-setting glass resin or epoxy, coat the hook's shank, especially the area where nylon strand and leaded bead eyes are. Allow ample time for complete setting of glue. (I usually build a dozen or more lures to Step 2, then cement them all at once. I store the extra ones, just like hooks, for future use.)

3. Tailwing: A) Replace the hook in tying vise and reattach the black tying thread to the hook, near the bend. Carefully select three pairs of saddle hackles, two pairs approximately three times the hook's shank length. The third pair should be one-half length shorter. For best results I select an entire grizzly saddle skin and dye it just for the eelworm pattern.

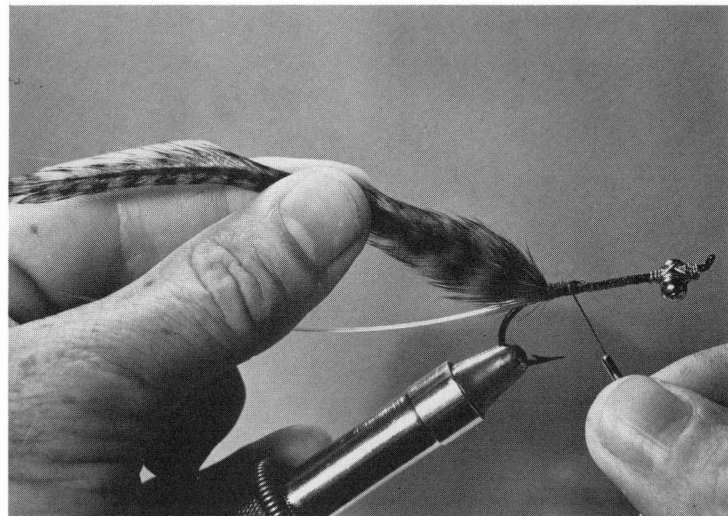

B) Just at hook's bend, tie both pairs of long saddles to the shank with bright sides facing out. The pairs should be same length. Natural curve should be downward.

C) In front of these, tie the third and shorter pair on each side of hook so that dull sides are out, creating a flare effect with them. A drop of Pliobond at the base of these hackles helps prevent feathers from turning or pulling out.

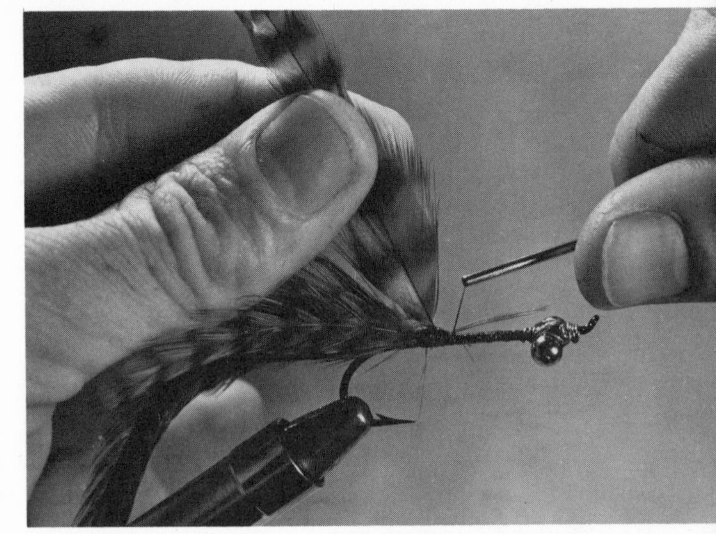

4. Rib: Just directly in front of tailwing hackles, tie in one or two soft, webby, saddle hackles with bright sides out. These will be used as a palmer-type rib over body and head later. Coat hook's shank up to eyes with Pliobond.

5. Body: To the tying thread immediately spin on a thick amount of dubbing. Proceed to form a very thick fuzzy body up to the eyes.

6. Ribbing: Take the rib hackle and spiral-wrap a palmer rib of hackle up to the eyes. Trim excess hackle tips after tying them down at eyes.

7. Head: Again spin on a bulk amount of dubbing and figure-eight-wrap dubbing over eyes and to front of them. Head is thus formed and should be slightly larger than body.

8. Loop snag guard: Bend the nylon strand around under the hook. You will have to remove it temporarily from vise jaws. Back in the vise, bring the strand underneath and through hook's eye. Take several turns with the tying thread to hold nylon strand in place. Measure the loop formed so that it goes about one-half hook's gape beneath the hook's point. This done, wrap the strand down tightly at hook eye and trim off excess length. Whip-finish head.

(Optional). At hook eye, attach orange fluorescent thread and build up the front over black thread wraps, then whip-finish off. I like this dash of color, as it helps me see the fly in dark water and makes certain fishing situations easier and more effective.

9. Coat the thread portion of the head with either epoxy or phenol-glass resin. With scissors, trim down palmer rib to just slightly longer than body or even with body. Fly is also effective not trimmed up and has an entirely different look and action if hackle is left long. Try both!

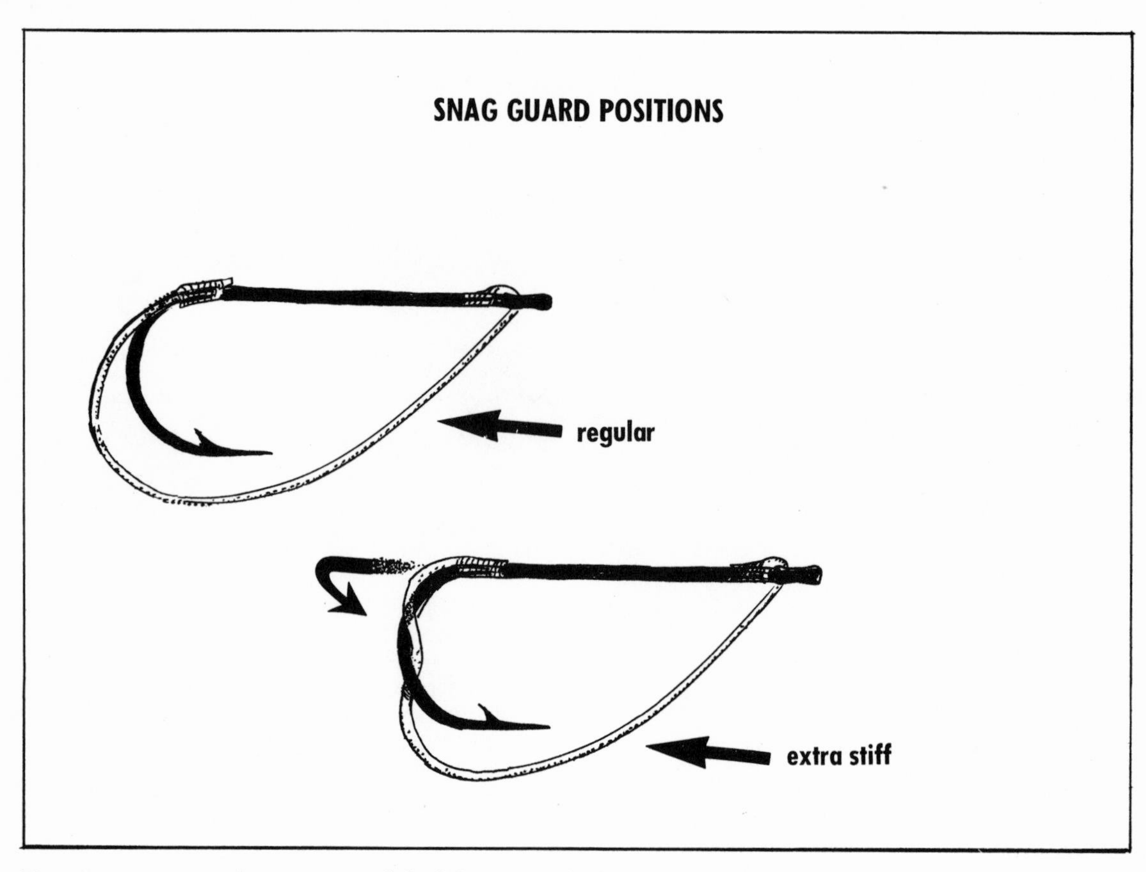

For extra snag guard protection while fishing Dave's Eelworm, Wiggle-Legs Frog, and Hair Gerbubble Bug bring the nylon strand inside the bend of the hook.

VI

The Materials of the Art

17

The Evolution of a New Fly Hook

by T. Donald Overfield

Take one tall dark sales manager of the English equivalent of a company like DuPont. Provide him with a background of more than thirty-five years of thoughtful trout fishing; ensure that his background covers the taking of trout from the Scottish Highland burns and streams when a boy through to the fine chalk-streams of England in later life. Now place him at a boring business meeting, the spring sunshine filtering through the windows while dull facts and figures become a background to thoughts of widening rings upon a stream. And now you have, if you happen to be Peter Mackenzie-Philps, the perfect setting for the design of a fly hook that looks fair to take the trouting world by storm, and consign the standard hook to the realm occupied by the gut cast, horse-hair line, and lancewood rod.

But let us not rush ahead. The past must be of interest here. Let us look at the evolution of the hook, and in particular the hook onto which one dresses the artificial trout fly.

The first use of the hook, undoubtedly of wood or bone, has not been set down with any degree of accuracy. Small wonder, for one would have to go far beyond the realms of recorded angling time. We do know that the Macedonians living upon the banks of the river Astraeus prior to the third century A.D. were taking fish by means of an artificial fly named in *De Natura Animalium* as the Hippurus fly. This pattern was most certainly tied upon a metal hook.

The first reference to the angler being able to buy hooks (as opposed to ending with bloody fingers as he tried to make such objects from his wife's sewing box, in the manner prescribed by Dame Juliana Berners in 1496) came with the publication of *The Secrets of Angling,* by John Dennys, in 1613. Within this priceless volume one may read:

> Then buy your Hookes the finest and the best
> That may be had of such as used to sell,
> And from the greatest to the very least
> Of every sort pick out and chuse them well,
> That hooke I love that Pegasus did make
> His shank should neither be too short or long,
> His point not over sharpe, nor yet too dull;
> The substance good that they may indure from wrong,
> His needle slender, yet both round and full,
> Made of the right Iberian mettell strong
> That will not stretch or breake at every pull,
> Wrought smooth and clean withouten crack or knot
> And bearded like the wild Arabian goat.

The hooks described by Dennys were produced in rapidly increasing quantities within the London area. One of the first makers was Charles Kirby of Harp Alley in Shoe Lane, the inventor of the hook bend that still bears his name to this day. Izaak Walton held Kirby's products in high regard, for in the second edition of *The Compleat Angler,* published in 1655, the old gentleman called Kirby "the most exact and best hookmaker the nation affords."

Charles Kirby started a veritable cottage industry. The number of hook makers grew apace with a rapidly growing sport. Though London was initially the mecca of the hook makers, two other areas of England soon became involved: Redditch in Worcestershire and Kendal in Westmorland. Redditch is still the home of top-quality hook making.

The basic design of the hook now settled down. There was little variation, other than in the shape of the bend, for the next two hundred years, fly-fishers being content to tie the hooks directly to a gut leader by whipping them with the tying silk prior to the tying of the artificial.

The first reference to a major change in hook design, the birth of the eyed hook, comes in 1849 when Hewett Wheatley, in his volume *The Rod and Line; or Practical Hints and Dainty Devices,* states (p. 79):

> I generally use them [flies] on hooks having a fine eye at the extremity of the shank; in fact, I very commonly make all flies, large and small, on similar hooks, a practice that will doubtless be much scouted by many anglers. . . . Should the good natured public ask for a second edition, I may perhaps give more details on the subject, for it is somewhat of a pet, though not exactly the child of my old age; rather the mistress of our youth and the friend of riper years.

From this we can safely assume that he had used eyed hooks long before the publication date of his book. Who made the hooks? Alas, we know not.

Certainly eyed hooks were made by Allcock's of Redditch, in the year 1867, but they would seem to have found little favor with the anglers of that period. In 1876 W. H. Aldam edited and published *A Quaint Treatise on "Flees and the Art of Artyfichall Flee Making."* It was a superb book, based upon an old manuscript written by an aged Derbyshire angler (name unknown), its major attraction being the actual artificial flies set into thick cardboard mounts. Only dressings of the large mayflies (drakes) were tied on eyed hooks; the others were tied to gut. (The patterns in the book had been tied by Ogden's of Cheltenham, Gloucestershire.)

We now come to the man who popularized the eyed hook, Henry Sinclair Hall. In the spring of 1877 he wrote to W. H. Aldam requesting samples of the mayfly hooks that had appeared in the book. These arrived on May 31, 1877—japanned hooks with a Limerick-shaped bend. Hall, in concert with his friend Bankart, carried out many hook-making experiments, all the while endeavoring to produce a light-wire, well-tempered hook with a finely drawn upturned eye. Such hooks were finally produced in salable quantities in 1880, and this time the sporting angler saw the advantage of such a pattern. The death knell of the hook tied to gut had been rung.

The only other modification to the eyed hook would come in 1886 when Cholmondeley Pennell came out with a down-eyed hook. Even then, fierce controversy broke out over the respective merits of the up-eyed hook and the down-eyed hook, the angling world eventually settling for a compromise: up-eyed for dry flies and down-eyed for wet flies. Once more, the ripples of contention faded away; anglers now took the eyed hook to their hearts. The design was to remain static for a further eighty-seven years, until one day in 1973 when Peter Mackenzie-Philps became bored, and started to draw, in side view, natural flies upon his scribbling pad.

Having drawn the fly, he doodled around, placing the hook bend and point where it would be least visible: between the legs of the natural. His pen continued to draw the hook within the outlines of the natural fly—and he suddenly realized that he was on to something quite new.

That very night Mackenzie-Philps went to work. Finding it impossible to soften tempered hooks, he resorted to a large pin and made a replica of his idea. His next step was to tie a fly upon the pin. The resultant fly floated beautifully. With its forward center of gravity, the body and tails remained clear of the water surface in a most lifelike manner. This initial experiment was followed by months of careful study and the making of hooks to the new design from untempered hooks. Many hours of fishing with these prototypes convinced him that he was indeed on to something new, and on July 11, 1973, he applied for, and was granted, a patent on his hook design.

Now came the question of hook manufacture, in the real sense. Mackenzie-Philps approached the top firm in the field of handmade hooks, Partridge Ltd., of Redditch, a very old, established outfit with an enviable reputation for hand-crafted hooks. His design met with unqualified approval, and so the initial production batch of ten thousand Dayfly hooks was started. Mackenzie-Philps's first worry was where he would unload so many hooks! He need not have worried. When news of the new hook design became known he was inundated with orders.

I consider myself fortunate to have been asked to participate in the prototype stream testing. Identical dressings, tied upon both conventional hooks and Fly-body hooks, were presented to the trout and grayling on all manner of streams and rivers. The Fly-body design passed the tests with flying colors. To ensure that the results were not just fortunate coincidences, the experiments were repeated over and over again, ringing the changes between standard hooks and the new pattern.

My one reservation was that the protruding body may be touched by the neb of the trout, at the critical moment of ingress as the trout's mouth closes over the fly, thereby pushing the fly away. This may have happened, undetected, on occasion; however, the preponderance of solid "takes" makes one conclude that this is a minor problem.

We now turn to the tying of a fly upon this new hook.

To date, four sizes have been developed:

The Dayfly: this hook has a bend size equivalent to a number 14 hook. The overall length, including the curved body wire, is 7/16" (11mm)—ideal for most of the duns. To tie smaller patterns, it is an easy matter to snip off a portion of the body wire with wire cutters.

The Mayfly: bend size equivalent to a standard number-10 hook. Overall length, including the curved body wire, is ¾" (19mm). The term "mayfly" is used in the English context, the size referring to the true mayfly species, *E. vulgata* and *E. dancia,* approximating in size the United States drakes. It is also useful for such patterns as sedges.

The Small Lure: bend size equivalent to a standard number-8 hook. Overall length 1" (25mm). Note that this hook has a straight, not curved, body wire. Used for streamers, muddlers, etc.

The Large Lure: bend size equivalent to a standard number-6 hook. Overall length 1¼" (31mm). Also straight body wire. Used for salmon flies, etc.

The advantage of the fly-body hook design must lie in its ability to assist in the simulation of the natural floating duns. Such simulation has been achieved by the Dayfly and the Mayfly sizes, these being the hooks that I have used to good effect; the Lure sizes may well be effective also.*

Reference to Figure 1 will show the general shape of the Dayfly and Mayfly series. It will be noted that the eye is in the vertical, not the horizontal, plane. Experience has shown that this radical departure from the normal design presents no problems.

**Editor's Note:* Since Don Overfield wrote this chapter, the Fly-body hook has entered a second generation of design. Sizes 6 and 8 have been discontinued (although they are still available from some suppliers), and sizes 12 and 16 have been added, together with other refinements in this promising new fly-tying hook.

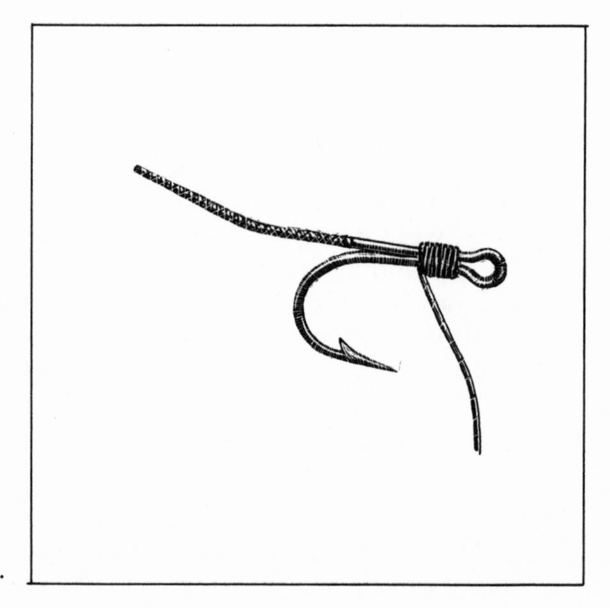

1. Start to wind the silk in the usual manner as shown.

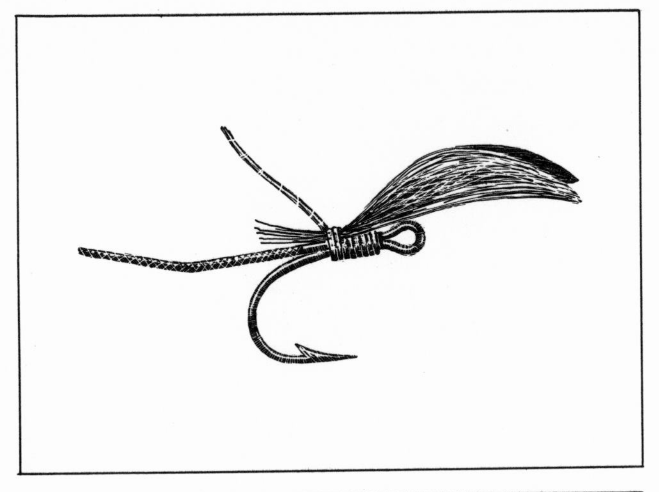

2. If you intend to wing the fly, tie in wing slips at this stage.

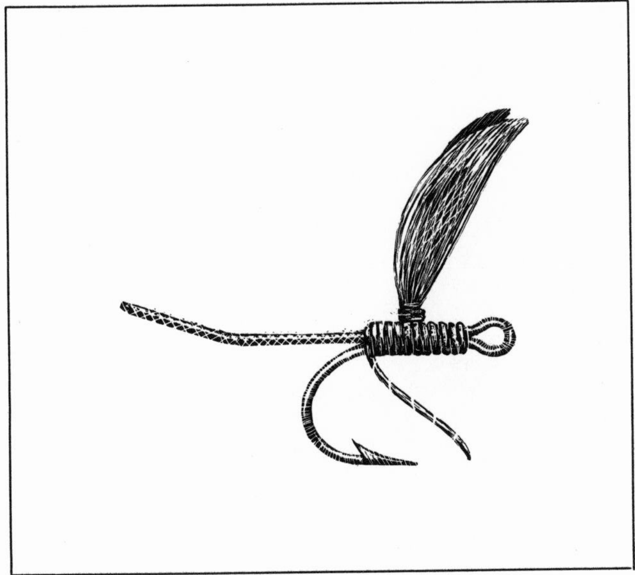

3. Holding the wings in an upright position, take two turns of the silk around the base of the wings, and continue winding the silk to a point where the bend and the body wire start to divide. Secure the silk with a half-hitch.

If you use a vise with the usual angled neck, you will now need to reverse the hook in the vise jaws.

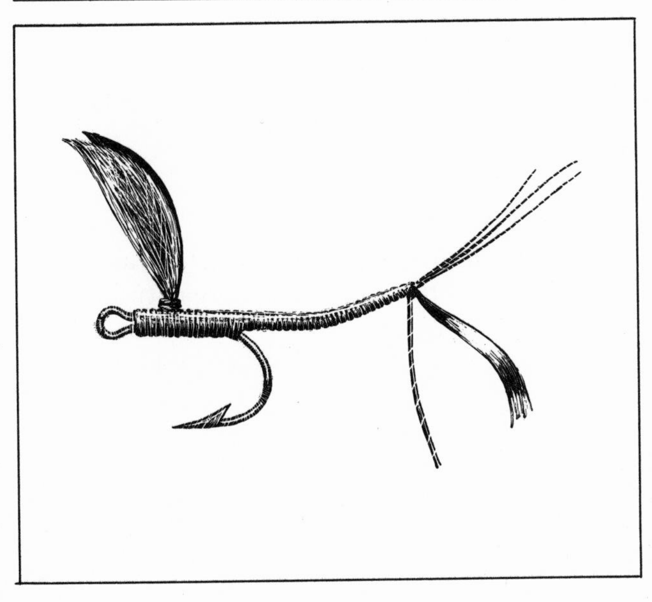

4. Wind silk down the body wire. At this stage it is a good idea to coat wire with adhesive to prevent body from slipping off rear of wire during a wrassle with a trout. To help further with this problem, Mackenzie-Philps has patented the idea of minute serrations, a crosshatch knurling effect, on the body wire, thereby providing a "key" for the silk and obviating the need for adhesive. This modification has yet to be incorporated on production hooks. Tie in tail whisks and body material.

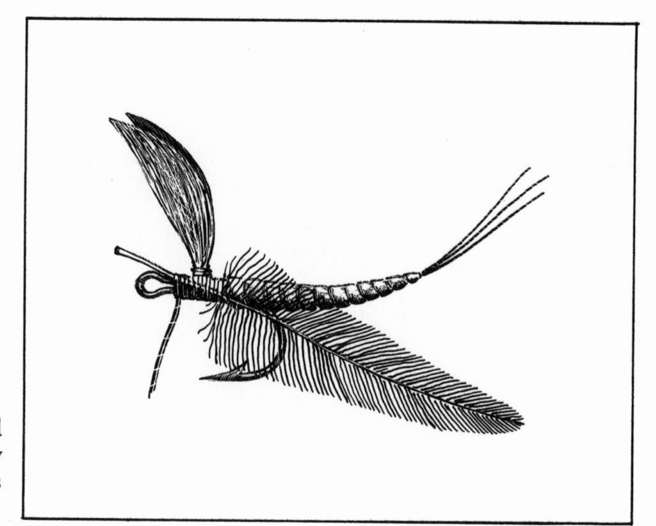

5. Proceed to wind silk back down the body, followed by body material, securing the latter in position by means of a half-hitch in the tying silk. Tie in hackle as shown.

6. Wind hackle behind and in front of wings. (You may initially find it difficult to wind the hackle because of the bend and point being in the way. However, one soon masters the technique of winding the hackle at an angle.) Complete the fly with a whip finish at head. The final result will be as seen here. (Optional): Cut off lower hackle fibers level with hook point as a further aid to precise flotation.

To sum up, the Fly-body hook offers the following advantages:

1. A far more realistic profile than has hitherto been possible.
2. The correct center of gravity with the major portion of the weight being forward of the bend, thereby allowing the artificial to sit upon the water in a more natural posture.
3. The bend and point are hidden within the hackle fibers, though this does not prevent a firm take when the trout rises to the fly.

Given these three advantages over the standard hook, one must assume that Mackenzie-Philps has come up with a major step forward in hook design. If nothing else, he will have provided the means for a controversy among thoughtful anglers, which in itself can be no bad thing.

A mayfly-sized fly-body hook pattern *(Ephemera dancia)* © by T. Donald Overfield.

Editor's Note: I sent several tyers these new hooks as soon as Don McGregor, manager of The Hackle House in Oakville, Ontario, sent me a decent amount of sample hooks. Don, like myself, was very excited over their potential and wanted to see how they would be accepted among North American flytyers.

René Harrop was one of the first to respond favorably to the hook. But besides his liking for the hook, he also ties on the hook with a method that is nearly perfect, I think. René simply places the hook's tail or shank (see illustrations) tip into the jaws of the tying vise enough to secure the hook. This allows a very standard procedure to be used, not unlike tying on any ordinary hook. Once the fly is completed, René cuts the little bare portion from the fly body. In almost all types of patterns, the loss of 10 percent of the body shank is insignificant.

This hook is now available through a number of United States and Canadian outlets.

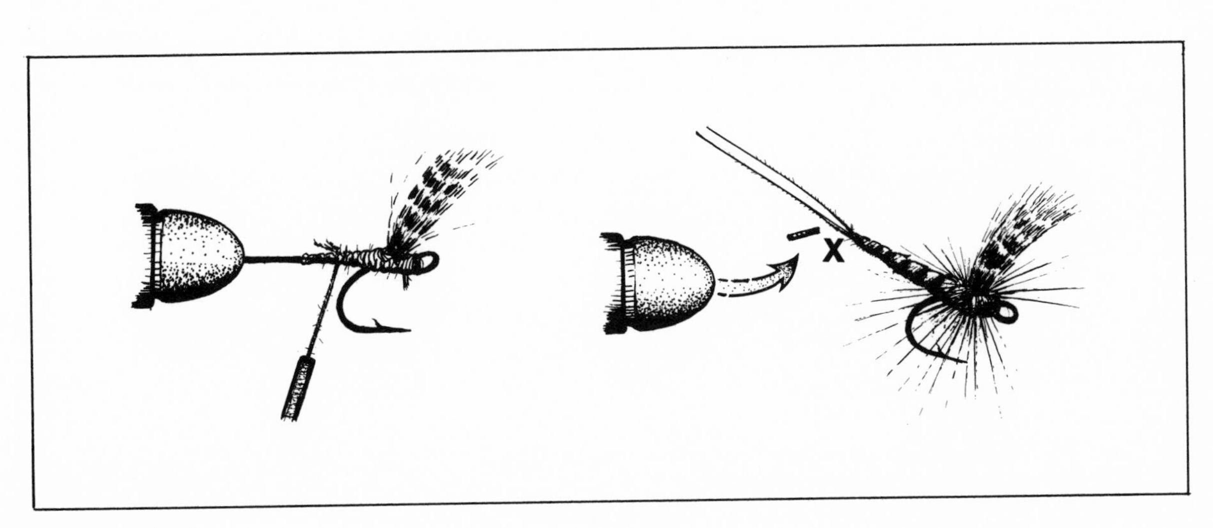

Harrop method

A caddis pupa, a nymph, a standard dry fly, and no-hackle spinner and dun tied on fly-body hooks.

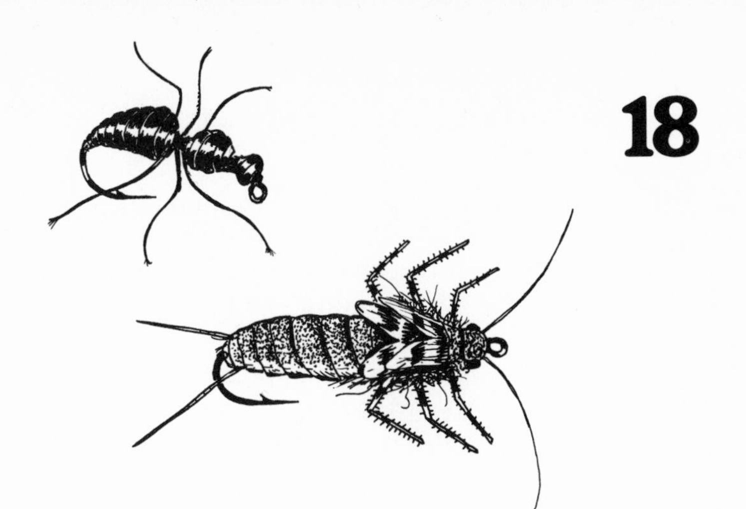

18

Liquid-Latex Bodies

by Bill Charles

For many years Bill Blades, a famous flytyer, and I worked to find a nymph body material that would be soft, translucent, and look natural all at the same time. Blades, now deceased, did come up with a body made of Duco cement and covered with raffia. But Bill admitted that it was neither translucent nor soft. When I received the news of Bill's death, I knew that he would want me to continue the search for a truly successful body material.

I continued working and in 1968 finally developed a soft and translucent material. I came across it quite by accident, like striking gold after a long search. It took three more years of experimenting to develop it fully, but now I am ready to tell interested flytyers how it is made. The effort it will take to produce liquid-latex body material will be justified by the results.

For this body material not only makes beautiful and natural-looking ant and nymph bodies, but also many other fly bodies that call for soft, translucent segments. A fish will not reject a soft and natural-looking imitation as quickly as a hard body. This gives you more time to set the hook. And you can make the body one color and rib it with another color; nymphs, ants, shrimp, bee and countless other wet-fly bodies can be made in realistic and durable patterns.

This body material is made from a liquid-latex rubber base that can be dissolved in water. That means that if you dye the water and mix it with the rubber-liquid base, you will get a colored rubber liquid.

The product is called Mold-Tex and is manufactured in Fort Worth, Texas. It is sold in many of the American Handicrafts stores in major cities throughout the country. Look in your telephone directory for the American Handicrafts store in your area (they also issue a free catalog). The liquid base comes in a plastic quart bottle selling for $4.95, and in gallon cans for $16.95.

Now I will tell you how to transform this liquid rubber into a solid mass of material so that you can wrap it on the shank of a hook.

When you receive the liquid, it will have the consistency of syrup, and you will want to thin small amounts to the consistency of milk—that is, slightly thicker than water. The only tools you will need are a one-ounce or slightly larger container, a small, flat stick to stir and spread with (an eye dropper would come in handy), and a flat, nonporous surface like a piece of glass, Formica, or plastic that you can pour the mixture onto. Be sure the surface is level before you start so it won't run off the side. For about a dollar you can buy four eight-by-eight-inch pieces of glass which will serve your purpose fine.

The right mixture is half an ounce of liquid rubber to a quarter ounce of dyed water; when mixed these amounts will yield three-quarters of an ounce of liquid body material. Stir with the flat stick until the rubber and water are completely mixed. Do not shake it—shaking will cause bubbles. After mixing the water and the rubber, the liquid might look light to you. Don't add more dye; the rubber will dry ten times darker than it appears at this stage.

Whatever dye you use, be sure to use only a small amount, and be sure the dyed water is cool before you mix it with the liquid rubber. Any dye that you normally use to dye feathers is okay. Liquid Rit works fine; just add a little to the quarter ounce of water and stir it well, then add the water to the half ounce of liquid rubber and stir it well again. Crystal Rit dye is good too. Put a quarter teaspoon of dye crystals in a clean, empty tuna can with about a half inch of water in it. Bring this to a boil, stir, and let it cool. Store it in a small bottle which you have marked for the color and the dye you used. Use this dye as the quarter ounce of water.

Food dyes also work fine. I bought a small box with drop-control vials—green, yellow, red, and blue—in a supermarket. To use food dyes, pour a quarter ounce of cold water (not dyed) into a half ounce of liquid rubber and stir it well. Then squeeze three or four drops of food coloring from the vial and stir the water–rubber mixture again.

You can use any dye that will mix with water, even tempera watercolors or waterproof drawing ink.

Pour the mixture onto the center of the glass, forming a circle. Spread the circle with the flat stick, to a rectangle five inches by seven inches. This size will give you the right thickness to produce sixty to seventy-five flies. The liquid rubber will dry on the glass in about six to eight hours, depending on room temperature. If you look at it periodically as it dries, you will notice that it dries much darker than when wet. You will be able to tell when it's dry if it all looks to be one solid color.

When you see that it has dried to one solid color, you can remove it from the glass. There are really two ways to do this. Even though it is dry, the latex is still so sticky that if you let one part touch another, you won't get them apart. Here is the way I think works best: spread some talcum powder evenly over the top of the rubber sheet. Using your thumb and forefinger, start peeling at one corner and, as you peel the rubber sheet slowly off the glass, pour talcum powder on the underside. After the sheet is completely off the glass, dust off the excess powder with a clean rag. Another way to remove the sheet rubber is to submerge the glass with the sheet on it in six inches of water, then peel the sheet off underwater. Stick it on the edge of a shelf to dry. If you find it still too sticky to work with after it dries, talcum powder it.

1. Stir the colored water and Mold-Tex together.

2. Pour the Mold-Tex–water mixture onto a clean glass.

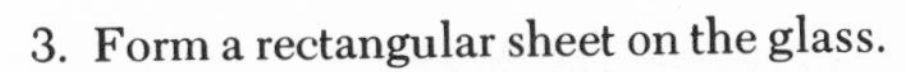

3. Form a rectangular sheet on the glass.

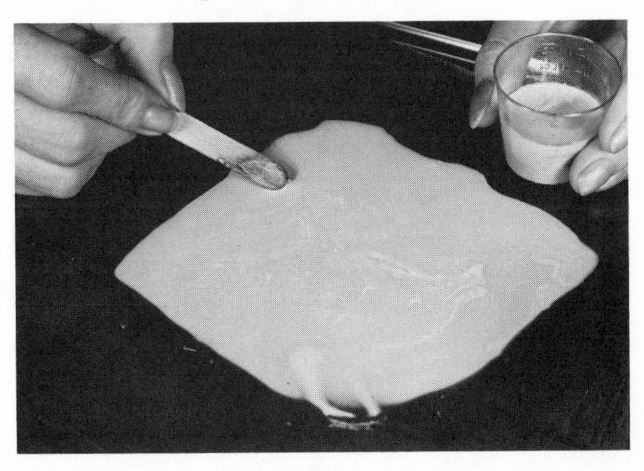

4. Remove the dried Mold-Tex sheet. The talcum powder prevents sticking. Note that the dry Mold-Tex sheet is almost as dark as the original dyed water.

You now have a flat, thin sheet of colored rubber material ready to be cut into strips that can be wrapped onto the shank of a hook. Cut the strips to widths according to the hook size you are planning to use: about one-sixteenth of an inch for a size 18 hook. The best cutting tool to use is a small paper cutter like the ones used to cut photographic paper; the next best is a good sharp scissors.

The Mold-Tex Ant

You don't have to be an accomplished flytyer to make ants with Mold-Tex strips. If you go through the effort to make Mold-Tex sheets following my instructions and make these ants, I know you will agree that it was the easiest fly you ever tied.

There is one special step for making Mold-Tex ants. When you pour the liquid rubber on the glass, you must spread it to a larger rectangle so that when the sheet dries it will be a lot thinner than the sheets you would make for nymph bodies.

Remember, Mold-Tex strips are very elastic and strong. A strip cut from a sheet to a size of one-sixteenth of an inch wide by about four inches long will make an ant on a size 12 hook, and the same-sized strip will also make an ant down to a size 24 hook. All you have to do is stretch the strip to the hook size you are using; the more you stretch it the narrower and thinner it will become.

You won't have to use head cement or tying thread to make this ant. And I won't mention color here, because there are red, black, brown, and other colors of ants, depending on what color you have made your Mold-Tex sheet.

These ants are not only effective for trout at the right time, but also take bluegills anytime. I have caught literally hundreds of them on ants I weighted with a few turns of lead wire under each hump. The Mold-Tex ant feels rubbery in a trout's or bluegill's mouth, so the fish won't reject it as quickly—and it is practically indestructible.

You can also use Mold-Tex to make durable, soft nymph bodies. Here is a pattern for the brown willow fly nymph found in many of our swift western rivers and streams, especially in Montana, Wyoming, Colorado, Utah, and Idaho.

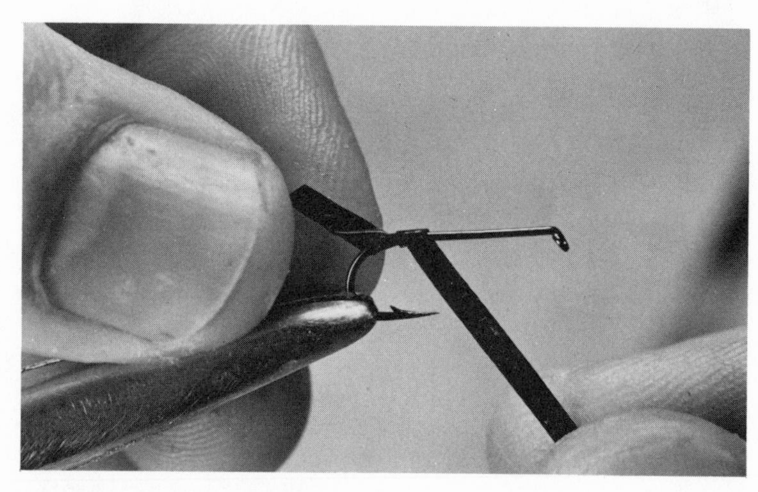

1. From your thin Mold-Tex sheet cut a strip four inches long and 1/16-inch wide. With one strip you are going to wrap the two humps. Start the rear hump on the shank of the hook at a point corresponding to between the barb and the point. To start the first hump, grasp a half-inch or so of the end of the strip between your left thumb and index finger. With the longer end in your right hand, wrap the first turn over on itself to hold the strip in place.

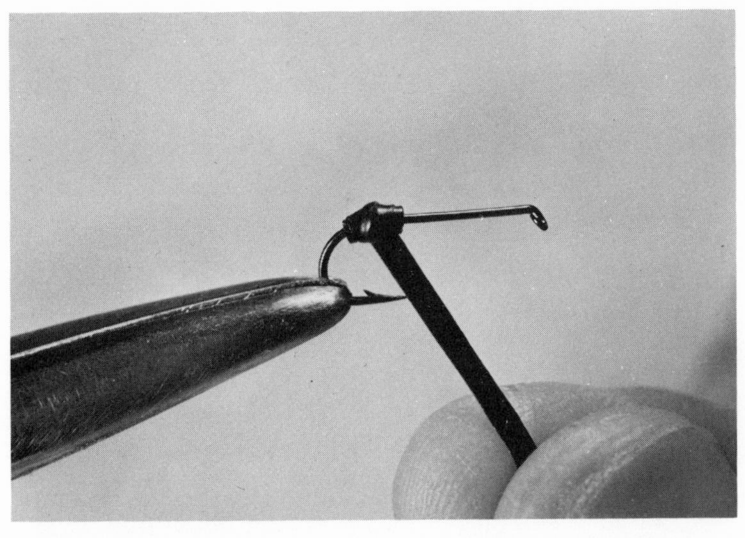

2. Grip hackle pliers on the long end to hold tension on the strip, leaving your right hand free to cut off the excess half-inch you started with. Remove the hackle pliers, and, being sure to keep tension on the strip, wrap about five turns on top of each other. Keep the strip flat and stretch it according to the size hook you are using.

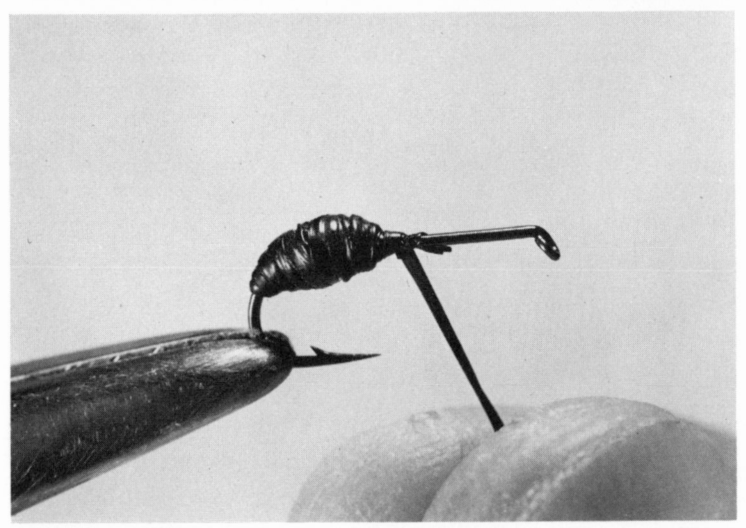

3. Next, to obtain the football shape of the humps, start making wraps around each end of the five wraps you had previously piled on top of each other. Bring the strip around the bottom and over the top of the right end, then around the bottom and over the top of the left end. It's just like making figure-eight wraps.

4. Keeping the strip flat and applying tension as you wrap it, wrap the front hump the same as you did the rear one. Leave a space between the humps for the legs, which will come later.

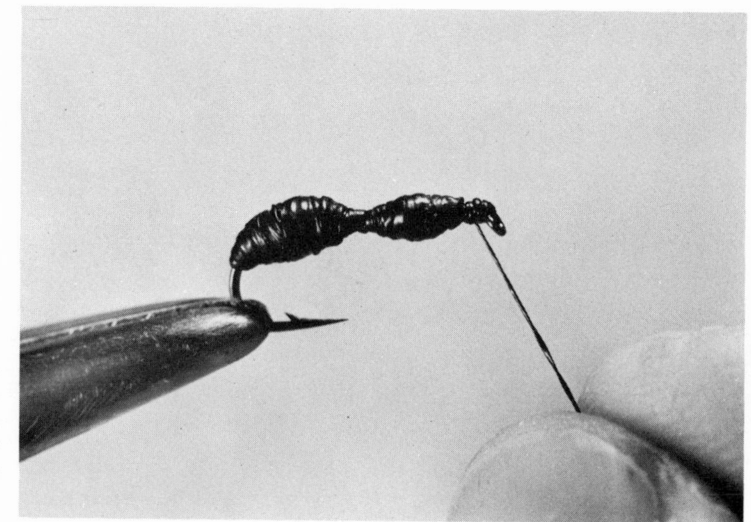

5. When the humps meet with your satisfaction, approach the eye of the hook; stretch and at the same time *twist* the strip. Keep twisting it until it looks like a piece of thread, and then make a couple of half-hitches behind the eye of the hook, and trim off the excess.

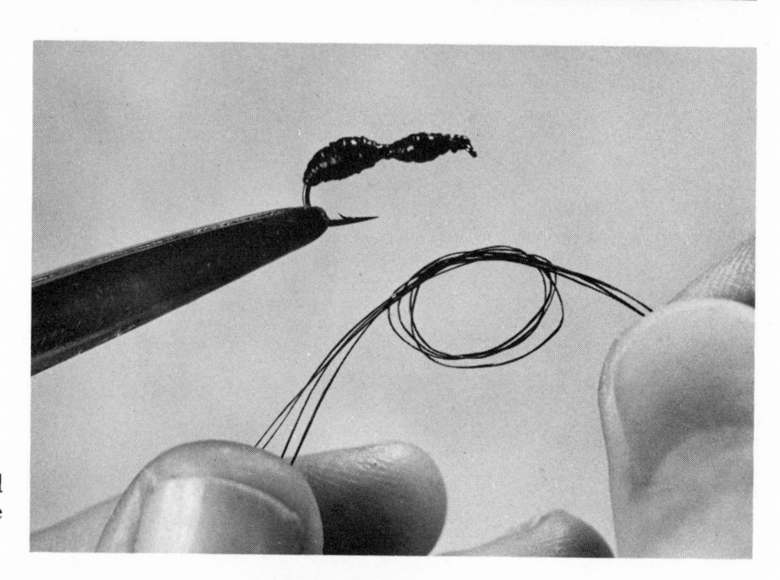

6. The legs are made from a long piece of thread doubled twice; make a simple overhand knot in the doubled thread, leaving a wide, open loop.

7. Slip the open loop of the knot around the midsection of the ant and pull it tight, with the knot on top.

8. Cut off both sides of the threads to the size legs you want. This will give you four legs on each side; of course, I know ants only have three legs on each side, but most trout don't take the time to count the legs. Put a small drop of cement on the knot and you have your ant.

Bill Charles's Stonefly Nymph

Hook:	No. 6 4XL
Weight:	.025 lead wire
Tail:	brown hackle quill
Body:	orange Mold-Tex strip
Wing Pads:	body feathers from Chinese pheasant, treated
Legs:	brown neck hackle quills
Antennae:	stripped hackle quills

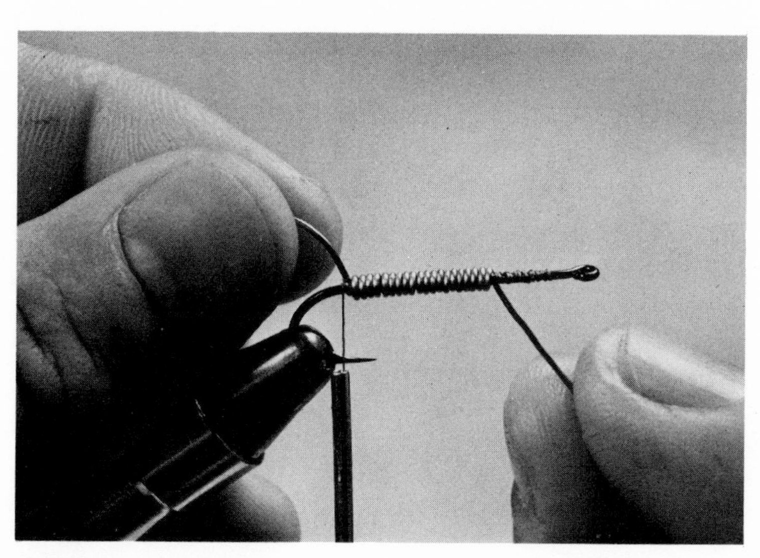

1. Start to wrap thread on the shank at a point above the point of the hook, and close the wrap at the eye. Now, starting at a point on the shank below the thread, wrap 21 turns of lead wire. The body should be wrapped a little wider where the wire is wrapped over the thread, and narrower where the wire was wrapped over the bare hook.

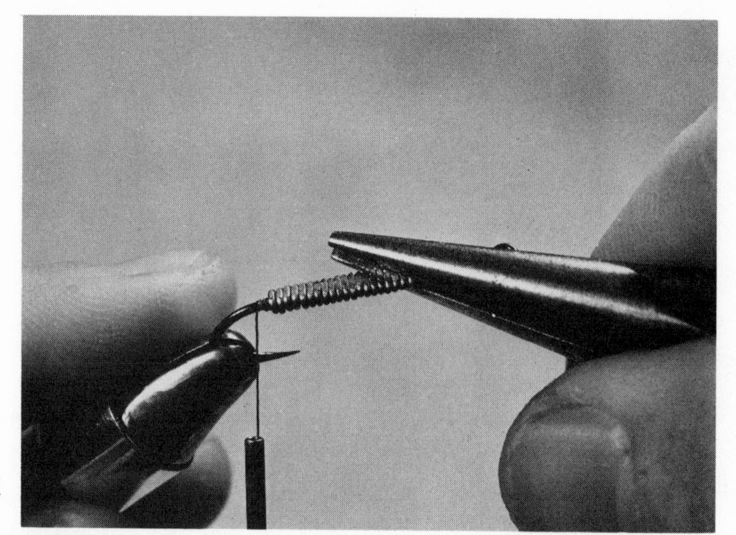

2. Flatten the lead body with a pair of smooth-jawed long-nosed pliers or a similar tool.

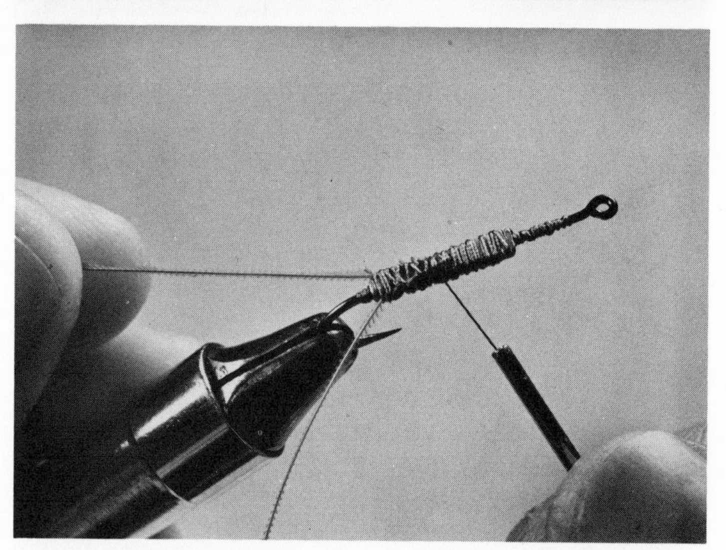

3. For tails, strip the fibers from the sides of two brown hackles. Flatten the center quills on the ends where they are to be tied on, so they don't roll or leave a hump. Color the hackle stems a dark brown with a felt-tip marker.

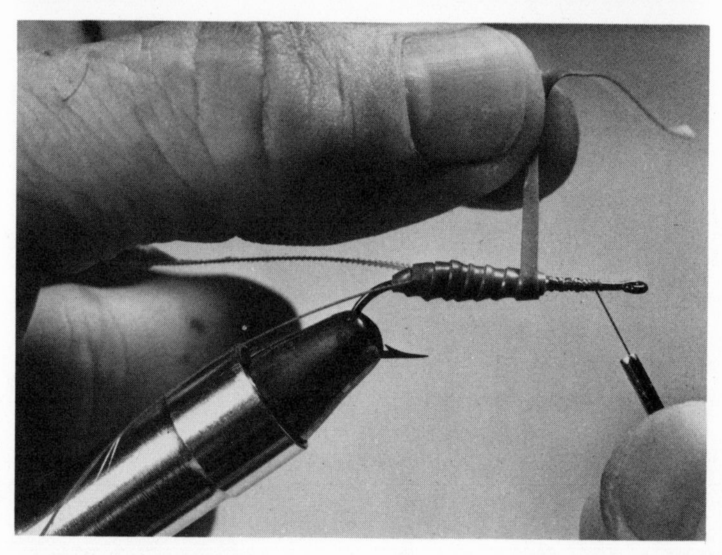

4. After the tails are tied in, wrap the body with an orange Mold-Tex strip, overlapping each turn slightly to create eight or ten segments. Then color only the top with a dark brown felt-tip marker, leaving the nymph with an orange belly—just like the natural.

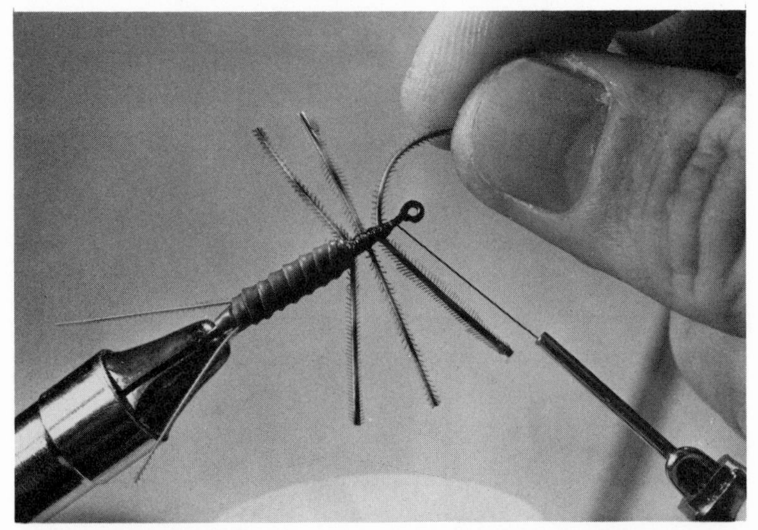

5. Make the legs from a wet brown neck. You want hackles with thick center stems. Trim the fibers on each side of the stem as close as you can without cutting them off completely (I use a straight-bladed toenail clipper). Starting with the rear legs, place the trimmed hackle stems under the shank and warp them over and under.

6. Wrap the thorax with brown dubbing around the body and between the legs. Now your nymph is ready for wing pads and antennae.

7. Dip Chinese pheasant body feathers in head cement and pull the cement through the feathers with your thumb and index finger; hold them until the cement dries. It should look like the second feather in the sequence above.

8. Cut two wing pads from the glued feathers. Tie them on top of each other on top of the thorax so that the bottom wing pad is twice as long as the top one. Color them dark brown.

9. Tie in two stripped hackle quills for antennae, bend the legs with tweezers, and you're finished.

19

Today's Materials and Tools

by Dave Whitlock

Today, fly-tying is paralleling fly-fishing's popularity, and, in fact, has sparked its own revolution in methods, materials, and tools. With the greater numbers of flytyers come more advances in tying techniques, diversity in patterns, and a new and larger demand on the materials market. And this growing market has been a stimulus to manufacturers and suppliers to develop and expand their range of products. Fly-tying services now border on big business.

Still, the manufacture of fishing flies remains, for the most part, a handcraft operation. Flies are manufactured by individuals, whether they are employed by companies like Dan Bailey and Orvis, are self-employed contract or retail tyers, custom tyers—or simply amateurs who tie for their own and their friends' needs. Of course this range of individual talent creates a wild diversity of needs and products. And, given all the different fish species we fly-fish for today and all the standard patterns for these fish (plus the variations or experimental ties), the complexity of needs is almost incomprehensible.

Ten years ago most supply catalogs were pamphlet-thin, offering a choice of a few basic tools, natural and synthetic materials, hooks, glues, and so on. Today the same businesses present in their catalog pages a staggering array of products for fly-tying, and new companies are appearing each year.

Before the fly-fishing revolution started in America and Europe, most materials (feathers, hair, and fibers) were derived indirectly, as byproducts of other manufacturing. Just as fly-tying demand began to grow for these materials, many became scarce, because of limited quantities or the nature of their availability. Civilization itself uprooted many sources by destroying natural animal and fowl populations.

Today this shortage dilemma is being solved either by developing domesticated populations of birds and animals or by seeking suitable substitutes from more plentiful natural sources. Initially, the idea was almost traumatic to grizzled traditionalists. But awareness of our ecological predicament has made it incumbent on the collectors, marketers, and buyers of materials to refrain from using the rare or endangered species that lend their hides to decorating our hooks.

As the regular supply of natural feathers has dwindled and the number of customers has dramatically increased, the stage has been set for producing these birds (animals, in rarer cases) solely for sale of their feathers as a primary product, with their potential meat sale as secondary. With the intelligent application of sound genetics and diet, superior feathers can be "manufactured" to meet the highest standards of flytying. At the present this is being done with domestic birds as well as with a few wild species. The prices of such unique feathers and hair will necessarily reflect the development investment and expenses of domestic confinement, feeding, and production.

Another alternative is the almost untapped source of wild furs and feathers from game killed by hunting sports. But it is doubtful that this waste of prime materials will ever be converted into market stocks, because of game laws prohibiting sales of wild game plumage and so forth. And we must be cautious not to encourage market killing by creating a lucrative sales demand for these skins.

However, flytyers can help themselves to make use of these materials by making local hunters aware of their needs and desires for these game overcoats. Probably 99 percent of the legally killed wood duck feathers go into the garbage. Many prime deer hides rot on the ground or deteriorate on some garage wall each year, while up the street Fred Featherbender orders small squares of the same hair from a dealer a thousand miles away to tie his muddler minnows. A visit to a local hunter's house, to his club meeting, or a few cards with your needs and phone number left with a local firearms dealer can almost overnight yield rich bounties of these wasting prime materials. Almost without exception, hunters are happy to give you what they otherwise have to dispose of themselves.

Similar excursions to small poultry processors, farms, trappers, fur-coat manufacturers, game farms, and taxidermists will yield good results. I have more than once dressed game for hunters as they left the hunting grounds, for the fresh feathers or hair. I also keep my eyes open for fresh roadside kills of small domestic and wild birds and animals. A couple of Ziploc bags and knives and scissors stored in your glove compartment will hold these roadside treasures in your trunk until you can clean them for use. Over the years I've collected owls, hawks, pheasants, grouse, prairie chickens, quail, squirrels, skunks, chuckars, cats, foxes, raccoons, chickens, mink, muskrat, coyotes, etc. that would have otherwise been wasted. They provided me with many fine materials unavailable from dealers at any cost. Some states might have certain laws restricting this type of collecting, but a call to your local warden will clarify what you may or may not do. He may also be able to suggest other sources of wild-game feathers and hair.

Feathers

Cock and hen chicken hackles have always been high on the list of important tying feathers. With the decline of the import market now, and with greater demands for rare and high quality hackles, a number of flocks are being developed around the country that should provide birds at least ample to meet the demands.

I have seen necks from natural blue duns, grizzly, cream, white, black, and ginger hackles that were bred and fed for the domestic hackle market, and they are simply beautiful in every respect. The hackles on these necks are shiny, stiff fibered, thin stemmed, beautifully marked, and almost without web. Besides being very long and narrow, most feathers have almost no taper. The best of it all is the size range: most have large counts of sizes 10 through 22.

For example, Dave Kashner recently sent me a blue dun neck as perfect as any I've seen since Bill Tobin of Cortland, New York, introduced his great strain of hackle some five or six years ago. Dave claimed he had a plentiful source of these beautiful natural duns for 1975 Orvis customers. I have several supergrade grizzly necks that Dave Inks of Creative Sports Enterprises sent me that are loaded with feathers from sizes 10 to 28! Such grizzly necks didn't exist anywhere ten years ago.

At the point of this writing, these special-purpose hackles from necks and saddle capes are coming on the market in increasing numbers. Their prices reflect the high-cost initial investment, development, and quality. But even at these prices they are worth it. I expect, moreover, that prices will go down some once the market demand is met and more competition develops.

Before these developments, there was talk, and some activity, generated by the idea of synthetic hackle. However, this project was temporarily postponed when it became obvious that breeders were becoming serious about developing "feather" flocks.

Turkeys, pheasants, ducks, geese, and some exotic species are also being raised for their plumage, for initial market consideration. When a jungle cock neck costs twenty-five dollars, or a matched pair of speckled oak-turkey quills costs seventy-five cents, or wood-duck feathers sell for twenty cents each, the opportunity and encouragement is provided for enterprising people to breed birds for feather sale. So I expect that we will have better days ahead as soon as breeders develop the product for the growing market.

Most of the quality material catalogs are stocking these pen-raised feathers in limited quantities. They are pretty easy to recognize by their prices—usually 100 percent to 150 percent higher than feathers from those birds that are still collected from sources other than feather growers.

Hair

The same dilemma we find ourselves in with regard to the world supply of wild birds for fly-tying applies to many fur bearers as well. But here, however, the outlook isn't so dismal, for there are increasing supplies of domesticated hair and fur, as well as increasing efforts to collect hunting kills for market use. And the populations of deer, squirrel, elk, muskrat, beaver, skunk, etc. are on the general increase, so these furs are therefore almost always available.

Synthetic fibers are also especially adaptable as fur substitutes, and are gaining acceptance with flytyers each year, especially substitutes for polar bear, otter, seal, and Australian opossum, which is almost impossible to find now.

The most noteworthy new natural hair source is the various deerlike hairs. I list them here, as I consider them in a new perspective; though they have been available for years, they have not received due attention by tyers.

Standard northern whitetail deer. Undoubtedly the most plentiful and versatile hair we have for tying today. It is available from all fly-material catalogs in natural dun brown, natural white, and dyed colors.

Southern whitetail deer. The identical animal to the northern whitetail except that the hair is usually more wiry and shorter, though colored and marked similarly, due to warmer climates. It does not flare as well, but it is superior for hackle, wings, and tail on western patterns, grasshoppers, and caddis.

Mule deer. A western plains and mountain deer that is usually more coarse and colored more grayish than whitetail. Excellent for tails, clipped bodies, hairwings.

Antelope. This rather coarse hair is either white with a gray base or a rich cinnamon-brown with a gray base. This hair dyes easily and flares better than any other I've seen. It is tender but has superior floating ability.

Elk. Elk is very dense dun gray, cream, light brown hair that flares very well and is somewhat more durable than most deer hair. It is tough to beat for hair-bass bugs, extended bodies, and wings. It takes dyes very well, but it—and the antelope hair—lack the interesting grizzled markings that mule and whitetail deer have. It varies greatly in length and texture.

Caribou. A fairly short dun-gray-to-light-cream dense hair that is extremely soft and light, but somewhat tender. It is particularly easy to flare with light pressure, and its texture is perfect for smaller deer-hair-bodied trout flies. It does not dye well because of its tender texture.

Dall sheep. A dense, pure-white hair that is soft and fairly tender. It flares well but is not particularly suited for general all-purpose use. It makes nice dense trout fly bodies and will dye light shades easily.

Moose. A very dark slate, dun-brown and black, coarse, tough hair that varies greatly in length. It is ideal for wings, tails, and bodies. It does not flare easily but does make great bass bugs if you use a strong thread to tie them with. It is ideal for ants and patterns that use special, knotted legs. Of course, the mane is a type of hair different from the body hair and is used for imitation quill bodies and insect legs.

Synthetic Materials

For years, flytyers have been willing to accept a few manmade materials for tying a limited portion of their flies. In the last five years however, the list of synthetics has dramatically increased. This increase and a new attitude toward fly-tying with synthetics has brought about a new era of fly development.

I have found a different, but keen, liking for many of these materials, and each one opens up new possibilities for creating new patterns or improving upon more-standard ones. Although many of these materials are manufactured for other uses, we are seeing more and more of them modified or adapted to fly-tying. For example, Doug Swisher and Dave McCann have been developing polypropylene fibers for several years in this manner. Some results of their efforts are the Poly II and a new grade of polypropylene loose wool matt ideal for nymph, dry-fly and streamer-dubbed bodies.

Polypropylene

Polypropylene is a derivative of petroleum. It is an oily plasticlike solid, naturally transparent and slightly lighter than water. For fly-tying, it is useful in thin sheets and filaments forming wool or yarn. It can be tinted any color. Light shades have an extremely lifelike sparkle and translucence. Polypropylene yarn is used in streamer wings, insect wings, and to form fly-bodies similar to those of floss. This year the yarn, called Polywing, is being made and sold for mayfly dun and spinner wings in natural shades of tan, gray and white, yellow, olive, and black. The combed-out yarn makes beautiful streamer wings, especially for saltwater patterns. It has superior action to bucktail or polar-bear hair, but it does have more tendency to tangle.

Polypropylene film or sheet. This can be cut into strips and used for nymph and shrimp backs, bodies, and wings. It is usually a translucent color, or clear. Most of the common disposal bags, zip-lock bags, and cleaner bags are polypropylene, and are quite useful in many ways for tying.

Polypropylene wool. This loose-fiber polypropylene is ideal for either straight dubbing or with other materials to form special dubbing blends. It is useful in all sorts of fly-bodies, from shrimp to dry flies. Fireside Angler calls their new poly wool Poly X, Leonard has Polyblend, Fly Fisherman's Bookcase has Poly-Dubbing, and Orvis a similar polywool dubbing. These are all stocked in a wonderful spectrum of useful colors that can be further expanded by mixing them in a blender, or with blend cards, to any shade desired.

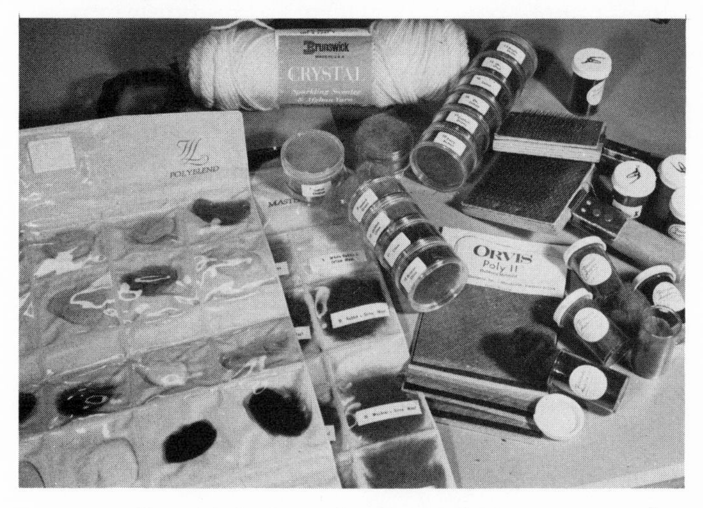

New synthetic fur-dubbing materials. *Left to right:* Leonard's Polyblend and Masterblend, Orvis Poly II, Orvis Spectrablend and Poly Body, Poly Wing Material, Crystal Orlon Wool, and Fireside Angler's Poly X.

Dave McCann has just this year introduced another improved polywool called Fly Rite that is a considerable texture improvement for most dubbing purposes.

David Beasley, Leonard's production manager, has informed me that the Leonard company is introducing a new special polydubbing especially blended with several textures of polypropylene to accomplish an underfur guard hair texture so popular in nymph body dubbing. It will be marketed by the name of Nymphblend. There are twelve initial colors, based on a color summary survey of Ernie Schwiebert's book *Nymphs.* These colors will be most useful for tying nymphs of the mayflies, caddis, and stoneflies.

Poly fiber matt. This is Poly II, an Orvis exclusive fabricated by Dave McCann. This year it is made available in several more useful colors, about seventeen shades in all. In my opinion these matt sheets are the most convenient poly-dubbing method for making a limited number of small patterns at home or on the stream. Blending is more difficult, but can be accomplished with blend cards or by hand. The matt will not separate and blend as well in a blender. These matt sheets store flat and carry very easily in the smallest streamside vest kits.

Orlon

Orlon is a petroleum product very similar to nylon. It is fabricated mainly for garments, as a lamb's-wool substitute, and to my knowledge is available only in yarn form. It has a texture most like natural lamb's wool, but somewhat softer. It has more sheen than wool and is perfect dubbing by itself or mixed with natural fur. I use it almost exclusively now to replace several hard-to-get or expensive dubbing furs. In yarn form it can be wrapped on a hook to form a compact, fuzzy body. It can be cut into ½- to ⅛-inch pieces and put into a blender to form an excellent dubbing wool matt. By itself or mixed with other fibers, it allows dubbing bodies to be wrapped with great ease. Because of its texture and particular shape it holds or meshes on itself or other fur extremely well. It is not available in most catalogs, but can be found at sewing-material or yarn shops. It comes also blended with nylon, giving it a natural-sparkle effect that makes for extremely interesting dubbing.

Nylon

Synthetic nylon has a great number of uses to the flytyer these days. Because of its physical character, it must be drawn into filament sizes to be useful for fly-tying purposes. It is transparent, but accepts dyes very easily and quickly.

Nylon monofilament. Larger diameters of round nylon monofilament (.006″ to .030″) can be used to form extended, wrapped, or woven fly-bodies, to hook snag-guards on flies, to shape certain bodies, heads, and wings, and as a whip-finishing tool.

Flattened monofilament. This is the shape that George Grant uses to overwrap his famous streamer and nymph bodies, and that Ernie Schwiebert speaks of so often in *Nymphs*. The Cortland Line Company makes it under the name Cobra.

Fine round monofilament (.006″ to .0001″). Of course, nylon filament thread is its greatest application to fly-tying. There is a wide scope of these threads, from single-strand to braided to twisted to flat multifilament thread. All colors, all sizes. These small filaments are also great as artificial hair for streamers and jigs. As I mentioned earlier, it is used as a blend with orlon wool, to which it lends an unusual sparkle effect.

A wide range of nylon products is listed in most catalogs, and it is available in tackle stores and sewing stores. Braided nylon rope can be unbraided, and straightened by stretching and steaming. This natural, transparent, straight, fine hairlike filament can then be used for wonderful wing material, giving a cross between marabou and polar-bear hair for action and color. Even women's discarded sheer-gauge nylon stockings make great wings on hatching nymph patterns. The uses for nylon are limited only by the flytyer's imagination.

Mylars

Mylar, a superstrength plastic film, is having quite an impact on fly-tying. It has mostly been known for its metallic finishes, similar to tinsel. However, unlike tinsel it does not usually incorporate metal, in order to achieve reflective effects. It is quite flexible, usually governed by the layer thickness. It is made in thin sheet form, and cut to any desired widths.

Mylar is available now in tinsellike materials that are easy to work with, strong and flexible. The colors are usually metallic gold, silver, copper, green, blue, yellow, and red. Besides these tinsels, it is also available in small sheets and in a large number of composite forms, such as braided piping, chenille, and ropes. Although there are a wide number of related tarnishproof plastics, I am referring to the whole family as mylars in order to avoid further complications.

Mylar sheets. A very thin, superstrong mylar, usually gold on one side, silver on the other. This sheet can be cut to any shape the tyer wishes for wings, ribbing, streamer bodies, and metallic, floating minnow bugs. Available in most material catalogs now.

Mylar piping. Mylar piping is a metallic-finished tubing braided over a cotton thread core. It comes in three or four sizes and can be used for streamer bodies, over quill-body floating minnows, etc. It creates an extremely realistically scaled minnow-finish effect. It is available in gold and silver in all material catalogs, and in crimson, red, and Kelly green. It is a bit tender to fish teeth or for rough handling, so it is best to put a vinyl or resin finish over it after tying it to the hook.

Mylar tinsel. An extremely tough, flat, oval strand of mylar that is a superior substitute for all metallic tinsel uses. Although most dealers will soon have these tinsels in stock, Fireside Angler of Melville, New York, has announced it to the market first in their "Firesel" mylar tinsel. It is stocked in popular widths with a gold-and-silver back-to-back finish that makes it extremely handy and economical. Best of all, it is supertough and resists the irritating breaks so common with flat metallic tinsels. It can be straightened with tension for incorporation in streamer wings and bug tails.

Ned Grey of Sierra Tackle, Montrose, California, also stocks a very useful mylar strip-tinsel that is excellent for flashy wing insertions or body ribbing. Herter's has a very good spooled, metallic, plastic mylar material. It is extremely flexible, but a bit too fragile. I use it a great deal, though, for saltwater-streamer wing flash.

There are almost countless other mylar materials that can be applied to fly-fishing. Look for these in fly-materials catalogs, sewing-material shops, and hobby and craft stores. Around Christmas time watch for a lot of unusual plastic, metallic decorations and wrapping materials. They are fantastic for fly-tying. Usually, you will find a lot of wild colors besides the common gold-and-silver finishes. Christmas tree icicles are made of plastic now and are super for fly-tying.

Latex

Latex is a natural-rubber compound, not actually new to fly-tying, but a great number of new ideas for its application have recently become popular. In sheet form, such as dental latex and balloons, or in a liquid form (such as Mold-Tex), it is an extremely easy, versatile, and durable material to create an infinite number of body-building methods on all types of flies. Raleigh Boaze popularized dental-latex sheet materials with his latex caddis-larva nymphs. This same latex sheeting is available in an excellent range of colors from Fireside Angler. Bill Charles of Chicago has perfected the technique of using water-based liquid latex into one of the most revolutionary techniques I've ever witnessed. We have asked that Bill describe his complete technique for the *Fly-Tyer's Almanac* in this section.

Seal-ex

Seal-ex is a synthetic Kodel polyester yarn product, an excellent substitute seal fur for dubbing fur bodies. Poul Jorgenson introduced this unique material to us and Fly Fisherman's Bookcase now distributes it. Alone or blended with other natural furs, it makes an outstanding medium-texture dubbing. It has perfect realistic translucence and the sparkle of real item seal, yet is much more reasonable in price, and infinitely easier to work with.

Fake straw or raffia

There is a synthetic decorative straw made from polypropylene, called Ribbon Straw, on the market now that is relatively new to most tyers. It was made originally for hobby crafts and decorative wrapping, but it has a luster and texture that promise infinite uses in fly-tying. The Polystickle streamer was one of the first patterns to use it, to form the minnow's body, back, and fins. It can be used as wrapped, segmented-body materials similar to raffia or peacock herl, minnow bodies, or as wings for duns, spinners, and nymphs. And it comes in an almost infinite variety of colors. Some catalogs might stock it by now, but you can also easily find it in hobby-craft stores.

Dyes

To my knowledge, there are no new dyes on the market today. But the new photodyeing *process* is the ultimate means of dyeing cock hackle to any desired shades of dun. Eric Leiser's book *Fly-Tying Materials* covers the photodyeing process quite well, and it alone is worth the price of Eric's excellent book. I'd advise anyone to learn it.

It should be noted here that besides these excellent commercial dyes produced by Veniard and Herter, the flytyer can also make great use of so-called fabric dyes sold in most local drug, department, or food stores. These are extremely convenient to use and work well on almost all synthetic materials, feathers, or hair. The three that are easiest to use and most readily available locally are Putnam, Rit, and Tintex.

Fly-Tying Threads

Today's threads are truly reflective of fly-tying needs in sizes, varieties, and colors to accommodate all our needs. Nylon, of course, has been developed to the extent that there is little need to rely on silk, cotton, polyester cotton, or rayon any more. Silk is still used by those tyers who love its texture and look. But for all practical purposes, nylon is our best fly-tying thread. The most popular nylons are: Danville's Herb Howard Prewaxed, Nymo, Monocord, and Buz's Super Mono. Almost without exception, all the materials' sources listed in the Appendix carry complete selections of nylon threads in wide size and color ranges.

Substitute Fly-Tying Materials

Over the last ten years, most flytyers have become more open-minded about substituting materials as many original or natural ones have become scarce, expensive, or unlawful to buy and sell or import. This dilemma also prompted flytyers to take a more objective and positive attitude toward materials and patterns. They have finally realized that, in most cases, there are excellent substitute materials, easily available, that either equal or surpass the standard materials for any given pattern. And in fact, most early fly patterns and materials were simply the result of using a naturally handy material that suited the requirements in color and fiber.

After all, why would a trout strike an almost inanimate fly but not strike leaves, particles, etc., of similar colors and sizes that were floating right alongside the fly? The popular explanation is that fish can somehow distinguish animal fiber from vegetable or mineral fiber. But tests have since shown that the fish has no true preference for natural materials if the fly is tied with synthetics that equal the animal hair or feathers in color, texture, and action.

Acceptance of these facts allows us to break from old sacred tradition, if need be, and search for natural or synthetic substitutes. Of course, most flytyers would love to duplicate the original materials and methods from a natural love for traditional art forms. But if a fly can be constructed to meet the imitation requirements (i.e., shape, color, textures and *action*), with different materials, then neither fish nor man can object. The substitutes listed here have proven equal to the original material. And I can say, without exception, that there are others that will prove to be even superior substitutes in the future.

Substitutes for feathers

Jungle-cock eyed hackle. Plastic or vinyl fake feather, pheasant shoulder feather coated with vinyl cement, and vinyl coated grizzly hackle trimmed to shape

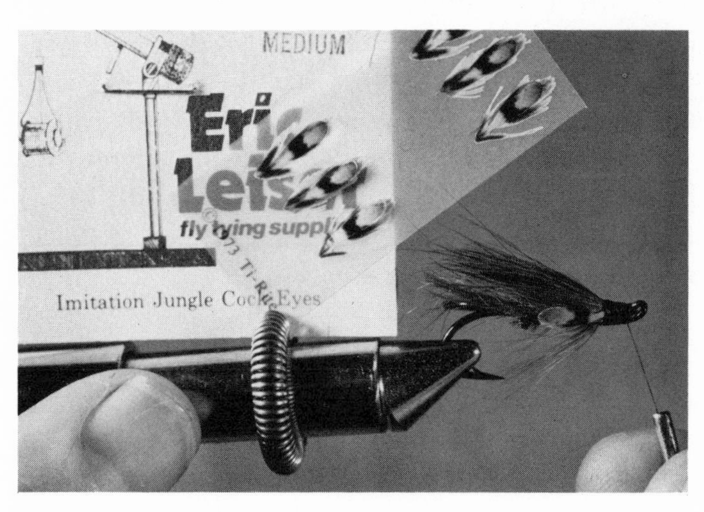

Synthetic jungle cock eyes, an Eric Leiser fly-tying material product.

European partridge. Western sharptailed grouse (Hungarian partridge), bobwhite quail, ruffed grouse, and hen pheasant

Prairie chicken. Hen pheasant, mallard hen, black duck drake and hen, grizzly chicken breast, dyed brown or gold, chukar partridge, and sharptailed grouse

Condor quill. Domestic or wild-turkey wing quill, wild and domestic goose-wing quill, blue-heron wing quill, buzzard wing quill, peacock-wing quill and tail herl, and moose mane

Wood duck barred flank. Mallard pintail, teal or gadwall drake barred-breast and flank, dyed wood duck or Egyptian goose flank

Hooded merganser barred flank. Heavy-barred teal, pintail, or widgeon-duck flank, dyed dark brown

Marabou. Wild or domestic turkey fluff-feathers from rump, flank, and beneath wings. Almost any large bird has some of these types of feathers on it beneath the outer, main posterior feathers

Oak-speckled turkey-wing quills. Cinnamon turkey quills dyed brown: natural, dark, domestic or wild turkey gray-and-white wing quills dyed brown. Speckled wing quill of cock peacock, hen pheasant tail

Wood duck white breast feathers. Bufflehead duck breast, domestic white-duck neck, and merganser duck breast

Substitutes for furs

Fitch tail. Most small tree-and-ground-squirrel tails; natural, bleached, or dyed. Also marten, mink tail, chinchilla tail

Beaver belly fur. Muskrat belly fur, otter belly fur, Poly II, Poly Blend, and Fly Rite

Seal fur. Orlon yarn, orlon–nylon yarn, polypropylene yarn, polar-bear underfur, fake bear-hair fur. Black bear underfur bleached, dyed, or natural. Seal-ex

Natural white polar-bear hair. White kip or calf tail, mountain goat neck hair, white combed-out polypropylene yarn, white or natural combed-out nylon rope, nylon hair, white fake bear-hair rug, some white dog hair, and fish hair

Dyed polar-bear hair. Black bear (natural, bleached, or bleached and dyed), calf or kip-tail (natural or dyed), fake bear-hair rug, dyed nylon hair, polypropylene yarn (combed out), and fish hair

Australian opossum. Bleached beaver-back, chinchilla fur, bleached woodchuck, natural and bleached raccoon, bleached gray fox, domestic long-haired cat, some long-haired squirrels, cottontail, swamp, snowshoe, and jackrabbit fur.

Fly-Tying Tools

The commercial market for fly-tying tools and materials is expanding almost daily, making it impossible for the average tyer to see samples or test all the goodies. For this reason I'm including a summary of the new items now or soon to become available to tyers. Consider this a Whitlock Buyers' Guide in that I'm only including those items that offer a real advantage over older items or similar new ones. It should also be realized that these represent only some of the new merchandise; it would be literally impossible to know and include all the available items. The authors will be able to update more perfectly and expand on new fly-tying areas with each future volume.

Vises

Since I wrote the material-and-tool chapter for *Art Flick's Master Fly-Tying Guide* (Crown, $10.00), several important new vises have been made available on the market. Two were discontinued; with the demise of the Flyfisherman's Shoppe, Inc., the Swisher-Richards pedestal vise and the Swisher-Richards Streamside Porta-Vise are no longer available. Both were specifically designed to accommodate the matching-the-hatch type of fly-tying.

As flytyers become increasingly keen on entomology, thanks to so many fine hatch-matching books, the average hook size must become smaller and smaller. Vises with positive long, narrow, pointed jaws are most practical for the sizes below 12.

The Thompson Model-A Vise, which seems to have slipped a bit in quality of materials, has a better-shaped jaw now for this purpose than my ten-year-old original Thompson. However, still-smaller jaws are needed for consistent tying of small flies in the 16-to-28 range.

Leonard has a version (as does Veniard) of the original Croydon type of vise that accommodates small hooks nicely. Leonard's is called Flybody Hook Vise, after the new Yorkshire Fly-body hook, and has the additional feature of reversing jaw direction to accommodate better one of the methods of tying with the Fly-body hook.

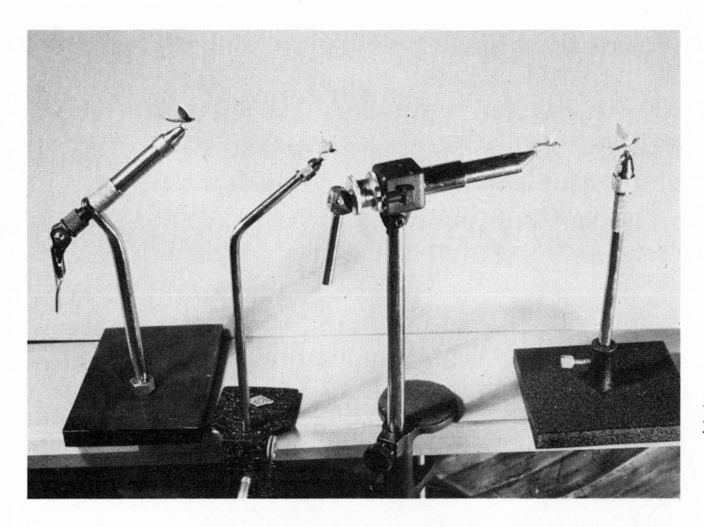

New fly-tying vises *(left to right)*: Fly Fisherman's Bookcase Special Pedestal Thompson A., Midge Vise, Orvis Vise, Leonard's Fly-body Hook Vise.

Leonard's versatile new Catskill Vise can be adjusted to 30, 60, and 90 degrees, as well as a vertical position, and accommodates a wide range of hook sizes, including flybody sizes. Designed with great simplicity, this vise is easy to adjust and operate, and since it includes an adaptor for streamside use, it holds great promise as an all-purpose vise.

The Veniard No. 5 Midge Vise has a standard C-style clamp which will also allow reversal of the jaw direction. (Fly Fisherman's Bookcase and Tackle Service stock this one.) Both these and the original little hand-held Croydon Hand Vise will easily accommodate hooks from sizes 1/0 to 28, and they give you the critical tenths-of-an-inch tolerance that allows for better access to these tiny fly-tying hooks.

Orvis's new superduper Custom Rotary vise also has a small jaw accommodation to make tying tiny bugs more practical than do heavier jaw standards.

For intermediate and large hooks, the Veniard Rotating Salmo Vise is fast usurping Thompson's past dominance in this area. This exceptionally sturdy, well-made vise is worth every penny of extra cost. Although most material houses stock the Salmo, there seems to be a shortage of them at times as the popularity of this imported vise increases.

The new Orvis Fly Tying Vise, just being delivered at the time of this writing, promises to be an outstanding, all-purpose, quality vise. With the hook locked in the jaw, the jaw can be rotated a full 360° for rotary use or complete inspection. Detent stops lock the law in position for regular, inverted, double-salmon-regular position, or double-salmon inverted. Adjustable for hook sizes 1/0 to 28. The jaw angle is fully adjustable, and the vise's height is adjustable from 1¼ inches to ¼ inch. Suitable for left- as well as right-hand use. Traditionally, Orvis has represented quality equipment, and their new vise promises to be a significant addition to our fly-tying needs.

In order to cope with the traveling C-clamp vise misfit-to-motel-table syndrome, the Fly Fisherman's Bookcase offers a Sunrise vise, similar to the Thompson model A, with a modified pedestal stand. The same vise will utilize standard clamps as well.

The little Leonard Fly-body Hook Vise also has a flat foot for erect standing on any flat surface, as well as an accessory streamside adaptor that can be screwed into a convenient streamside log or fencepost. I wouldn't recommend attaching it to your leg or your wife's kitchen table.

Besides the popular pocket-sized hand Croydon vise, there are several styles of locking hemostats that serve fairly well as streamside hook benders as well as hook removers.

I have heard that it is possible to machine or grind down standard vise jaws to accommodate more closely the requirements of midge-size-hook tying. If this is possible, and I feel certain it is on most vises, the purchase and modification of a second set of jaws for your present standard vise could increase its hook range somewhat. A local machinist would probably be equipped to restructure the jaws without harming the temper or closure angle.

In the future, I hope we can have a vise available to flytyers that better accommodates the tyers using the upper-size range of hooks regularly. The increase in bass and saltwater fly fishing will certainly justify such a husky, heavy-duty vise.

Bobbins

I think of a good bobbin as simple but functional, light but durable, designed to thread easily—not to tangle or fray the tying silk or nylon, regardless of the size. A bobbin that is too heavy or has too coarse a drag on the thread spool is almost useless for smaller flies. A bobbin should easily adapt to any standard-sized thread spool without a lot of adjustments.

Considering all these qualifications, the Matarelli bobbin, developed in 1953 by Frank Matarelli of San Francisco, is the ultimate bobbin. Frank originated this type of bobbin, which, in many opinions, is certainly the best on the market. A number of companies carry Frank's bobbin under his name, but some others stock it under their

Special new Fireside Angler floss bobbin and New Matarelli Tinsel Bobbin.

own company names; unfortunately, since this makes it easy to get the wrong bobbin. Many of these look-alikes don't measure up to Frank's craftsmanship and quality. When ordering, I'd suggest you either buy those that have Frank's name or ask the company if they are Matarellis.

André Puyans gave me a couple of bobbins produced for Creative Sports Enterprises. These bobbins are quite similar in design to the Matarelli except that both ends of the thread barrel have a flared opening. This simple improvement discourages clogging and practically eliminates thread breakage or fraying.

Frank Matarelli also makes a unique and useful bobbin tool—a bobbin threader and tube cleaner for his own bobbins. It is a two-part tool with a special spring-wire loop on one end for threading. The other end, attached to the loop threader with several lengths of ball chain, is a tempered section of metal rod that just fits inside the bobbin tube for cleaning it out.

Fireside Angler and the Hackle House have a new bobbin (at least it is new to me): a floss bobbin. Although I haven't tried it, the idea is really terrific, since floss is so hard to handle barehanded without fraying, discoloring, or tangling it. This bobbin should also save a lot of tidbits of floss from becoming waste ends. The floss bobbin is designed like the Matarelli thread bobbin, an additional plus for it.

Matarelli has also developed a new use for his famous bobbins. When I heard of the idea of using a bobbin for floss, I suggested to Frank that perhaps a tinsel bobbin would also be extremely practical and useful for the new superstrong and durable mylar tinsels. Frank sent me several designs and my initial tests have proved them to be simply great for flat and oval tinsels like Fireside Angler's Firesel, which comes on small plastic spools. Other tinsels can easily be loaded onto similar spools.

Scissors and other cutting tools

Scissors have always been a tool that varied greatly in quality and durability. At the time of this writing I know of no new revolutionary design. All catalogs stock a variety of good foreign-made scissors that are adequate for fly-tying cutting purposes.

My advice is to look for models that have large finger holes, fine, delicate points, and are made by a recognized firm. Be willing to pay four to six dollars for them—and be just as willing to take care of them. Use at least two sizes, for coarse and fine cutting, to prolong their life. Keep them hidden from wife and kids with an instant alarm system on the cabinet, and learn how to sharpen their blades, or take them to a good cutlery-sharpening man.

I also use razor blades, a hunting knife, X-Acto knives, and Wiss Quick-Clip Speed scissors to supplement my cutting needs. For removal of fuzz around and in a finished fly eye, a hot needle or butane lighter and hackle guards beat the tiniest, sharpest scissor blades.

Hackle pliers

The need remains for hackle pliers that handle tender or tiny feathers without cutting the stems or allowing them to pull free. Unfortunately, this ideal pliers has not yet been manufactured. The best all-around general-use hackle pliers I've found are the Herb Howard models, which come in two sizes. They are simple, sure-gripping pliers. Flyfisherman's Bookcase on the East Coast and Buz's Fly Shop on the West Coast catalog these fine tools under Mr. Howard's name. Several other companies carry them, sometimes, however, hidden under other names.

The minihackle pliers carried by Fly Fisherman's Bookcase are excellent tools for very small, delicate hackle feathers. I like these almost as much as my original Herb Howards for delicate work.

If you have more than your share of hackle-plier problems, you might try tying the hackle-tip first to the hook shank and then grasping the butt stem with your pliers or your fingers. It usually works quite well, and allows you to make use of most prime areas of small hackles. You might also try soaking hackle feathers in water or humidifying them before tying them. This softens the stem and swells fibers, which gives the hackle more flexibility and allows a better grip to the jaws of the hackle pliers.

Fur blenders

The blending of natural animal furs, fake furs, and other synthetic hairlike fibers into dubbing felts for all kinds of fly-bodies has become very popular. I first mixed or blended underfurs into dubbing by hand, which worked OK but never got them truly blended, and it took a long time for enough just to tie a dozen or so nymphs. All that is changed today. Dubbing can be made by hand, in water and detergent shaker bottles, blend cards, electric blenders, dry and wet, and ready-made blends.

Blend cards and electric blenders are new to most tyers—and the best way to go, in my opinion. The blend cards, introduced this year by Fireside Angler, make manual blending of small amounts of fur quick and efficient, especially compared to the hand or water-bottle methods. They are an inexpensive set of specially designed curry combs that mix the various furs into a dubbing blend at the home tying table, or at camp. I find them less messy than the other methods. They are noiseless as well, and create far fewer domestic problems than does use of electric food blenders. Full instructions come with each set of cards.

Three basic methods of blending fur: Leonard's Miniblender, Standard food blender, and Fireside's Blend Cards.

But electric blenders are the ultimate way to blend all types of fur into dubbing. Until recently, however, this usually meant having his-and-her food blenders. Several materials companies now offer a perfect solution for the tyer who doesn't need large amounts of dubbing, yet doesn't want to go manual. This Mini-Blender perfectly accommodates the amateur or pro tyer's blending needs. Their size precludes making commercial amounts of dubbing, but this same size is perfect for creating a limited amount in many color variations, or for economical experimenting with various recipes or materials. Its size also allows for fairly easy portability and storage. It is 110 AC, not battery operated. All this and a fair price—between thirteen and eighteen dollars—makes it a most worthwhile investment.

A standard household food blender can be used as is, or with an aluminum screen-wire insert to reduce the volume. Another way to reduce the volume is to use a half-pint or pint blender jar which comes with some brands of blenders. Purchase an extra blender jar, top, and blade, if you use your wife's blender, to avoid bad scenes. If you are purchasing a home-size blender for yourself, be sure and look at the new ones with a built-in lid stirrer. They're best for blending over a half handful of fur at one whack. Also purchase a spray can of one of the electric-dryer static-electricity depressors for blending use. They make blending much easier, especially on days when the room humidity is very low.

There are quite a few tools on the market that make a lot of tying operations much easier, quicker, or simpler. The more adept you get at using tools, the more speed and consistency you will acquire as time goes by. I've found that, teaching myself how to tie flies some twenty-eight years ago at the age of twelve, I developed a lot of bad manual habits that I had to break later when I became a serious commercial tyer. Without exception, the substitution of good tools to do jobs I had formerly bypassed or done without the required tools has resulted in far better tying for me. Accessory tools that seem unnecessary or clumsy at first to the tyer, will, if the tyer persists, usually gain great favor with him.

Whip-finisher

Almost every fly is best finished off with the whip-finish method. Commercially made whip-finishers are rather gadgety-looking affairs, but they are not hard to learn to use well. Many tyers still use a hand whip-finish which is harder to learn, and can be tough to throw on certain types of tiny or material-obstructed fly heads.

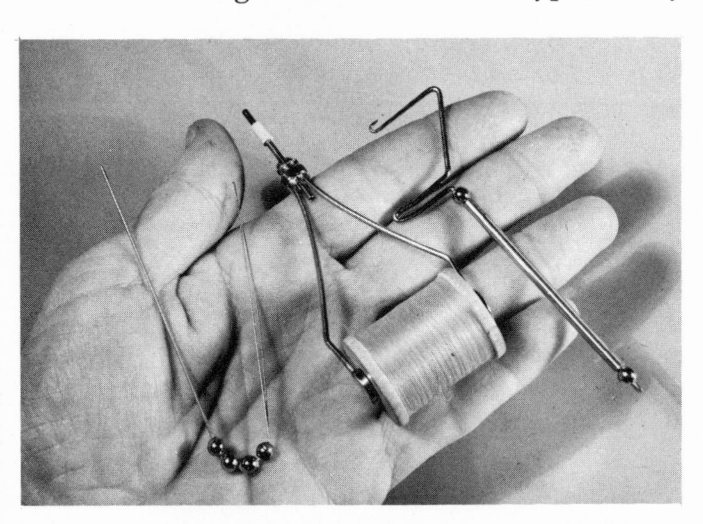

Frank Matarelli's new Whipfinisher, bobbin with special new tube, and unique Matarelli Bobbin Threader and Cleaner.

All the supply companies listed at the end of this chapter have one or more whip-finish tools, varying in size and manufacture. The new Matarelli Whip-finisher and the Mini-Whip-Finisher are my first choices for whip-finishing tools. I spoke with Frank about his new stainless-steel hand-crafted whip-finisher, and he emphasized that his unique tool was supplied with a very specific set of instructions. They should be closely followed to achieve the tool's full design potential.

A simple nylon monofilament loop on a small stick, a large needle head, or a piece of old rod make an extremely simple and easy-to-use manual whip-finisher, and are the type I use for most of my fly-tying. For various sizes of tying threads, I match the nylon monofilament loop diameter with about .002″ for good results. This method is exactly the same used by rod builders to wrap and finish off rod guide wraps.

Pliers

There are simply countless uses in fly-tying for various types of special-jawed pliers. X-Acto, maker of the famous changeable-blade knives, has a complete set of high-quality pliers to meet almost any conceivable need. Most hobby shops that have the X-Acto blades and knife sets will have these neat little pliers also.

Dental-clasp pliers are another extremely useful pliers especially for straightening and bending wire and hooks. Ask your dentist where you might purchase a pair.

Hemostats come in all sizes and jaw designs, and make wonderful fly-tying tools. I find them much better for picking up and gripping small objects than tweezers, with the exception of larval tweezers or insect forceps.

Larval forceps or tweezers are so well balanced that they can pick up an insect egg without crushing it.

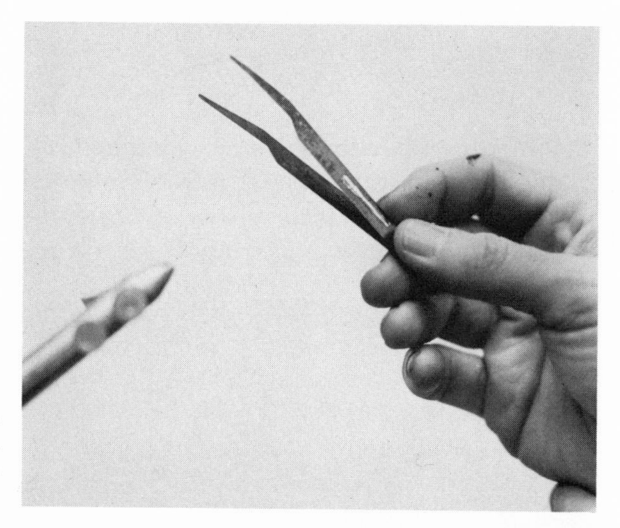

Larval forceps are the ultimate tool for delicate tying and work with naturals. They will quite literally pick up an insect egg without crushing it. *Photo by R. Hoebermann*

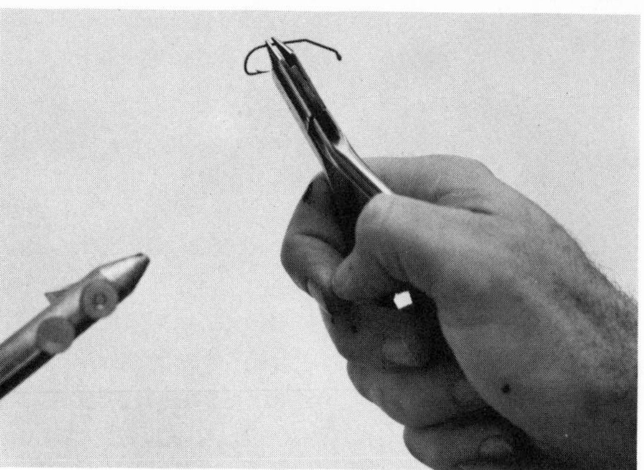

Dental pliers make easy work out of bending hooks. *Photo by R. Hoebermann*

There are plenty of tools to use to tie flies, but practically none to clean up the mess created in the aftermath of a day's tying. Flytyers have always used the brush broom and home vacuum cleaner, which blow, sweep, and scatter wanted and unwanted materials very well. So I'm pleased to see the market at last responding to this problem with a number of marriage-saving products.

The Waste-Trol, designed and manufactured by Darwin Atkin of Porterville, California, is not a totally new product, but I definitely feel that it deserves to be mentioned. The Waste-Trol is a unique waste-catcher that attaches directly to the vise and table. It catches about 95 percent of all the wastes, dropped tools, and spilled liquids the average tyer will experience during any tying session. A rectangular wire frame holds a standard-sized disposable plastic bag above the lap, which catches anything dropped accidentally or intentionally around the vise. The plastic bag also attracts hair, lint, and feather particles by static electricity. When not in use it folds beneath the tying table or is easily removed.

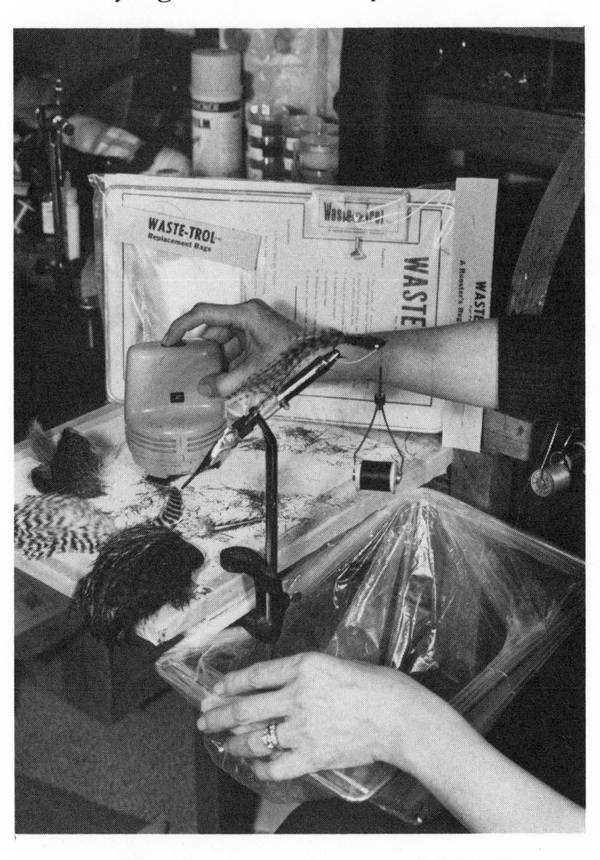

Cleaning aids in use at tying desk, including Mini Vac and Waste-Trol.

The Waste-Trol is available this year in three designs—regular, miniature, and one with two side-pockets for special tying operations. It is available through material catalogs at a very reasonable price. I can think of no more useful or valuable aid to the tyer, with the exception of the vise and bobbin.

There are a number of house-current and battery-operated miniature vacuum cleaners that really mop up the mess on your lap, table, and floor. But they're a little more inconvenient than the Waste-Trol for keeping tidy during the actual tying time. These tiny vacuum cleaners do, however, beat the broom or duster for efficient cleaning. Fly Fisherman's Bookcase catalogs Waste-Vac, a battery–operated hand-size portable model, which stores on the home table or travels lightly to camp. Several of the small electric brooms and portable car-vacuum cleaners are also ideal. They can be purchased at most department or discount stores and auto-accessory parts stores.

Material clip

A material clip has always been popular for holding various materials in position so that they do not interfere with the tying operation being done at that moment. Several companies make a clip that embraces the vise-jaw sleeve with a spring-clamp foot. But it has some drawbacks, so that it at times actually interferes with tying operations.

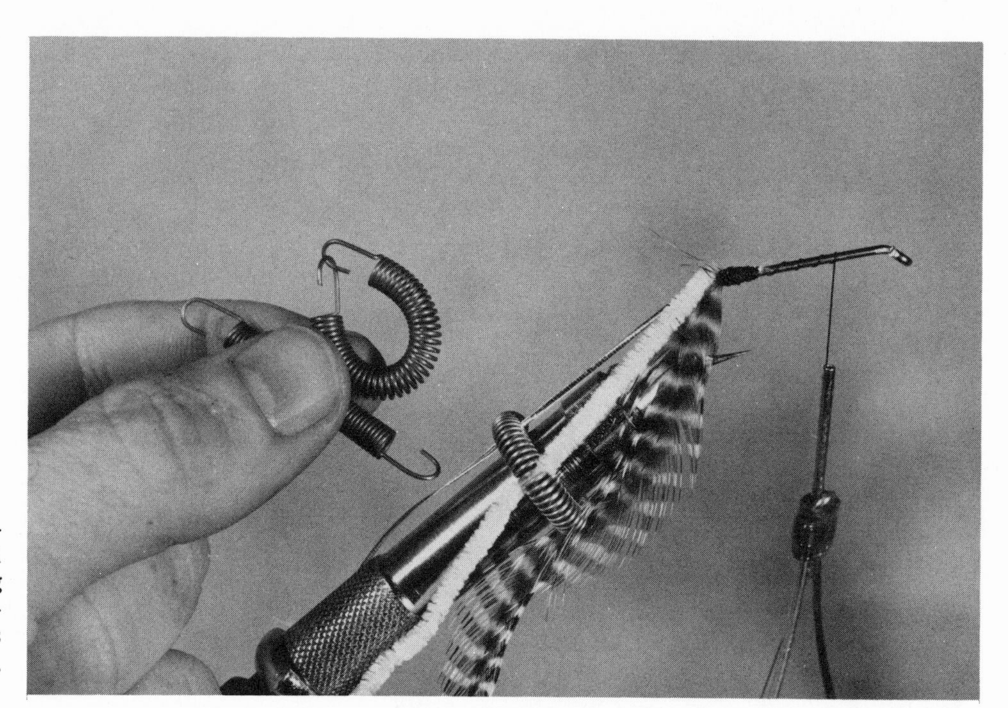

Composite shot of Paul Collier's amazing spring material clip. Contains uncoiled spring and coiled spring; in use on tying vise holding three materials at the same time—tinsel, hackle, and chenille.

Paul Collier, the Federation of Fly Fishermen's President, from Culver City, California, sent me several material clips he likes. After I used one I was immediately convinced it was vastly superior to any on the market today, and free of drawbacks. It is a simple coil-spring, 1⅛-inch long and 3/16 of an inch in diameter. This little spring, which resembles a miniature screen-door spring, is from a soda vending machine. It circles the vise-jaw sleeve and hooks back onto itself. The curvature around the sleeve opens one side of the spring. Any size or amount of materials can be clipped onto the spring from any angle! It hugs the vise from out of the way, and doesn't snap off suddenly as the spring-clamp types will do. I'm sure any similar spring with open eyelets on each end for hooking onto itself would work.

Hair stackers

Various devices and gimmicks have been used for straightening or aligning various guard hairs for tails, wings, and collars—lipstick holders, film cans, metal tubes, etc. However, the "Stacker" ™ made by Laggies Fish Catching Company is unique and useful for this purpose for the average flytyer. It is simple to use and does an excellent job on bucktail, deer hair, bear hair, squirrel tail, and so on. It is available from most West Coast material catalogs and some eastern companies.

Cements, Coatings, and Paints

In recent years there have been a fantastic number of new products for bonding and coating available to the flytyer. Although few, if any, of these Space Age products have been produced with flytyers in mind, most of them fit our needs perfectly. In the past year or so, some have begun to be stocked by materials houses, and others can be found elsewhere.

Epoxy adhesive

Epoxy glues are the ultimate in strength and variable rigidity for bonding bug bodies to hooks. There are many types of epoxies which work very well for a wide range of cementing and armor-coating jobs on fly heads, bodies, and wings. I favor two types. The medium-fast-setting Hobby Epoxy, which sets up in fifteen minutes, allows faster working time and seems to be just as durable as the longer-curing types. It is available from most hobby shops. My other choice is 3M Scotch Brand Epoxy. This is a superstrength twenty-four-hour-curing adhesive that I use to cement bug bodies to straight or humped-shank hooks and for most of my epoxy junctions of leader to fly-line. Curing can be accelerated by heating. By varying the ratio of adhesive to hardener, a rigid or flexible set can be obtained. For a more flexible set, use less hardener than the one-to-one ratio mix on the directions. Excess or spillage will wash away with water before it hardens.

Heat mixed 3M Epoxy and paint it over a foam-plastic-, cork-, or balsa-bodied bug to obtain an armor-plate finish. The same goes for tinsel, mylar, mylar tubing bodies, and fly heads—especially for saltwater use! This epoxy is usually stocked in local paint or hardware stores that carry other 3M products.

Epoxy enamel paint, which comes clear and in a variety of pigment colors, is a terrific paint for the tyer who wants durability, as for lead-jig heads, bass-bug bodies, and saltwater streamers, for example. I use Herter's English Marine Epoxy Enamel. Unfortunately, Herter's sells it in quart cans only; I have seen the same type of paint in smaller amounts at local paint stores. Inquiries to material dealers might result in their stocking small bottles of this useful paint. Perhaps one or more of our fly-material catalogs will soon stock a complete line of these cements and paints.

Polyester finishing resin

Here is another wonderful coating that, like epoxy, is set up by the reaction of mixing two components. It gives silky, glass-hard finishes on bugs, streamer bodies, wrappings, and fly heads. It is much more reasonably priced than epoxy and cures in 40 to 120 minutes' working time. It is transparent, or can be pigmented, and holds a paint overcoat very well. The most popular seems to be Titan Finishing Resin. It comes in pint, quart, and gallon cans. There is a paint dealer in most cities who will carry it, or write to Titan Finishing Resin, California Titan Products, Inc., Santa Ana, California 29707. Titan also makes a new surfacing agent that gives a better set and surface finish for the Titan Resin.

I have also had similar excellent results using Herter's Resinote Finishing Resin, which is even more reasonably priced, although not quite the same consistency as Titan, and a bit more sensitive in setting up.

Liquid vinyl cement

Vinyl cement is a very useful water-clear flexible cement that is as tough as stainless steel. I much prefer it to standard head cements, as it takes less to build up a smooth, glossy, durable head. It is also great for coating special feathers to increase their durability without discoloring them. Duck-quill-section wings on no-hackle-dun patterns last much longer with a thin coat of vinyl cement over them. Jungle-cock eye feathers coated with it stay flexible and durable and will not split up with fishing use. I quite often use this vinyl cement as a base cement on fly bodies, as it dries fairly slowly and penetrates well into materials. It is great to use to reinforce the flattened lead wraps of nymph bodies. Its uses are almost endless.

Orvis was the first, to my knowledge, to stock it. Besides Orvis, most of the other dealers catering to flytyers stock it in tubes or bottles. You can also purchase it at most auto parts or upholstering shops, as it was originally made to patch vinyl cloth materials and products. Locally I have found it in a plastic dispenser bottle labeled "Classic Vinyl-Fix." Classic Products Limited, 1101 Avenue G, Arlington, Texas, is the manufacturer.

Goodyear Pliobond rubber cement

Although Pliobond rubber cement has been around for a long time, it is just becoming popular with flytyers. This smelly brown-and-white sticky liquid is as useful as it is ugly. It is fantastic for cementing certain bug and fly underbodies, and makes a very good head cement if thinned properly with acetone. One of its unique uses is Everett Drake's method of coating his famous bubble-head deer-hair bugs. Everett applies several coats of thinned Pliobond to the deer hair. When it dries, it renders the head almost indestructible, yet flexible. I now use it at the base of each bunch of deer hair I flare for bass hairbugs, and on my sculpin head instead of rod varnish. It is outstanding as a penetrating, sticky, slow-drying undercoating for fuzzy-dubbed nymphs.

Plio-head, especially stocked by Fly Fisherman's Bookcase, is a special formulation of Pliobond cement that is somewhat easier to apply to the fly body and head. Pliobond rubber cement is usually available in small bottles in most fly-material catalogs, or can be purchased at any Goodyear Tire Store in large bottles or cans at a considerable saving. But you must keep the lids tight and keep acetone handy to thin it when needed.

Contact cement

Recently I have been experimenting with contact cements, and have found them to be very useful in accomplishing otherwise difficult or impossible gluing jobs. A light coat of contact cement on any two surfaces instantly bonds them together at a touch. For example, when tying beetle or jassid-type wing backs, contact cement on the underside of the back-wing feather and along the top of the body will bind the wing down to the body to conform to the shape of the compacted wing of a beetle or jassid without the prolonged holding that other types of cements require. It also ensures a nonsplitting durable wing.

The 3M Company manufactures Scotch Brand Contact Cement in small, convenient, brush-top bottles. It is available in most stationery, hardware, and food stores. The brush top is extra-convenient, since this stuff is rough to clean out of ordinary brushes. Three-M also makes contact cement in spray cans equipped with a special small-area directional nozzle for great convenience in limited areas.

I have experimented some with the dental contact cements, which are fast and strong, but expensive to use.

Dowell silicone rubber cement

Silicone rubber cement stays almost jello flexible yet tough as boot leather. It is proving to be as useful in fly-tying as it is to hold car windows and aquariums watertight. It can be used as a flexible cement on bodies or as a body itself, such as one pattern of the sea-arrow squid does to shape its head. It is a transparent white that can be tinted or will reflect colors from underneath. It is available at most pet shops, paint stores, and auto-glass shops.

Decorative enamel paints and lacquers

Dope lacquers, once so popular, have been for the most part replaced by spray and liquid decorative enamels. They dry a little more slowly, but have much greater body and durability. They come in convenient little spray cans or tiny one-quarter-to-one-fluid-ounce bottles. They are stocked in standard metallics, pearls, clear, and fluorescent colors. They can be used to paint plastic, cork, balsa bodies, heads, and eyes on streamer heads, and over certain feathers.

Look for these special enamels in art and hobby stores or department stores. The most popular brands are Testor's and Pactra. I like both and find them very reasonably priced and convenient to buy locally. Herter's also stocks a fairly complete line of paints suitable for fly or lure painting. Most of the other fly-materials dealers stock very limited choices of these enamels but still stock the lacquers. Local tackle stores usually stock the Weber Finish Lacquer and Fire Lacquer which is daylight fluorescent.

Plastic spray fixatives

There are a great number of clear acrylic, varnish, enamel, or lacquer sprays on the market today that have uses in fly-tying. Finishing bug bodies and coating feathers are the most common uses. I've experimented with a number of them in the last six to eight years, with varying success.

About three years ago, Harry Parker, a friend and fly-tying associate from Tulsa, introduced me to Tuffilm.™ This acrylic spray made by Grumbacher, the quality art-supply manufacturer, is a fixative for various art and drafting media. However, it has other uses, as Harry discovered when he tried spraying turkey-wing quills in preparation for tying Dave's Hoppers. Applied moderately it did not alter the feather's color, shape, or general texture, yet the flues could hardly be pulled apart! We've used it on many other feathers since, including delicate starling- and duck-wing quills, without the slightest problem. You can tie extremely durable, perfect wing quill segments, no-hackle and standard dry- and wet-fly wings, as well as super caddis and hopper wings with feather treated with Tuffilm. I also use it on my nymph wing-case feathers, and spray streamer-shoulder feathers with it before painting on an eye, gill, or the like.

You can purchase Tuffilm at almost any art-supply shop or stationery store in two spray can sizes. If you cannot locate this spray locally, write to M. Grumbacher, Inc., 460 W. 34th St., New York, N.Y., 10001, for information on purchasing it.

Waterproof Inks

Besides the various paints I've mentioned, there are also a number of waterproof inks that are useful in marking or coloring feathers, hair, body materials, and fly heads. The most convenient and popular are the modern felt-tip pen inks that John Veniard wrote about several years ago. These now come in a very wide variety of waterproof colors including standard colors, wood stains, and fluorescents. They apply neatly, easily, and dry almost instantly. I use Flair's El Marko pens and Eagle's Prisacolor pens, along with Magic Marker pens. One or all of these are available in most stationery and art-supply stores.

Robert Boyle suggests the use of waterproof drawing inks for very fine detail and subtle colorations on nymph bodies, wing cases, heads and so on. The best ink for this job is Pelikan drawing ink, made in Germany, an extremely dense, high-quality durable ink. This water-based ink comes in a wide range of colors and shades and can be mixed to create even more. You can use either a small paintbrush or ink pen to apply it to surfaces. I recommend that after it dries it be overcoated with a clear vinyl, Tuffilm, or varnish to assure durability. There are several other India drawing inks available with similar properties. You will be able to buy most of them at art supply and stationery stores.

Hooks

Hooks are one fly-tying component that have not kept pace with the development of other manufactured fly-tying products. Almost everyone complains about quality, models, prices, and availability of fly-tying hooks—while doing very little actually to design or encourage new and better hooks.

What is the problem? As I see it, most of us want better hooks, but know practically nothing about hook manufacture and marketing. When flytyers, fly-tying groups, organizations, and dealers become educated and concerned and are willing to pay the price for new and better hooks, I feel the manufacturers will respond favorably. As long as we remain ignorant of their manufacturing requirements and problems and are willing to pay but a cent or two for hooks, we must continue to take what we can get.

Fly-tying hooks make up just a fraction of the total number of hooks manufactured, but this number is growing as flytyers increase in number. The future looks promising if we just become serious enough to help manufacturers accommodate our needs.

Here is a report of recent developments.

I have learned from Dave Kashner that Orvis was forced to discontinue their great line of supreme and premium dry-fly hooks. The problem was one of procurement, not lack of demand—an unfortunate circumstance to those of us who have found these hooks so valuable. Perhaps in the near future Dave will be able to find means to offer Orvis customers these or similar hooks again.

New Hooks

Mustad Midge Hook Number 94842. This regular-weight dry-fly hook with a perfect bend and turned-up eye comes in five sizes from 20 through 28. It is a great midge hook and is also excellent for small nymphs, no-hackle duns and spinners, and standard dry flies.

Mustad Number 94831. This one is a new hook (perhaps only to me). It is a 2X fine, 2X long, perfect-bend, turned-down-eye hook that is outstanding for hoppers and light tippet nymphs.

Keel hooks. Keel hooks aren't brand-new on the market, but they are back on the market after a brief absence and are much more widely distributed now. They are still in need of remodeling to improve hooking, and the facilitation of more types of flies. This hook is made in both a freshwater-bronzed type and stainless-steel saltwater models.

Yorkshire Fly-body Hook. This is truly a new-design hook that has created quite a bit of excitement lately. The hook's originator, Peter Mackenzie-Philips, has informed me that the hook is in a second generation design stage now which has considerably improved its hooking percentage. The hook sizes 6 and 8 have been discontinued and sizes 16 and 12 added to sizes 10 and 14 now available. Don Overfield discusses this hook at length in this section.

Buz's Special Hook. This turned-down eye, Limerick-bend, 2X strong, 1X and 3X long hook was at one time made by Allcock, and is now being made by Wright and McGill. It is made for and handled exclusively by Buz's Fly Shop of Visalia, California. Finished in bronze, gold, and nickel, it is a versatile heavy-duty hook for fresh and salt water. Although not new, it is relatively unknown in the Midwest and East. I tie almost all my sculpins, Whit nymphs, steelhead, and Pacific salmon flies on it.

Stainless-steel hooks. There are a number of new stainless-steel hooks on the market today that can be used for tying saltwater flies. Although early stainless-hooks were not as satisfactory, recent changes in the wire stainless alloys being used for fishing hooks have improved. You'll most likely find the Wright and McGill stainless-steel hooks most readily, as they are available from many catalogs and in most tackle stores. Stainless-steel hook models popular with flytyers are the Wright and McGill Number 25455, Keel hook Number 6655, Mustad Number 34007, and Shakespeare L-126c.

Visual Aids

Good lighting and magnification are extremely important for tying many flies—regardless of the tyer's age. A good pedestal or clamp-mounted fluorescent lamp gives a natural light that is cool and economical. Luxo and Dazor both make round- and straight-bulb models that are worth every penny of the cost. The small, high-intensity portable lamps are great for road tying, but they're not practical for daily home use, in my opinion, as the bulbs are expensive, hot, and the lamps are very sensitive to breakdowns. Some tackle catalogs stock one or more of these lamps, or you can find them locally at stationery, electric fixture, business furniture, or department stores. A little shopping will pay off, since prices vary greatly from source to source.

You can buy all sorts of magnifiers that will assist in viewing small or difficult jobs, but two are especially practical for flytyers, I feel. One of the most practical is the Magni-Sighter. Worn on the tyer's head, this device is optically adjusted for the average focal length a tyer works at between his hands and vise and his eyes. There are several power selections to accommodate your particular needs. They are available in several popular catalogs.

The ultimate visual aid is a workable combination of light and magnification. Using the round fluorescent bulb in combination with a magnifying glass, Luxo and Dazor have come up with lamps that meet this ideal. These combinations do, however, require a short period of adjustment before you can go ahead full speed.

VII

Scientific Papers-
Odonata and Caddis

Anyone who takes the time to explore the scientific literature describing the flora and fauna of the United States will soon be struck by the fact that three states, Illinois, Connecticut, and New York, have made many of the most thorough studies. The publications of the Illinois Natural History Survey, the State of Connecticut Geological and Natural History Survey, and the New York State Museum and Science Service stand in a rank by themselves.

By curious happenstance, one entomologist, Philip Garman, contributed to both the Illinois and Connecticut surveys. In 1917, the *Bulletin of the Illinois Natural History Survey* published his report on "The Zygoptera, or Damsel-flies, of Illinois," and a decade later the Connecticut survey brought out his study on dragonflies. To this latter work we turn now, for although Garman deals primarily with Connecticut species, many of them are to be found elsewhere in the United States, and moreover, Garman's study is of such character that some researchers prefer it to all others.

The selection given here is from pages 11 to 33 of Garman's "The Odonata or Dragonflies of Connecticut." To avoid confusion, it should be noted that Garman uses the term dragonflies to include also the damselflies.

Both extracts have been slightly edited to conform to the publisher's style.

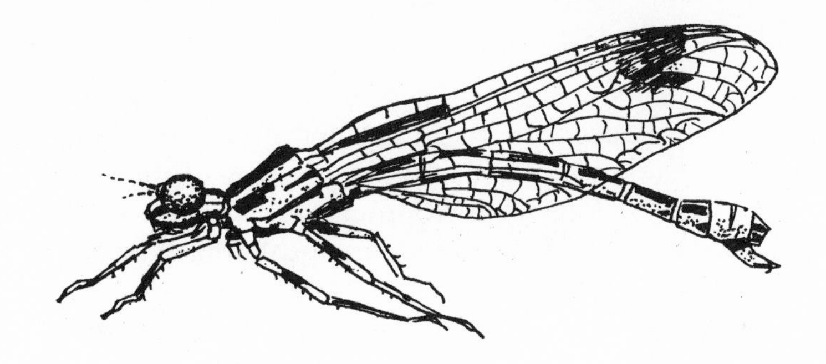

20

"The Odonata or Dragonflies of Connecticut"

by Philip Garman

Dragonflies or Odonata form a branch of Insecta frequently encountered and often considered in biological work. They have been much studied by naturalists, perhaps as completely as any other order of insects, and the present work does not purport to establish anything especially new or original. Its main purpose is to bring together as much information about dragonflies in Connecticut as is possible (within reasonable limits) at the present stage of our knowledge, and to present it in usable form . . .

Dragonflies are among the most beautifully colored and delicately constructed of all insects. They deserve consideration by the amateur naturalist as well as the professional. Moreover, they are desirable tenants in mosquito-plagued districts and, if they could only be reared in large numbers, would form a natural arm of defense against a universal nuisance. Few insects combine such a useful career with the natural beauty that we find in dragonflies, and so it is hoped that the present small contribution will help some one at least to know the dragonfly better and to appreciate its many admirable qualities.

Habits and Life History

All except a few dragonflies are aquatic when young. They feed mostly upon mosquitoes, small flies, and other insects, and are beneficial. Cases have been reported where the nymphs fed upon small fish, and still others in which trees were injured by oviposition, but such instances are rare, and the amount of destruction occasioned is negligible . . .

As far as known, there is never more than one brood of dragonflies per season in Connecticut, while the larger Aeshnids probably require three or four years to develop. Zygoptera or damselflies begin to emerge early in spring (April), and some species continue to emerge until fall (September). Some of the larger Anisoptera are more frequently seen in July, August, and September, their emergence taking place during late summer. Cordulines and Gomphines are most abundant in June.

Most damselfly nymphs may be taken among vegetation of one sort of another, but a few occur under rocks or rotten logs in swift currents. The Anisoptera may be found mostly in the mud at the bottom of the stream or lake, where they conceal themselves by attaching rubbish to their bodies, or by burrowing in the mud itself. Some, of course, inhabit floating vegetation.

Odonata are fond of unpolluted water and do not thrive where there is much contamination. Ponds and lakes about which cows or horses are allowed to graze are frequently without dragonflies, or with only a few of the more hardy species. The gradual pollution of fresh water in the New England states and elsewhere has, moreover, reduced the relative numbers of dragonflies so that one should collect in many localities to obtain a complete collection of these interesting creatures. Fortunately, many lakes have become public property and included in parks and estates, while still others have become reservoirs for the supply of towns, cities, and villages, and the sources of contamination removed or abated. For this reason the dragonfly's prospects for the future are better, though evidently they are not as numerous as a half-century ago.

Many families of dragonflies select their environment, and some species may nearly always be found under certain ecological conditions. For instance, the nymphs of the Agrionidae, among which the black-wings are perhaps the most common examples, are found in clear woodland or meadow brooks. The nymphs of Argias are most frequently found in running or moving water under stones, logs, etc., and the Lestinae, most frequently in bogs or freshwater ponds with considerable vegetation. Among the Anisoptera, selection of environment is not as evident, but we find many Gomphidae in shallow, slow-flowing streams; a species of Libellulid (*Erythrodiplax berenice)* confined to brackish water along the seacoast; Sympetrum species frequenting bogs and marshes, and so on. Adults of certain species may be found fairly close to their nymphal environment, but some wander long distances from their former aquatic home. Aeshna species may be seen frequently a mile or so from the nearest water, and it seems likely that they fly many times this distance away from their natural haunts. Other species are known to congregate in sunny spots away from the water on the approach of cold weather. Still others prefer pasture lands as a hunting ground or the clear expanse of a lake or pond. The congregation of species may perhaps be connected with the migration of such as *Anax junius, Libellula pulchella,* and *Libellula semifasciata,* which takes place northward in spring and southward in fall. Mr. C. R. Ely reports that he has witnessed the migration of dragonflies several times at his summer home in East River, Connecticut, the migrating insects being collected in a dense swarm, and moving along the seacoast . . .

Emergence from the water usually takes place late in the afternoon or evening, or early in the morning, though a great deal depends on the location. Damselflies emerge throughout the day, and require only a few hours to develop enough to fly. The Anisoptera require longer, but even they are ready to begin the hunt again in an incredibly short time. Many species, however, do not obtain their full coloration until some days afterward, and individuals thus immature are known as *teneral.*

The food of adult Odonata consists of small insects such as mosquitoes, gnats, beetles, and moths. The larger Aeshnids are particularly active feeders and may be seen to capture insects of considerable size. Some species have been known to feed successfully on honey bees.

The nymphs of all species eat other insects, mainly the larvae of small Diptera, but the younger nymphs subsist on protozoa and crustacea, such as Cladocera and Copepoda. Probably others of the smaller groups are also eaten. We thus find the damselfly feeding upon mosquito wrigglers in the later nymphal stages and hunting down the mosquito itself when adult. No nymph, however, is fastidious in selecting its food, and there is hardly one which will not devour with apparent relish the members of its own family. Probably some of all aquatic families of insects are eaten as well as other aquatic animals not belonging to this class.

Nearly all damselflies lay their eggs in the stems of plants. Of the Anisoptera, the Aeshnidae lay eggs in plants or soft mud, and the Cordulinae lay gelatinous masses containing many eggs which are draped over aquatic vegetation or other support. The remaining families for the most part drop their eggs into the water directly.

The damselflies often descend several inches below the surface of the water, but *Lestes* are said to oviposit above the surface. Libellulidae may frequently be seen skimming close to the water and occasionally dipping the tip of the abdomen, thereby releasing the egg, which sinks to the bottom.

The following interesting account of the oviposition habits of *Enallagma aspersum* is taken from an article in the Maine *Naturalist* II, p. 133, by William Colcord Woods:

> After a sufficient trial of our patience, we saw a couple "land" on a pipewort stem nearby. They alighted head upward. The male released the female from his grasp, clung to the stem some ten or fifteen minutes, and then flew off to join his companions in their patrol, but his mate, rapidly executing an about-face and folding her wings closely about her, hurried fearlessly down the stalk into the water. She crawled down the stem, and then explored the weed-grown bottom, poking her abdomen here and there, doubtless in the act of oviposition. From time to time she thrust her abdomen between her wings, which had a glistening silvery appearance under water, and we wondered whether she may have used air imprisoned there for respiration, for this species can remain under water a remarkably long time for an aerial species. She had ranged at least two feet from the stem on which she made her descent, and had been submerged more than twenty-five minutes when we disturbed her. Would she just stay down there and die? What would be the outcome of her plunge? It was not our patience but our noontime which was exhausted, for we had not been sent down there to study blue damselflies, so reluctantly one of us thrust in a stick and poked the busy mother. Immediately she loosed her hold, and floated at once to the surface, when to our utter astonishment down swooped a watchful male, who, catching her by the nape of the neck, drew her out of the water. As soon as she had been lifted above the surface film, she was able to use her wings, and the pair flew off together.

Parasites and Enemies

The dragonfly, although itself predaceous, has enemies. Chief among these are fishes and birds. Fishes are particularly fond of the nymphs, which are reported to form 25 percent of the food of a bullhead (Baker, 1916); 25 percent of the food of the grass pickerel (*Esox vermiculatus*); and about 13 percent of the food of crappies (*Pomoxis annularis* and *P. sparoides*), and pirate perch (*Aphredoderus sayanus*, Forbes, 1888). The size of the fish, however, is important in determining the amount of Odonate food eaten. Wilson (1917–18, p. 229) claims that very small fish do not eat Odonata nymphs at all but that they are very fond of the eggs. Fish under 9mm. in length eat no nymphs whatsoever, while fish such as the largemouth bass, bluegill, common sunfish, and calico bass reach 22–25mm. (about 1 inch) before they begin. Fish 75–105mm. (3–4 inches) were found by Wilson to feed almost entirely on dragonfly nymphs, under some conditions.

Dragonfly nymphs are reported to be in demand as fish bait in several localities. Wilson (*Ibid.*, p. 225) says that small boys in the vicinity of Torrington, Connecticut, collect and sell them as "perch bait," and in other localities they are used as bait for trout, rock bass, and perch. He also reports that adult damselflies are more frequently eaten by fish than is supposed, and that fishes will snap up quickly any damselfly that has been injured and is unable to rise from the water.

Birds are next in importance as enemies of Odonata, and their greatest success lies in capturing tenerals. English sparrows, robins, red-winged and yellow-headed blackbirds, shrikes, cuckoos, king birds, fly-catchers, and herons have been observed by various authors to eat Odonata. Herons feed upon the nymphs, the remainder upon adults. Shrikes, cuckoos, and king birds, especially the last, are said to be quick enough to capture fully mature adults. Walker, in fact, reports (1912, p. 36) that the appendages of *Epiaeschna heros,* one of the largest and swiftest dragonflies, have been taken from the stomach of the chuck-will's widow.

Turtles, terrapins, and frogs (bullfrogs and cricket frogs) are enemies of Odonata. Bullfrogs are reported to feed upon nymphs and adults, and the cricket frog upon the adults of damselflies.

The larger species of Odonata destroy the smaller and are therefore enemies. Aquatic Hemiptera and Coleoptera are vigorous insect feeders and will feed on Odonate nymphs when they encounter them. *Dytiscus, Zaitha, Ranatra, Belostoma,* and *Notonecta* have been reported in this connection, while ants and robber flies *(Asilidae)* are sometimes able to capture and overpower adults. Several egg parasites have been observed (Hymenoptera and Diptera), and the eggs of the damselfly family *Lestinae* are especially liable to attack, being exposed above the water line (Needham, 1903).

Spiders are confirmed enemies of most insects and have been found to capture dragonflies . . .

General Characteristics of the Odonata

The Odonata include insects, the adults of which have biting mouth parts and net-veined wings. The legs are weak and used mainly for support when at rest, though sometimes for grasping and holding prey.

All species have an incomplete metamorphosis, the aquatic nymph developing by successive stages until the last instar,* when the insect leaves the water and the adult

*A glossary of entomological terms, especially as they apply to Odonata and caddis, can be found in the Appendixes.

emerges. The transformation in changing from nymph to adult is almost as great as we find in orders with complete metamorphosis, but there is no true pupal stage and they are known as hemimetabolous . . .

Odonata, Plecoptera (stone flies), and Neuroptera (ant lions and dobson flies) are more closely related to one another than to other orders of insects; but although similar in many points, are readily distinguished in nymphal and adult stages. The basis of separation of adult Odonata from the Neuroptera and also the Ephemerida lies in the presence of the nodus in the wing of all representatives of the dragonfly group. The nymphs are easily distinguished from others of similar form and habits by the possession of a hinged labium which folds beneath the head and is capable of being extended beyond the tip of the latter. The Neuroptera have no vestigial wings in the earlier stages, differing in this point from the Odonata.

Geologically, the dragonflies are one of the oldest orders, dating back to the Carboniferous period when related forms occurred with a wing spread of more than two feet . . .

Scientists have recognized 2,400 or more species of dragonflies throughout the world (Tillyard, 1917; p. 300). Muttkowski in 1910 listed 494 species from North America, and of these, some 160 occur in New England. Many of them have a wide range and may be expected to be found almost anywhere in the United States.

Compared with Coleoptera or beetles, for instance, dragonflies are few in numbers. A recent publication has described 1,084 species of weevils from the northeastern United States, and one author states that nearly 4,000 species of beetles probably exist in the State of Indiana. Our *Check List of Connecticut Insects* records 1,452 species of Lepidoptera (moths and butterflies) within the state and only 101 Odonata or dragonflies—showing the relative scarcity of dragonflies as compared with other insects. The number of species of dragonflies captured in Connecticut to date totals 112 and leaves about 50 of these herein described yet to be found . . .

The External Anatomy of the Dragonfly

The parts of the skeleton of any insect are similar, even in widely separated groups; but through the process of evolution many parts have been lost or so modified that they are only to be recognized by means of "landmarks" in the structure of the body wall. Moreover, the features used in classification are often so different in different orders that specialists do not agree as to the proper nomenclature. It is therefore important to note the "landmarks" for the recognition of the parts of the skeleton as well as to provide a means—with figures and general descriptions—for the guidance of the beginner . . . In all descriptions, the insect is regarded as in a natural position with feet on the ground and body parallel to the surface.

The body of all Odonata is divided into three main divisions, known as head, thorax, and abdomen. Each division is in turn composed of a number of rings or segments, more or less modified, but homologous with the segments of its wormlike ancestors. The external skeleton is provided with pigment and divided into sclerites or plates that are similar in different families and suborders. The lines separating the sclerites are called sutures.

The Body Structure

Adult

Head.—Surrounding the mouth opening are projections of the body wall and appendages designed to aid in capturing other insects and preparing them for its use. Just above the opening is found a broad, emarginate piece known as the labrum, which is about twice as broad as long. Above it is a fixed sclerite known as the clypeus.

Above the clypeus and between the large, compound eyes occupying the sides of the head is an area known as the front. It bears the jointed appendages called antennae. The front extends to the small ocelli or simple eyes and is usually bounded by a suture on each side below the compound eyes. The epicranial suture extends from the rear of the head to a joint just behind the ocelli where it forks and extends laterad to the compound eyes. The posterior surface of the head, on either side of the foramen or body opening, is commonly known as the occiput, and contains three sclerites, the occiput and two postgenae, more or less fused.

Below the mouth opening there is a hinged organ, the labium, which in most individuals covers the entire lower surface of the head. Beneath the labium (or above it when the head is in position) are found the two maxillae, one on either side, and between the tips of the latter is a circular pad, the hypopharynx.

The compound eyes are always large, frequently contiguous above, and they contain a large number of hexagonal facets, sometimes of two different sizes. The antennae vary in shape and also in the number of segments, there being usually seven. In the Odonata the labium is unique because of its large size and great mobility. It varies in form in different families and is important in classification.

Thorax.—The thorax is composed of four rings or body segments. Immediately behind the head is the microthorax, a very small incomplete ring composed of a small plate on either side. Following this is the prothorax, a larger segment, to which is attached the first pair of legs. The region of the prothorax, or in fact all parts of the thorax above, on either side, and below, may be known in a general way as notum, pleura (singular, pleurum), and sternum . . .

The mesothorax and metathorax (following the prothorax) are always fused in Odonata, and the dividing line is traceable with difficulty in adults. Except for the attachment of the second and third pair of legs and the wings, there is little to separate them to a casual observer.

It is important to bear in mind that the thorax and abdomen of all dragonflies are greatly modified and different in many respects from other insects. There are, however, the usual "landmarks" which facilitate a comparison of the sclerites in different groups. In the thorax these consist of processes or points of articulation of the appendages, particularly the legs, invaginations of the internal skeleton, and breathing pores.

The proximal segment of the legs, for instance, articulates with the body in concave sockets that have lanceolate or somewhat circular margins, with a lateral point or projection on each. The point may be easily located by following the lateral ridge of the coxa to the margin of the socket . . .

Wings and Legs.— The wings and legs of Odonata are comparable to other insects, and the nature of both appendages is of great importance to systematists. The legs are composed of the following segments beginning with the proximal: coxa, trochanters (two segments), femur, tibia, tarsus (three segments). There are always two claws attached to the tip of the tarsus. Various shapes and sizes of setae are borne on femora, tibiae, and tarsi.

The wings are apparently complexly veined, but analysis of the system of venation proves it to be homologous to that of other insects. The great number of supernumerary cross-veins is indeed confusing at first sight, but it is possible with a little study to follow the course of the larger primary veins and, when once acquainted with the general scheme, to find the characters for identification . . .

Abdomen.—The abdomen is composed of ten complete rings or segments variously modified and pigmented. The spiracles of the segments (except the first) are hidden completely by the overhanging terga and the pleura reduced to small membranes beneath the lateral edges. The sterna or sclerites of the ventral surface are often reduced to a line, or hidden entirely by the approximated terga, while on segments two and nine the sterna are modified to form the genitalia. The male genitalia of segment two, known as accessory, are unique, being found in no other order of insects . . .

The ovipositor of the female . . . is frequently reduced to two small plates on the ventral surface. Attached to the tip of the tenth segment are the anal appendages. Their structure varies a great deal in the male sex and offers another important feature of classification.

Nymph

The nymph differs from the adult in many features. In the head, the appendages surrounding the mouth are essentially the same, but the labium is different, especially the shape of the labial palpi . . . The ocelli are never present in the nymph, and the compound eyes not often contiguous. The antennae are also different from the adult, especially in the families Gomphidae and Agrionidae, where certain segments are greatly enlarged.

Thorax.—The prothorax usually consists of a simple ring with a pair of legs attached. An indistinct line on the mid-dorsum divides the pronotum. The pleura are divided by a line running dorsad from the coxal processes. The legs are not usually provided with heavy setae as in the adult, but the tibiae sometimes possess small scales at the tip. Meso- and metathorax are essentially the same as the adult in form, though sutures are not usually as distinct and the wings are, of course, undeveloped. All signs of wings are wanting in the first instars.

Abdomen.—The lateral margins of the abdomen are produced in the form of keels and variously adorned with spines and setae. The mid-dorsal line is likewise produced and sometimes ornamented with very large hooks. At the tip of the abdomen there may be found either short, spinelike projections or long, leaflike gills.

It should be remembered in studying dragonfly nymphs that there is more variation in the younger stages of a species than is usually found in the adult, and that in species the adults of which are closely allied, there is no feature known which will put the nymph in its proper place. It therefore behooves the student, if he desires a more accurate determination, to rear the specimen considered, whenever the individual belongs to a group of closely related species . . .

Variability in the Odonata

There is sometimes considerable variation in the Odonata, both in color and size. Specimens described from Connecticut may be smaller or larger than those found in other localities, but as a rule this variation should be within five millimeters of the dimensions given. Occasional examples will naturally occur that may be stunted from lack of food or, having found conditions more favorable, may be larger than those described. Even wing veins show variation in number, especially cross-veins, which is to be expected, since this part of the dragonfly has undergone rapid evolution. It is well known that dragonflies change color as they become older, the brighter colors being replaced by duller hues, which in turn often become pollinose, due to waxy secretions. Preserved specimens may also present a totally different appearance from the freshly collected specimens, especially if means are not taken to prevent discoloration. Such variations in the Odonata should make one cautious about determinations, and he should base them primarily upon structure wherever possible.

Collecting and Preserving

To collect adult dragonflies, a light and stout net should be available. Landing nets of convenient size are on the market, the best of which consist of a handle of two sections and two flat pieces of spring steel which fold together longitudinally and open out to make the rim of the net. This net is about fourteen inches in diameter with a handle two to four feet long, according as one or two sections are used. The bag itself should have a margin of heavy cloth to fit over the rim, since most of the wear comes at this point, and should be composed of good-quality bobbinet or bolting cloth. Bolting cloth makes a very satisfactory outfit. Such a net should be about eighteen inches in length and should taper gradually from mouth to tip.

For collecting nymphs, a fixed, solid, semicircular rim is preferred to a jointed one such as the landing net just described. This may be welded to a piece of two and one-fourth inch coupling and a pole screwed into the pipe, or may be attached to the handle, preferably a long one, by various means. . . .

If much collecting is done, some sort of carrying satchel should be provided. Williamson constructed an ideal bag which is composed of a leather case (7½ x 11 inches by 8½ inches high) into which he fits a series of tin boxes of assorted sizes, allowing him to shift them with ease and still keep his material separate. He has attached to the rear of the bag a ring which fastens to the belt and keeps the bag at the back when stooping or running. Small hunting bags which serve the purpose fairly well may be had on the market and are suitable for collecting dragonflies.

It is well to give more attention to preserving specimens after they are collected, however, than to waste too much thought and time over the manner of collecting.

Nymphs are well preserved in 80% alcohol. Formalin should not be used, or heat, except perhaps 1% formalin in 80% alcohol. Adults, if placed in 80% alcohol, are preserved admirably, including colors. Reared specimens should be preserved in alcohol, since nymphal skin and adult may be kept together more easily than if pinned. Dr. Calvert, however, mounts exuviae of damselfly nymphs on a square of mica, covering the whole with transparent cement, and pins it with the adult. If specimens are reared, care must be taken to allow full color to develop in the adult. Some workers while collecting keep on the alert for emerging nymphs, which may often be found along the banks, on weeds and shrubs; these they place in paper bags until fully colored and developed and do not kill until then. One cannot be too careful, however, in this kind of collecting to associate the proper exuviae with the adult that emerged from it.

For killing adults, bottles about two inches in diameter and four in height should be obtained. Sodium cyanide in pieces the size of a pea or smaller should be scattered over the bottom and sealed in place by pouring in plaster of paris and water about the thickness of cream. If desired, sawdust may be placed over the cyanide and held in place with circles of cardboard. Smaller killing bottles may be constructed of thick-walled test tubes with sawdust and cyanide kept in place with cardboard or heavy blotting paper cut with a gun-wad punch.*

Care must be taken not to allow killing bottles to become moist, since dragonflies coming in contact with moisture saturated with cyanide are quickly spoiled. To this end, bottles should be aired before using, allowing the plaster to set and become hard and the excess moisture to escape. Still further care should be taken to clear out the cyanide bottle or tube frequently while collecting, removing the contents to envelopes or small boxes.

After killing, all specimens must be dried thoroughly and may be stored then in boxes or triangles of paper. If it is desirable to spread the wings, a setting board such as is used for moths and butterflies is convenient. The length of time required to thoroughly fix the wings depends upon the size of the specimens and the place where they are kept; but the process may be hastened by placing in an oven and heating gently. If heat is not applied, at least two weeks should be allowed for the specimen to dry. It is essential to dry all specimens quickly in order to preserve their colors, and drying by artificial heat is to be recommended for this reason. It is important, before finally mounting, to support the body by running a fine bristle or pin through the head, thorax, and abdomen. This keeps the various sections of the body together and prevents breakage, which is one of the worst troubles in maintaining a collection of dragonflies.

Williamson dries all specimens in triangles of paper, later pinning those which he desires through the base of the wings. To dry specimens while on collecting trips, he has constructed a box with a funnel-shaped cloth which fits on the bottom. This he hangs on a tree over a lantern.

For rearing Zygoptera, jelly tumblers may be used conveniently and successfully. There should not be more than one individual in each tumbler, since the nymphs will kill one another, and a small piece of water weed taken from the habitat of the nymph should be placed in the water. Sphagnum moss also serves this purpose, and is adapted to the needs of Zygoptera. Anisoptera require larger jars or cages, but unless the cage is large, only one individual should be placed in each. Various kinds of cages have been used in rearing dragonflies in the field, most of them consisting of a simple wire cage placed in shallow water.

Mosquito larvae may be used for food for the nymphs, or any soft-bodied aquatic larvae. Ephemerids are particularly desired by many species. Full-grown nymphs are better for rearing than the younger stages and may be distinguished from the latter by means of the wing pads, which are well filled out in the older stages.

**Editors' Note:* We do not recommend cyanide because of the danger involved in handling this substance. Ethyl acetate is a safe substitute.

Representative Illustrations of Dragonflies and Damselflies

The following illustrations of dragonflies and damselflies have been taken from Garman's study, reprinted in part in this book, and from two papers by C. H. Kennedy.

The Structure of Damselflies (Zygoptera) (from Garman)

Nymph of *Ischnura verticalis.* Maximum length 14 mm. without gills. Length of gills 7 mm. Color: green or brown. Found in slow streams, ponds, marshy bays from Newfoundland south to the Carolinas and west to Texas. Among the first damsels to emerge in the spring, as early as the first week of May in Ontario.

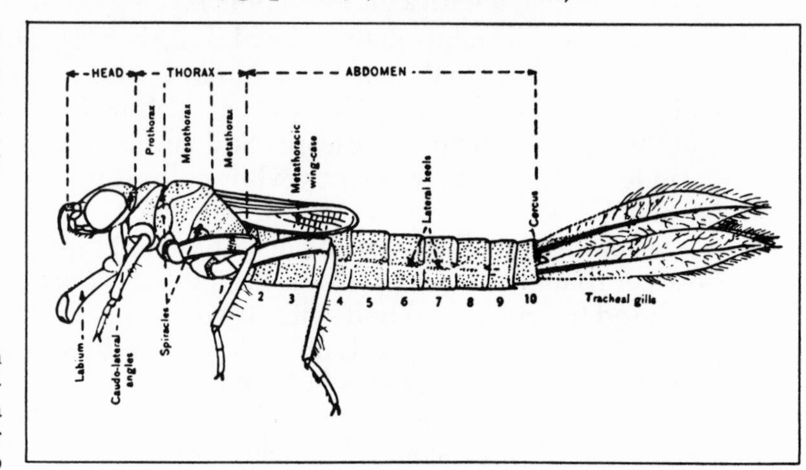

Adult Damselfly, *Lestes vigilax.* Maximum length 47 mm. Color: head, dull green or black; thorax, metallic green-yellow; below: abdomen, green; terga 1–8, 9–10 dark brown or black. Found in bogs or bog-margined lakes from Quebec to Florida west to Iowa.

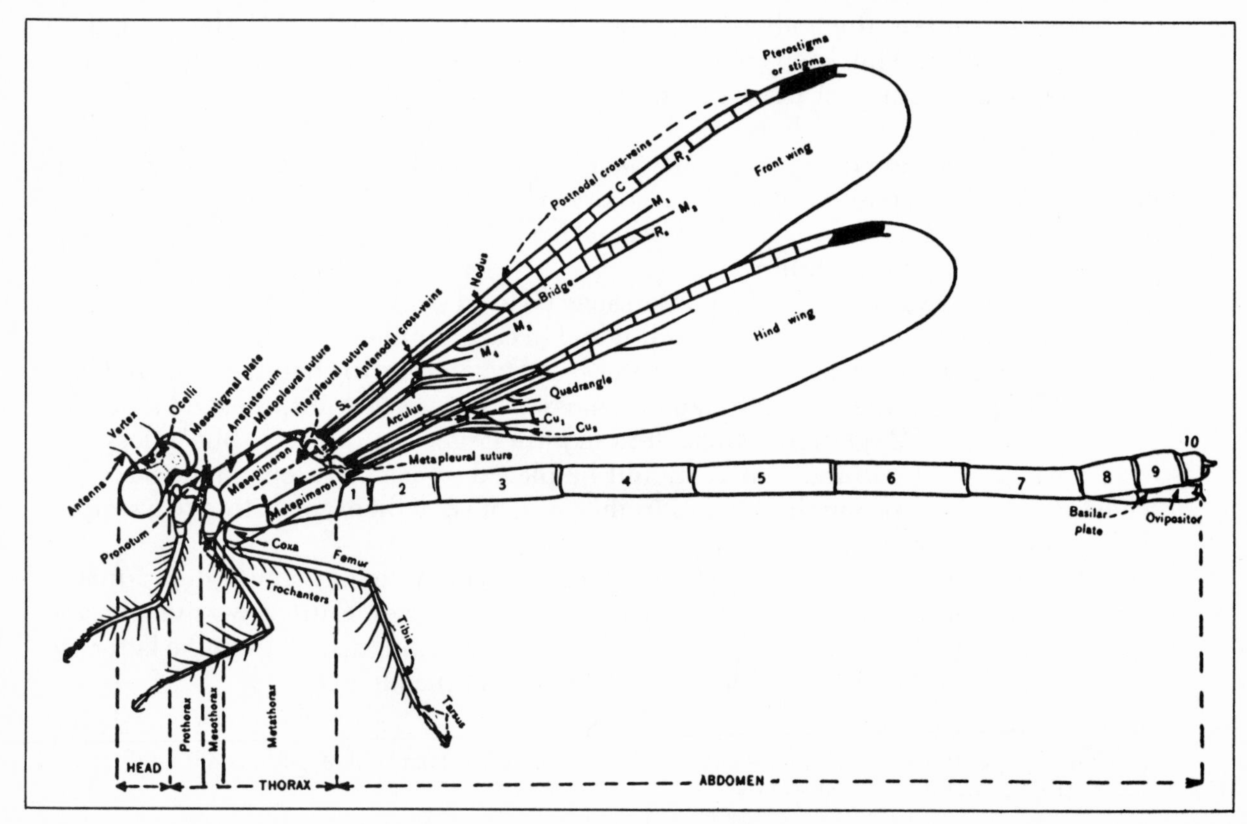

Two Views of a Damselfly Nymph (from Kennedy, "Washington")

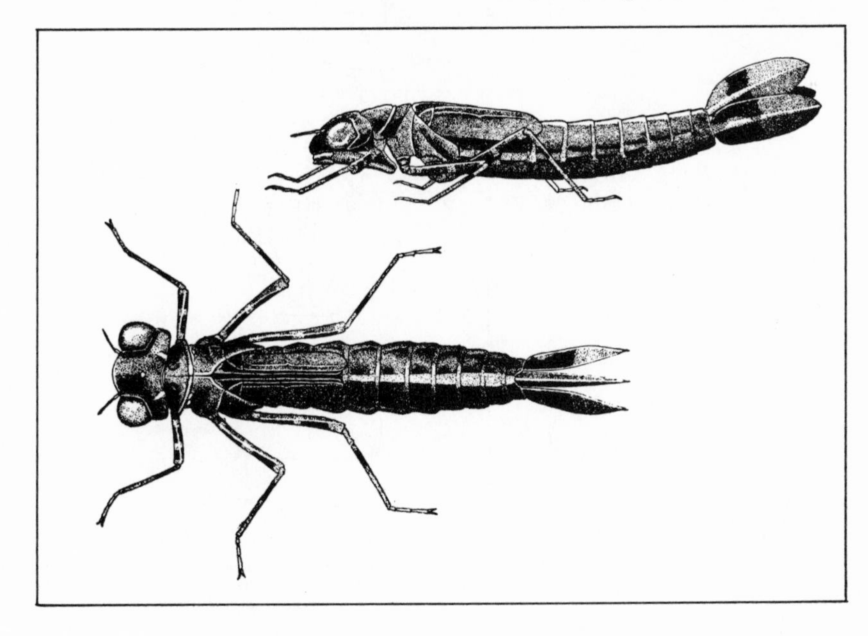

Argia vivida, a relatively robust damsel nymph reaching a length of 12 mm. without gills. Length of gills 3 mm. Very dark except for the broad white stripe down the mid-dorsal line of the abdomen. A west-of-the-Great-Plains species, found in spring-fed streams and pools from Mexico north to British Columbia.

Two Views of a Damselfly Adult (from Kennedy, "Washington")

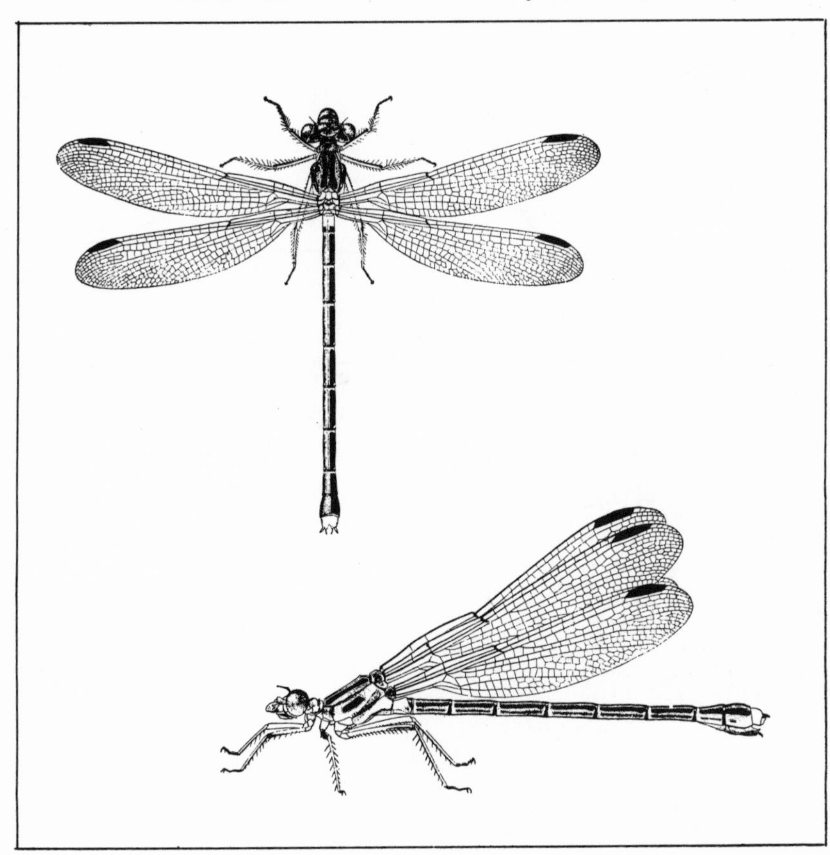

Archilestes californica, female. Kennedy does not give the length, but it is probably about 30 mm. He found it along the Yakima River from late July into October. Color generally brownish, becoming darker with age.

The Structure of Dragonflies (Anisoptera) (from Garman)

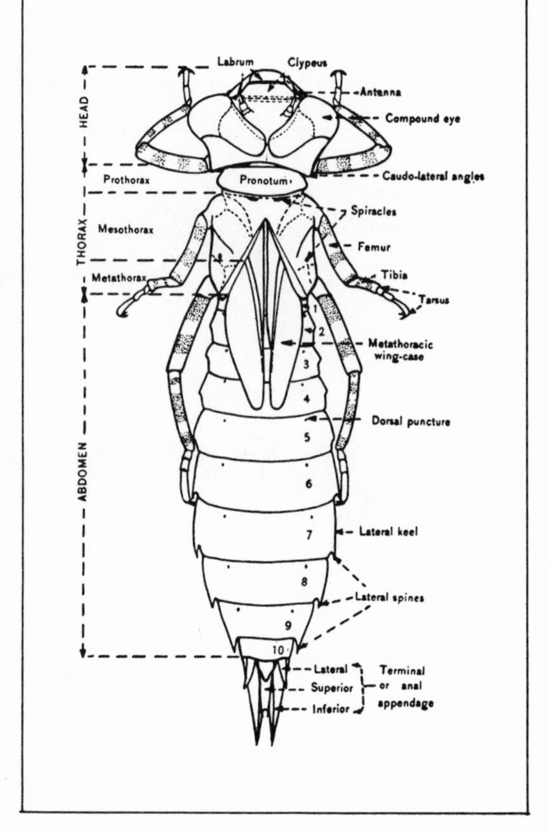

Nymph of *Basiaeschna janata.* Maximum length is 32 mm. Color is brown. Ranges from Nova Scotia south to Florida and west to Oklahoma.

Adult of *Anax junius,* "the king of June." Maximum length 80 mm. Probably found in every state, including Alaska and Hawaii. Yearround in Florida. See color photograph of imitation.

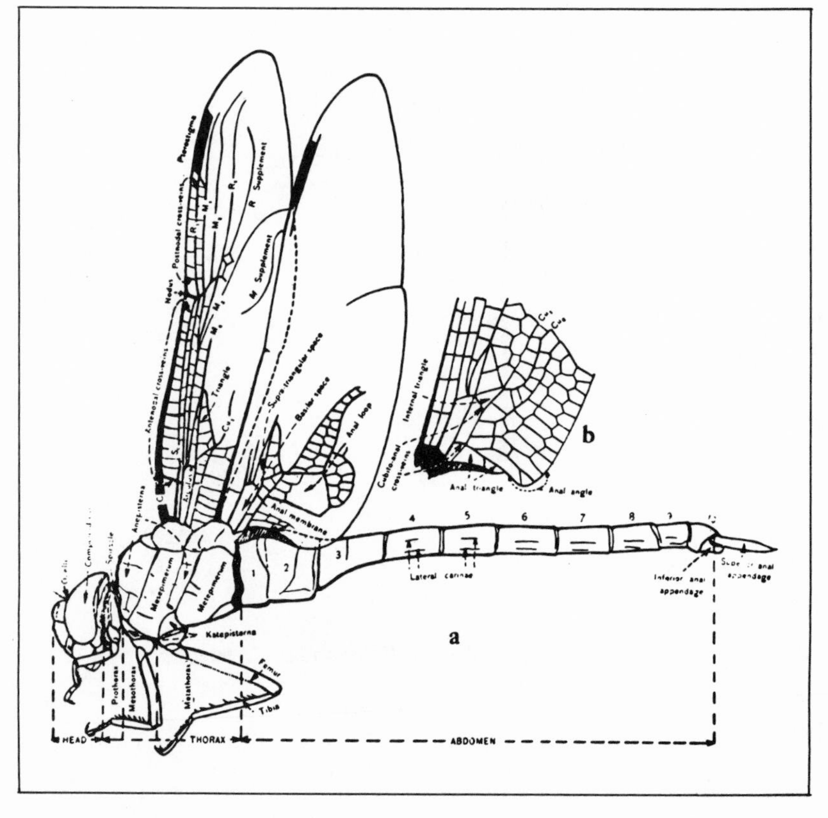

Two Views of a Dragonfly Nymph (from Kennedy, "Washington")

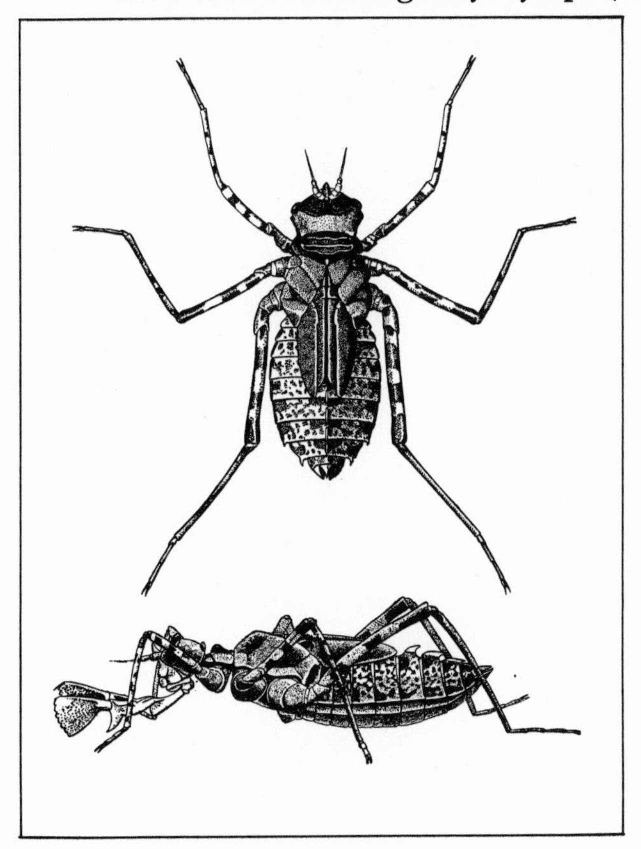

Macromia magnifica, the lateral view showing the nymph with the labium extended. This species is found in streams and ponds in the Far West, ranging from Arizona north to British Columbia. Dirty olive in color and reaches a length of about 30 mm.

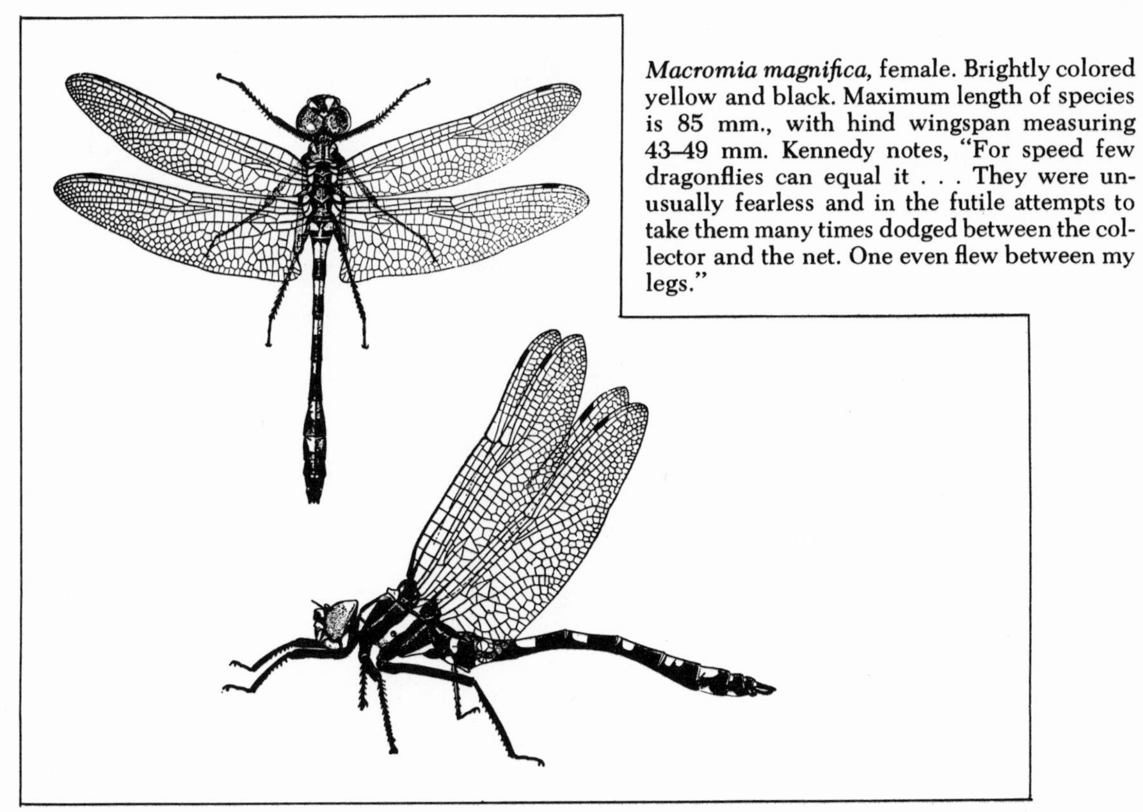

Macromia magnifica, female. Brightly colored yellow and black. Maximum length of species is 85 mm., with hind wingspan measuring 43–49 mm. Kennedy notes, "For speed few dragonflies can equal it . . . They were unusually fearless and in the futile attempts to take them many times dodged between the collector and the net. One even flew between my legs."

Dragonfly Life Cycle (from Kennedy, "California")

This drawing sums up the life history of a stream-dwelling dragonfly, in this instance *Cordulegaster dorsalis,* found in British Columbia, California, Nevada, and Utah. Figure A shows the nymph with a protective coat of algae; B, the exuviae or shuck, and C, the female laying eggs in the stream bed.

21

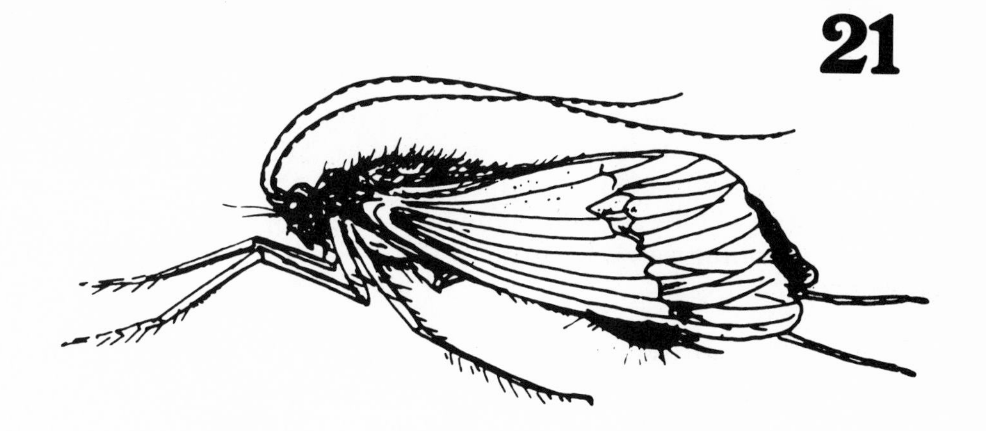

"The Caddis Flies, or Trichoptera, of Illinois"

by Herbert H. Ross

The caddis flies, or Trichoptera, are for the most part medium-sized to small insects resembling moths in general appearance. Their larvae are aquatic in habit and caterpillarlike in appearance. The order Trichoptera contains over 750 species, ranking about seventh among the insect orders. For Illinois, we have now recorded 184 species, the largest known list for any state. It must be remembered, however, that Illinois does not have the same wealth of diverse aquatic situations as some other states, the lists of which will be greatly increased with intensive collecting. . . .

Biology

The bundle of sticks crawling about in the water, green worms under stones in the stream, swarms of "flies" around the lights along river and lake—these are forms of caddis flies familiar to the general insect collector. They are but a few isolated phenomena, however, in a picture of life histories and interrelationships varied in pattern and interesting in detail.

Life cycle

In general, the life history of caddis flies follows this pattern: The eggs are laid near or in the water, each soon hatching into a worm called a *larva,* which lives in the water and may build a case of sticks, sand grains, and other small objects. When full grown, this larva makes a cocoon in which it changes into a transformation stage called a pupa. The adult structures (e.g., wings and genitalia) develop within the pupa. When the adult structures are fully developed within it, the pupa cuts its way out of the cocoon, swims to the surface, crawls out of the water and attaches itself firmly to a stick, stone, or other object. The adult then bursts the pupal skin, wriggles and crawls out of it and flies away free. Mating flights follow; a period ensues for maturity of the eggs within the body of the female, which then lays the eggs in the water, beginning the cycle again. . . .

Eggs and oviposition

Caddis flies lay many eggs, the number probably ranging from 300 to 1,000 per female. Considerable information is known regarding the manner and place in which these eggs are deposited, but a tremendous amount remains to be observed.

The adult females of Rhyacophilidae, Philopotamidae, Psychomyiidae, Hydropsychidae, and Hydroptilidae enter the water and there lay strings of eggs on stones or other objects. These strings are usually grouped to form irregular masses, each containing from a few to 800 eggs. The eggs are surrounded by a thin, cementlike matrix.

Females of other caddis fly families usually extrude the eggs and form them into a mass at the end of the abdomen before depositing them. These masses are usually irregular or ovoid, but in some genera are very definite in form, as, for example, the genus *Triaenodes,* in which the eggs are arranged in a flat oval. . . . In all egg masses the matrix surrounding the egg is gelatinous and swells upon absorbing moisture.

The Leptoceridae, Phryganeidae, Molannidae, and Brachycentridae usually attach the egg masses to submerged stone, logs, or vegetation. The females of some of these have been observed entering the water or putting the abdomen into it for this purpose. Other families, such as Helicopsychidae, Goeridae, Lepidostomatidae, and Sericostomatidae, deposit the egg masses in or near the water, apparently as frequently one way as the other. When not laid in the water, the masses are usually placed near it.

The family Limnephilidae has been the subject of interesting observations and speculations. The egg masses are deposited above the water on plants or stones which protrude above it, on objects along the shore, or sometimes on twigs high in trees. In this last case the gelatinous mass may liquefy with rain, and the drops so formed run down the twigs and drop into the water, carrying young larvae with them. Evidence of actual migration to water of young larvae hatched from egg masses far from the water's edge has not been demonstrated. Rain probably plays an important part in this phenomenon.

Larval habits

Mode of Living. Possibly the most interesting, and certainly the most startling, aspect of caddis-fly biologies is the construction, by many species, of houses in which they live. Not all species have these houses, and many of the houses are of different types. Much has been written regarding possible classifications of these habits, including the formulation of complex systems and explanations. I believe, however, that the following brief synopsis will present most of the pertinent data.

Free-Living Forms. The larvae of the genus *Rhyacophila* are completely free living, having no case or shelter; they lay a thread trail and have many modifications for free life in flowing water, including widely spaced, strong legs and large, strong anal hooks. For pupation they form a stone case or cocoon.

Also free living are the early instars of many Hydroptilidae . . .

Net-Spinning Forms. Larvae of Hydropsychidae, Philopotamidae, and Psychomyiidae spin a fixed abode which is fastened to plants or other supports in the water, sometimes in still water but more frequently in running water. Three common types of these structures are found, all of them spun from silk and forming some sort of net; when taken out of water they collapse into a shapeless string. There is always an escape exit at the end of the tube.

1.—Finger nets . . . These are long, narrow pockets of fine mesh, with the front end anchored upstream, the remainder trailing behind with the current. They are built by the Philopotamidae.

2.—Trumpet nets . . . In this type the opening of the net is funnel shaped, and the end is fastened in such a way that the water movement distends the net into a trumpet-shaped structure. This type of net is used extensively by the Psychomyiidae.

3.—Hydropsychid net . . . Peculiar to the family Hydropsychidae is the habit of erecting a net directly in front of a tubelike retreat concealed in a crevice or camouflaged by bits of wood, leaves, or similar material. These nets may be erected between two supports in the open, as in the case of *Potamyia,* or the net may be constructed as one side of an antechamber, as in the case of many species of *Hydropsyche.*

In all these types, the caddis-fly larva cleans the food and debris off the net, ingesting anything edible swept into it by the current. Normally the larva spends most of its time with its head near the net ready to pounce on any prey. When disturbed, it backs out of the net or retreats with great agility. The flexible body structure enables the larva to move backward rapidly, but it can move forward only slowly.

Tube-Making Forms. Some psychomyiid larvae, notably of the genus *Phylocentropus,* burrow into sand at the bottom of streams, cementing the walls of the burrow into a fairly rigid structure which may be dug out intact. The mechanics of food gathering in this group are not well understood.

In both the net-spinning and tube-making forms, pupation takes place in the end of the tube or retreat. The larva constructs a cocoon of leaf fragments, stones, or whatever other material is available, lining it with silk. The pupa is formed here.

Saddle-Case Makers. Larvae of the rhyacophilid subfamily Glossosomatinae make a portable case which consists of an oval top made of stones and a ventral strap made of the same material. The larva proceeds with its head and legs projecting down in front of the strap and the anal hooks projecting down at the back of the strap. For pupation, the strap is cut away and the oval dome is cemented to a support, the pupa being formed in the stone cell thus made.

Purse-Case Makers. Following exactly the same principle as the above are many cases of the Hydroptilidae. In general appearance they resemble a purse. . . . The larva occupies the case with the head and legs projecting out of a slit in the front margin while the anal hooks project out of a slit in the posterior margin. For pupation, however, the case is cemented along one side to a support and the slits are cemented shut to form the pupal chamber. Not all Hydroptilidae have cases of this type, some of them having true cases.

Case Makers. All caddis-fly larvae except those listed above make portable cases which the larvae drag with them in their daily movements. These cases are usually made of pieces of leaves, bits of twigs, sand grains, or stones which are cemented or tied together with silk. Rarely the case is made entirely of silk. Case construction varies a great deal from one group to another, from one species to another within the same genus, and frequently within the same species. In general, cases subject to greatest stream current are the most solidly constructed, whereas those in small ponds where there is scarcely any water movement are the most loosely constructed.

For pupation the case is anchored to a support and a top added to the case; the pupa is formed inside this shelter and no additional cocoon is made.

Feeding Habits. Most caddis-fly larvae are practically omnivorous, eating whatever comes to hand. Such forms as the Hydropsychidae and Limnephilidae eat a preponderance of plankton, sessile diatom growths, and other small organisms, but if opportunity affords they will eat insect larvae and often each other. When their populations become crowded, caddis-fly larvae are cannibalistic to a high degree.

Certain genera are primarily predaceous, the most notable ones being *Rhyacophila* and *Oecetis.* Examination of stomach contents shows that both of these are voracious eaters; we have found forty to sixty Chironomidae larvae in single individuals of *Rhyacophila,* the alimentary tract being crowded with these midge larvae from one end to the other. In these two genera the mandibles are long and narrow, apparently fitted for grasping prey of this type. Such mandibles do not occur in phytophagous forms which may be cannibalistic.

The order Trichoptera as a whole, however, may be characterized as one in which the minute aquatic life is assimilated and converted to units of larger size which are in turn usable by a variety of larger organisms.

Respiration. This function in the Trichoptera is accomplished by cutaneous exchange or by gills. It varies greatly within families and genera. Usually the larvae of greater size have the larger or more abundant gills, and the small larvae have no gills at all. This is by no means a general rule throughout the order. In those species having gills, gill pattern and type is almost uniform throughout the entire period of larval growth, from the youngest to the full-grown stage.

Adult habits

Caddis flies include many strong fliers, such as *Macronemum,* but they also include other genera that fly only short distances. A few species have brachypterous or apterous females which cannot fly but which run with great agility.

In daytime, most of the caddis flies rest in concealed crevices or on foliage in moist, shaded glens bordering streams. At dusk the adults fly quite freely, often skimming back and forth across a body of water just above the surface. These flights are probably mating flights, since males are frequently involved; observations indicate that these flights are not correlated directly with oviposition.

The adults have mouth parts that are adapted for the ingestion of liquid foods and have no hard grinding parts for mastication of hard foods. In some families such as the Phryganeidae the end of the labium forms a large, terminal membranous lobe similar in general appearance to the proboscis of higher Diptera. Records indicate that in spite of having no other means of getting food, adults of many species normally live one or two months, and probably in all species nearly a month.

Oviposition is discussed in connection with the eggs. . . .

Collecting and Preserving

Caddis flies have such diverse habits and habitat preferences that several kinds of collecting are necessary to get representative samples from a given area. In most cases these same methods are equally effective with other aquatic groups, including stoneflies, mayflies, and midges. The adults are aerial and the larvae aquatic; further, it is more the rule than the exception that at any one place the adults in the air and the larvae in the stream belong to different sets of species. Collecting for one phase must not be stressed to the exclusion of the other.

With one exception, caddis flies, both immature stages and adults, should be collected in liquid, preferably 80 percent grain alcohol. The exception is adults of the genus *Leptocella,* readily distinguished in the field by a long, narrow shape, extremely long antennae and white ground color. . . . In this genus it is necessary for specific diagnosis to use color patterns formed by the delicate wing hairs, which rub off with remarkable ease. Specimens of this genus should be killed in a cyanide or other dry bottle, a few at a time, and carefully handled to avoid rubbing in transit and in pinning.

Adult collecting

Adults of most caddis flies come to lights readily on warm nights having neither wind nor a bright moon. Collecting at lights is thus a profitable source of material. In towns, illuminated store windows and signs attract many of these insects and provide convenient collecting points.

Vapor Glow Tubes. Adult Trichoptera are attracted very strongly to blue light and hence are to be found most abundantly around blue neon lights, or glow tubes. Fortunately for the entomologist, many of these blue lights can be found in towns and these will serve as good concentration points for caddis flies. At points where such lights are not available we have had very good success with a portable mercury glow-tube which emits a strong blue light and is very attractive to Trichoptera and many other insects. This is described in detail by Burks, Ross & Frison (1938).

Automobile Headlights. Another type of night collecting we have found effective at points away from towns is as follows. Drive an automobile to a spot overlooking a stream or lake and turn on the bright lights. Into a shallow pan, such as a pie pan, pour enough alcohol to cover the bottom with from one-eighth to one-fourth inch of liquid. Hold the pan directly under a headlight. If aquatic insects are on the wing, they will come to the light and eventually drop into the liquid, which traps them. With a small piece of wet cardboard, scrape the entire insect contents of the pan into a small bottle of alcohol, which should then be labeled, location, name of collector, and place being given.

If few insects fly to the car lights, it is convenient to dispense with the pan. In this case the caddis flies may be picked off the light easily by dipping an index finger in alcohol, "scooping up" the insect rapidly but gently on the wet surface and then dipping it in the bottle. An aspirator, or sucker, also can be used with success.

Sweeping. For daylight collecting, sweeping often proves effective. Resting places differ widely with the species, but most caddis flies prefer shaded, humid places. For these, sweep vegetation overhanging the water, whether it is herbage nearly trailing in the water or boughs which hang above it. I have noticed that many times the flies seem to prefer (for resting places) coniferous trees near the stream, and heavy beating of these is usually profitable. Sometimes the flies are numerous in bark crevices of large tree trunks along stream banks; here they are extremely difficult to detect, for they mimic bark to a remarkable degree when their wings are folded. Be sure to have your net ready when you examine a tree trunk, because the flies dodge and fly with surprising speed when alarmed.

Bridges. One of the favorite resting places of adult Trichoptera is the shaded, damp, underside of a concrete bridge. When other collecting fails it is sometimes possible to pick up from a few to many caddis flies resting under a highway bridge. Here again the flies are wary, and must be approached with caution and a ready net.

Along the Water's Edge. Frequently the adults may be captured on stones, sticks and vegetation in the water. This is true especially of the Rhyacophilidae. A method which sometimes gives good results is to press floating vegetation, such as watercress, until it is slightly submerged. Any adults resting in this foliage will swim to the surface in a moment or two.

Collecting larvae and pupae

All Nearctic caddis flies are aquatic in the developmental stages. For this reason almost any water habitat has possibilities for the collection of larvae and pupae. These should be preserved in liquid, preferably 80 percent grain alcohol, as with the adults. If vials are filled with larvae, the liquid should be changed a few hours after collection.

The easiest way to start a search for these immature stages is to turn over stones and logs in riffles and rapids; if present, larvae and cases may be found without difficulty in these situations. Handfuls of drift, weeds from the stream or river bottom, and debris may be laid on the bank, and the caddis-fly larvae may be picked out as they begin to move, at which time they are easily detected.

Cocoons of caddis flies may generally be identified because they are securely fastened to some object. These should be removed very carefully, in order to avoid breaking the silk membranes more than necessary. Where conveniently situated, they may be cut away from both sides with the sharp ends of a pair of forceps.

Representative Illustrations of Caddis

The following illustrations dealing with caddis have been taken, by permission, from studies by such authorities as J. T. Lloyd, Cornelius Betten, H. H. Ross, Alvah Peterson, and others. The source of each illustration is identified by the name of the author in whose study it originally appeared. For further information, see the Bibliography of Scientific Books and Periodicals.

The Structure of Caddis Flies

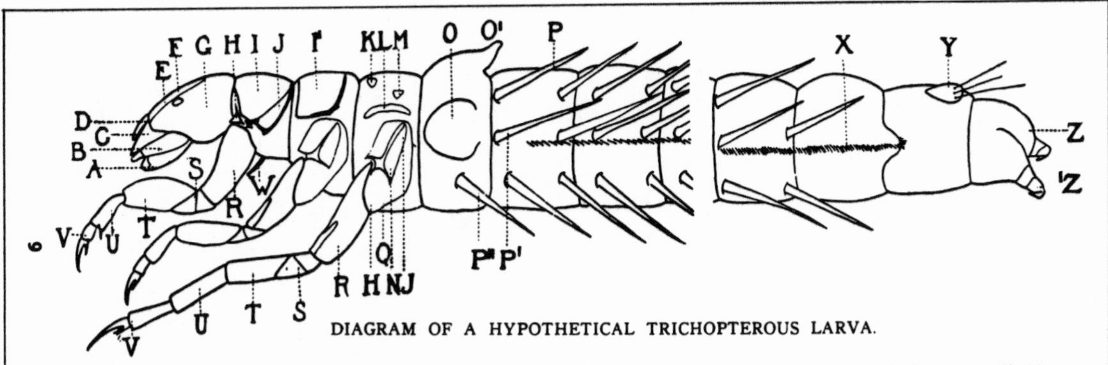

DIAGRAM OF A HYPOTHETICAL TRICHOPTEROUS LARVA.

A—Labium; B—Maxilla; C—Mandible; D—Labrum; E—Frons; F—Eye; G—Gena; H—Episternum; I—Pronotum; I′—Mesonotum; J—Epimeron; K—Cephalic chitinous plate; L—Lateral chitinous plate; M—Caudal chitinous plate; N—Pleural suture; O—Lateral spacing hump; O′—Dorsal spacing hump; P—Sub-dorsal gill; P′—Lateral gill; P″—Sub-ventral gill; Q—Pre-axal swelling; R—Coxa; S—Trochanter; T—Femur; U—Tibia; V—Tarsus; W—Prosternal horn; X—Lateral fringe; Y—Chitinous plate; Z—Proleg; Z′—Drag hook.

Diagram of a hypothetical caddis larva (from J. T. Lloyd, "The Biology of North American Caddis Fly Larvae").

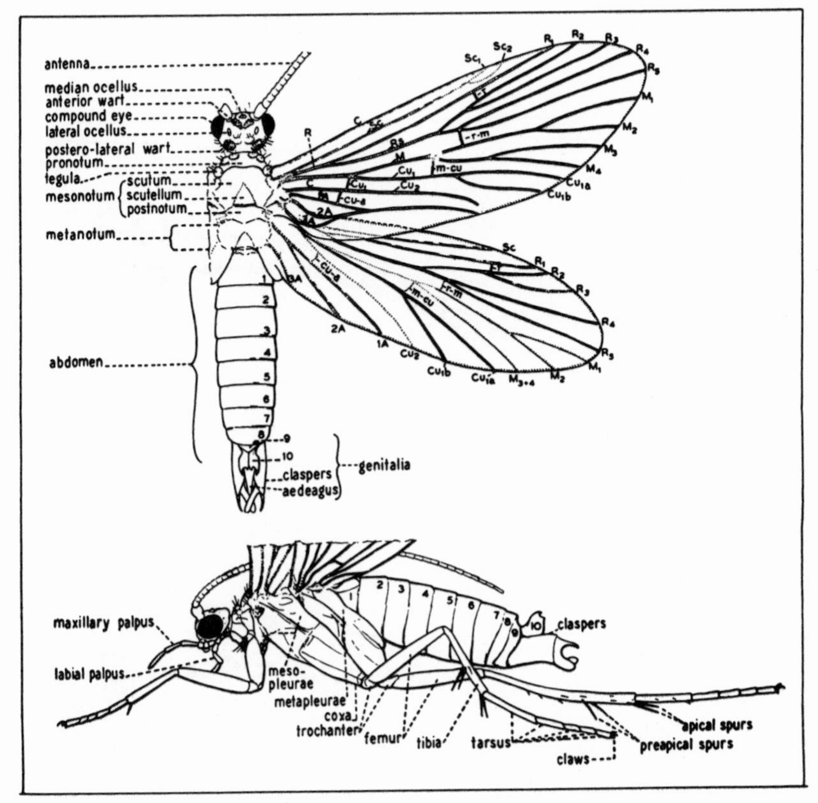

Rhyacophila lobifera, adult male, illustrating the terminology of parts. Maximum length 13 mm. Note that the wings are spread to show venation (from Ross).

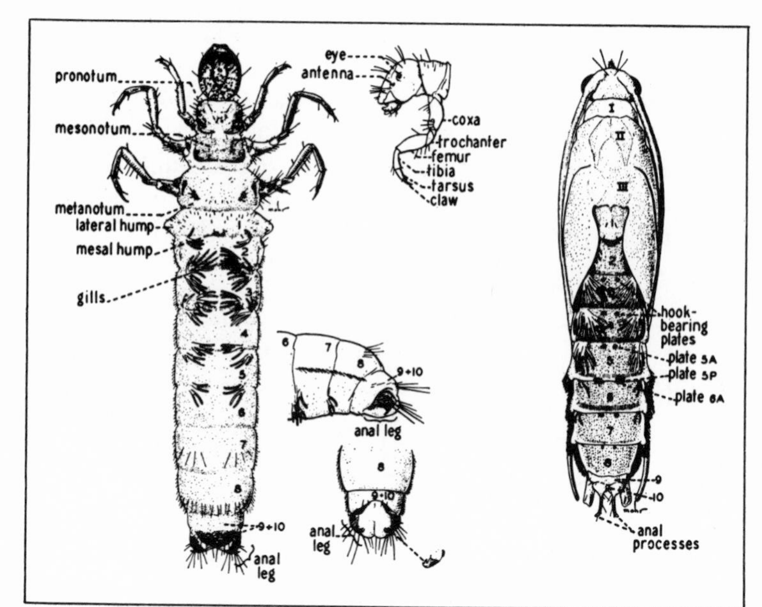

Limnephilus submonilifer, larva and pupa, illustrating terminology of parts. Maximum length of larva 17 mm. (from Ross).

Caddis Larvae

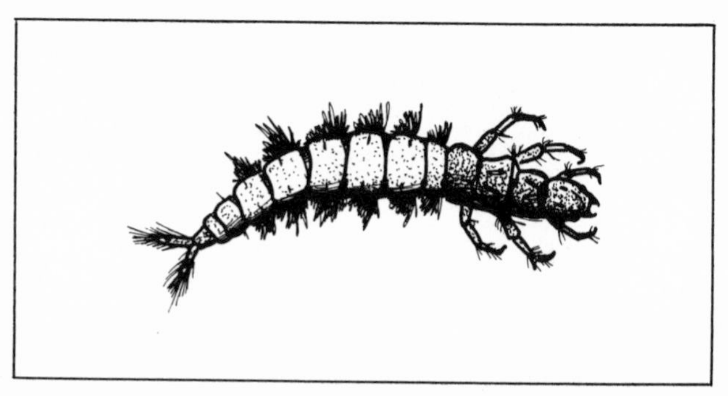

Hydropsychodes analis. Head dark brown except for light yellow areas surrounding each ocellus; abdomen yellowish tan; 11.5 mm. long (redrawn by D. W. from Elkins).

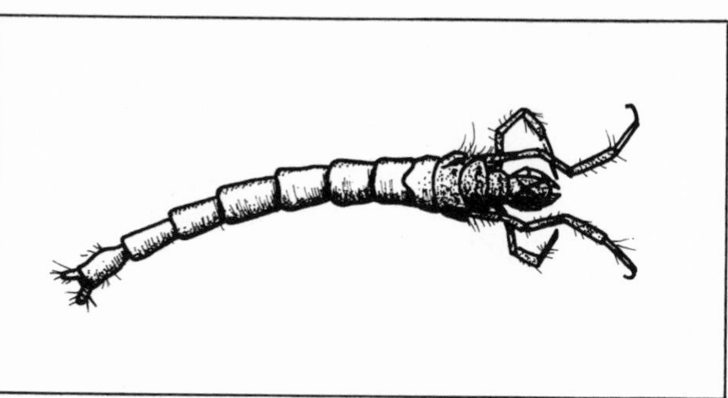

Leptocella albida. A river and lake species widely distributed in North America. Length 13 mm. Head brownish yellow gray with black fork; abdomen green with double row of bright yellow spots showing on sides (redrawn by D. W. from Elkins).

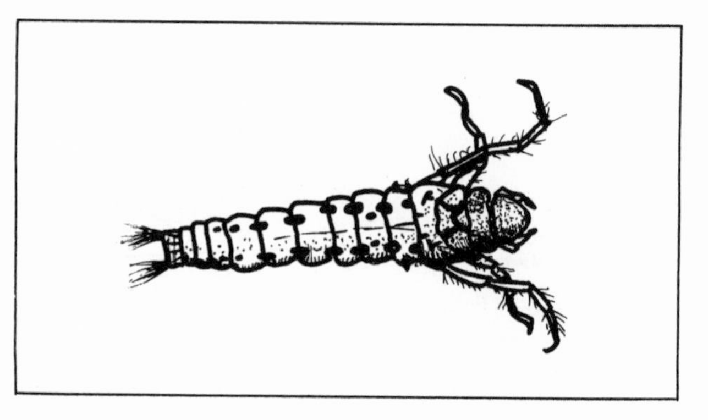

Leptocerus cancellatus. Ross calls species *Athripsodes cancellatus.* A stream species distributed as far west as Oklahoma. Length 6 mm. Head light brown, abdomen white. Note the small head and the hind legs three to four times as long as the forelegs (redrawn by D. W. from Elkins).

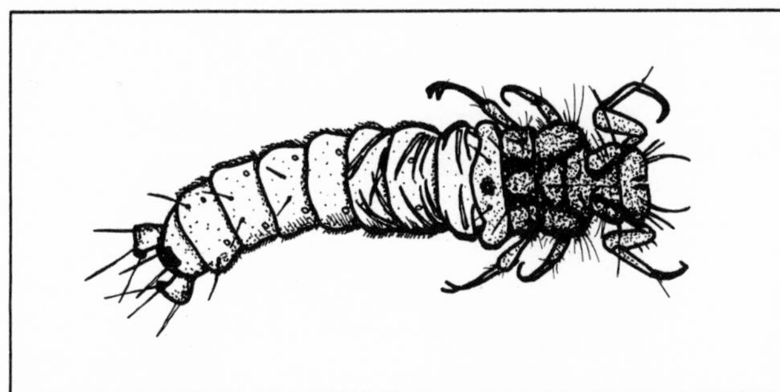

Agrypnia straminea. Apparently a lake species. Length 17 mm. Head orange to light tan or yellow with dark brown stripes. Abdomen green (redrawn by D. W. from Elkins).

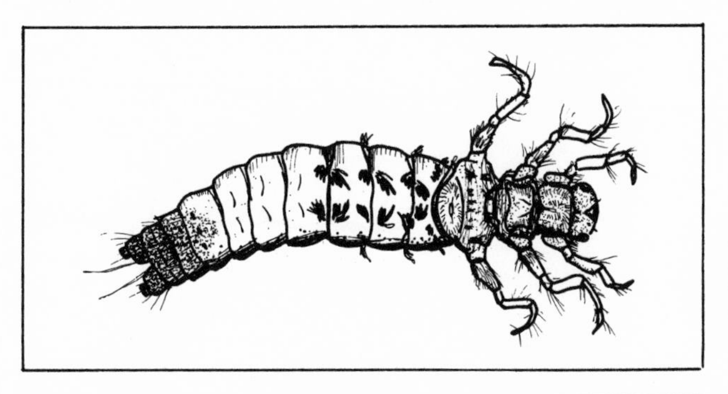

Hesperophylax designatus. A river species widely distributed throughout the northeast and Middle West. Length 15 mm. Head and prothorax darkish brown, abdomen yellowish or greenish white (redrawn by D. W. from Elkins).

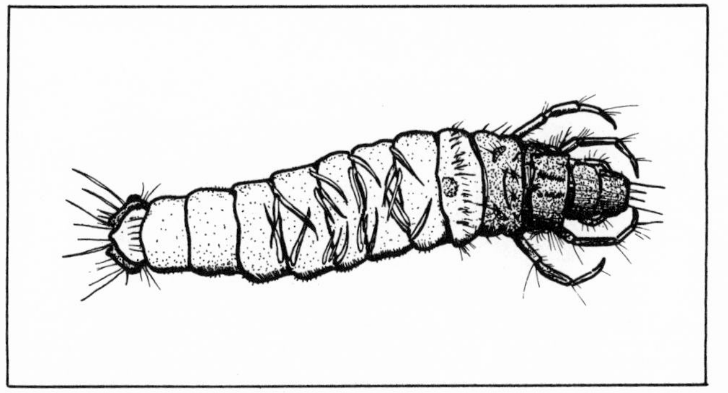

Stenophylax subfasciata. Lake species but may inhabit very sluggish rivers. Length up to 23 mm. Head, prothorax, and mesothorax dark, legs dark brown, abdomen greenish white, slightly reddish on dorsal side (redrawn by D. W. from Elkins).

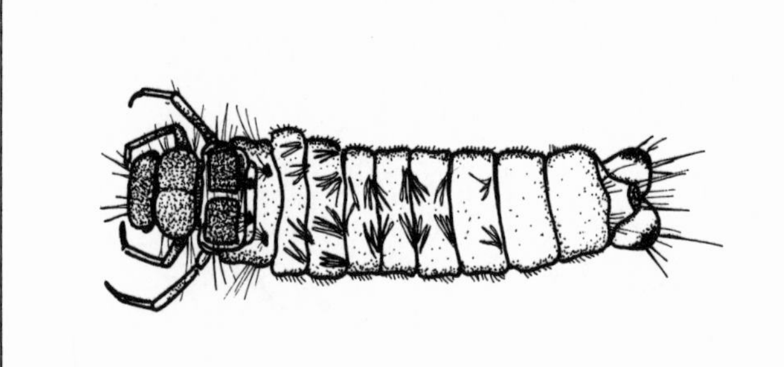

Limnephilus combinatus. Species called *L. rhombicus* by Ross, who shows a sketch of larva in case on page 190. Larvae up to 20 mm. Head and thorax yellow with black and brown markings; abdomen yellowish. A stream species, ranging from Greenland to Illinois (redrawn by D. W. from Elkins).

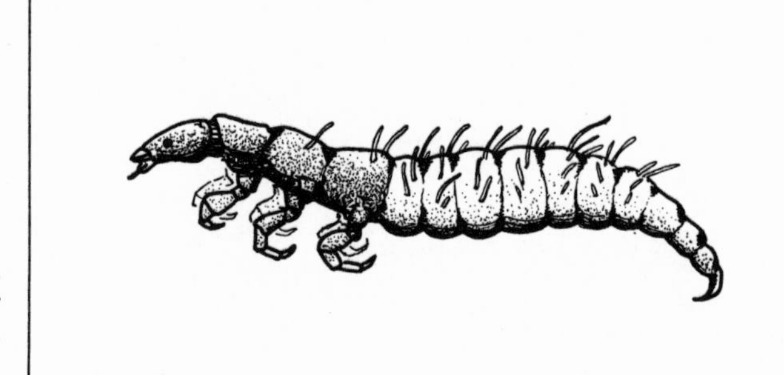

Noncasemaking form of larvae (species from *Rhyacophilidae*). Note the lack of hump and fewer gills as compared with the casemaking form (redrawn by D. W. from Dodds and Hisaw).

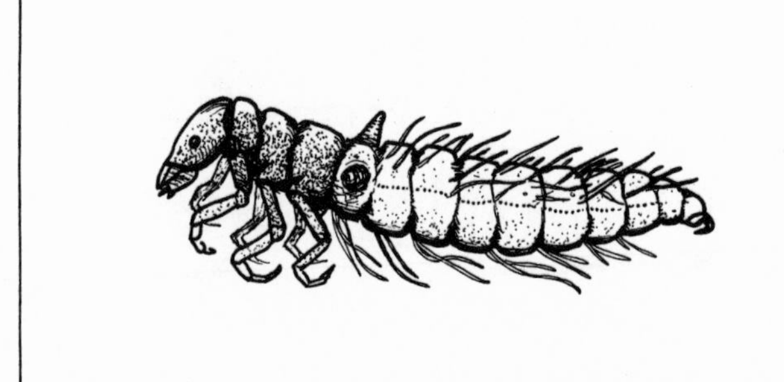

Casemaking form of larvae. Note the hump and many gills (redrawn by D. W. from Dodds and Hisaw).

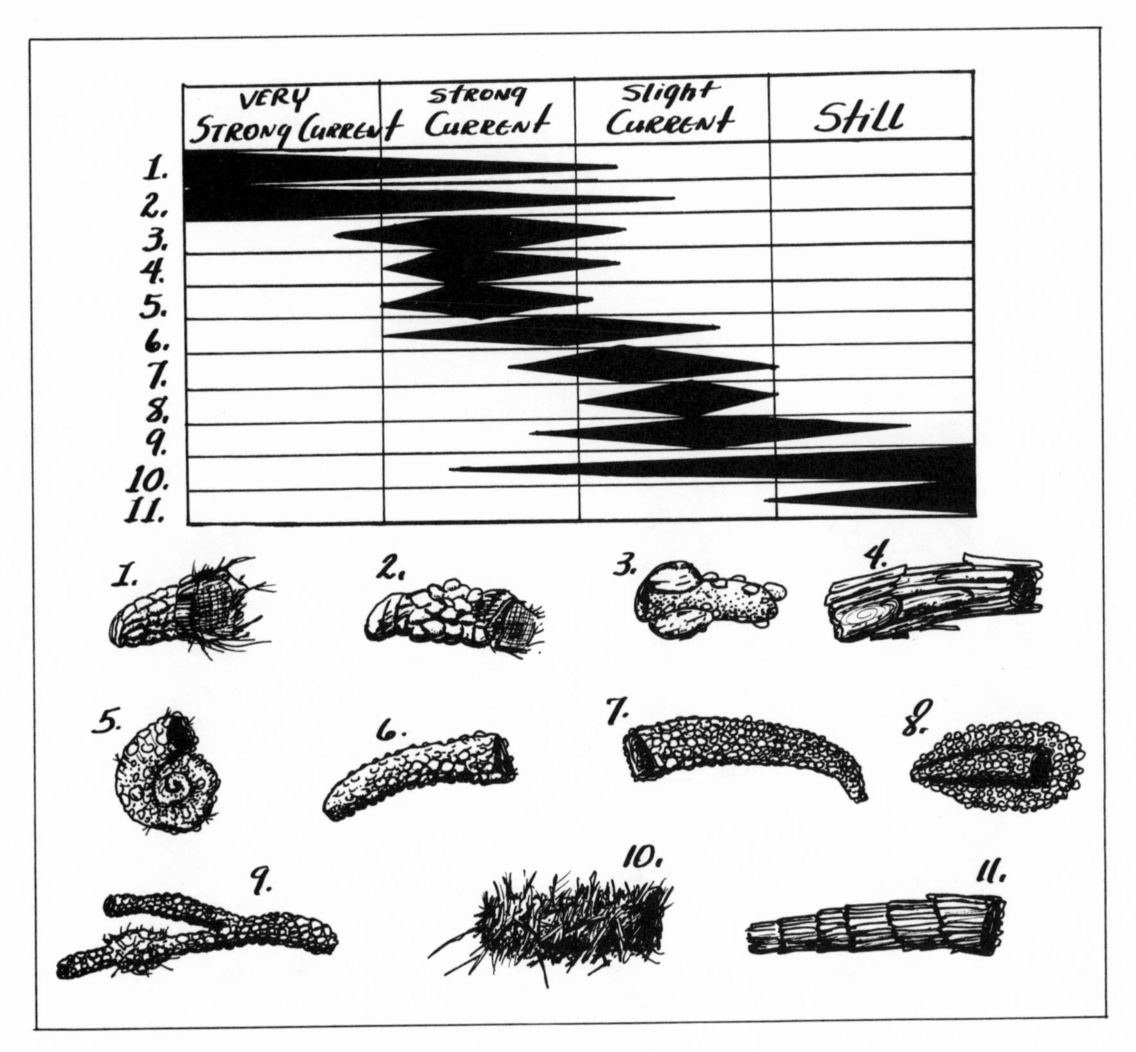

Caddis Casemakers and Net Spinners in Relation to Current Flow in Northern New Jersey

1. *Hydropsyche analis,* a net builder
2. *Hydropsyche scalaris,* a net builder
3. *Goera fuscula*
4. *Astenophylax argus*
5. *Helicopsyche annulicornis*
6. *Psilotreta frontalis*
7. *Notidobia americana*
8. *Molanna cinerea*
9. *Phylocentropus lucidus.* Branched case of sand, nonportable, burrowed and embedded in the stream bottom. On occasion as long as 65 mm.
10. *Platycentropus maculipennis*
11. *Phryganea interrupta*

(Adapted by D.W. from Sleight, "Relations of Trichoptera to Their Environment")

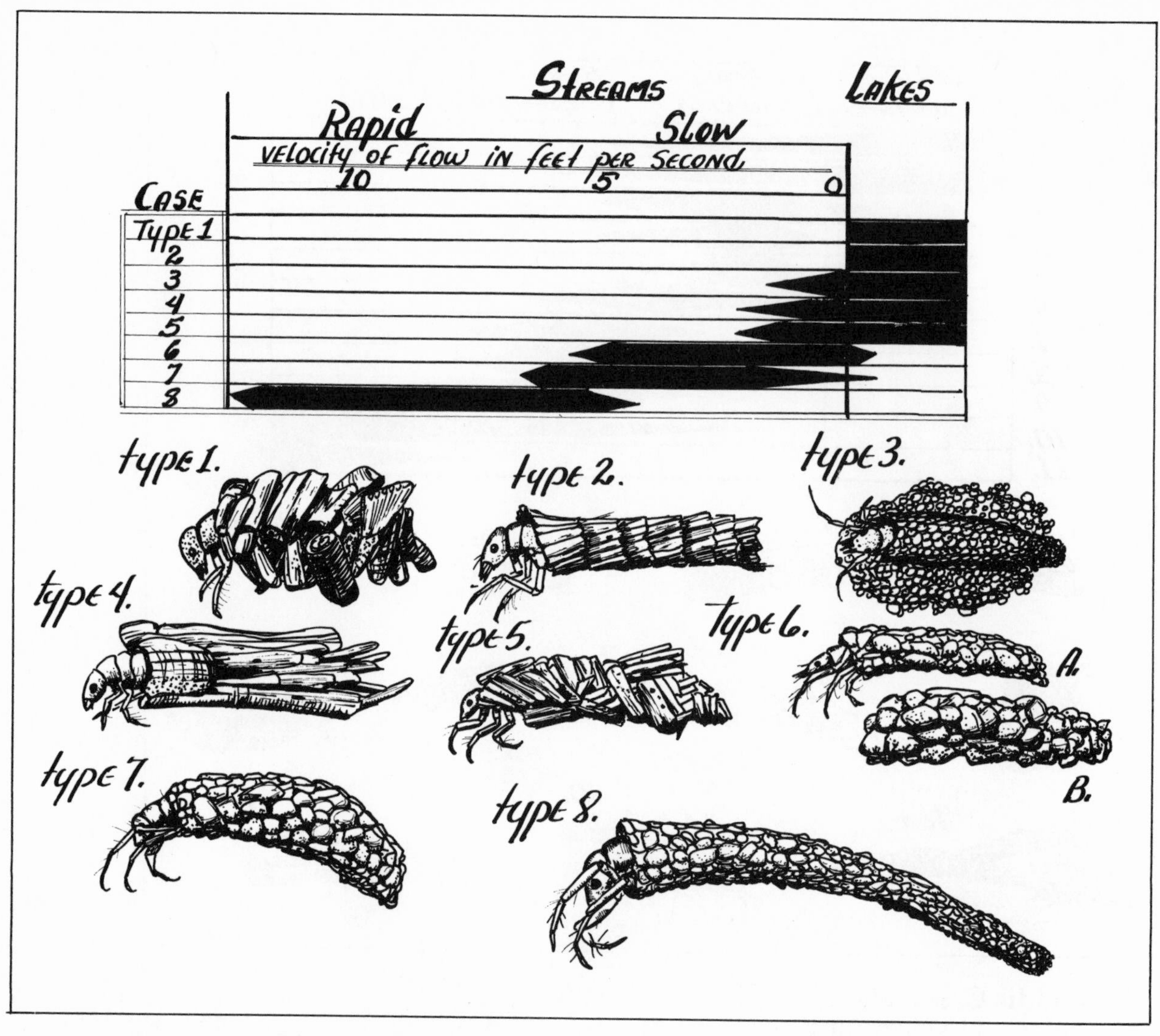

Types of Larval Cases in Relation to Current Velocity in the Colorado Rockies

Type 1. Species unidentified
Type 2. *Glyphotaelius hostilis*
Type 3. *Molanna flavicornis*
Type 4. *Anabolia maculata*
Type 5. Species unidentified
Type 6. *Hesperophylax designatus.* a) larva; b) pupa
Type 7. *Dicosmoecus gilvipes*
Type 8. *Neothremma alicia*
(Adapted by D. W. from Dodds and Hisaw)

Caddis Larvae (from Peterson)

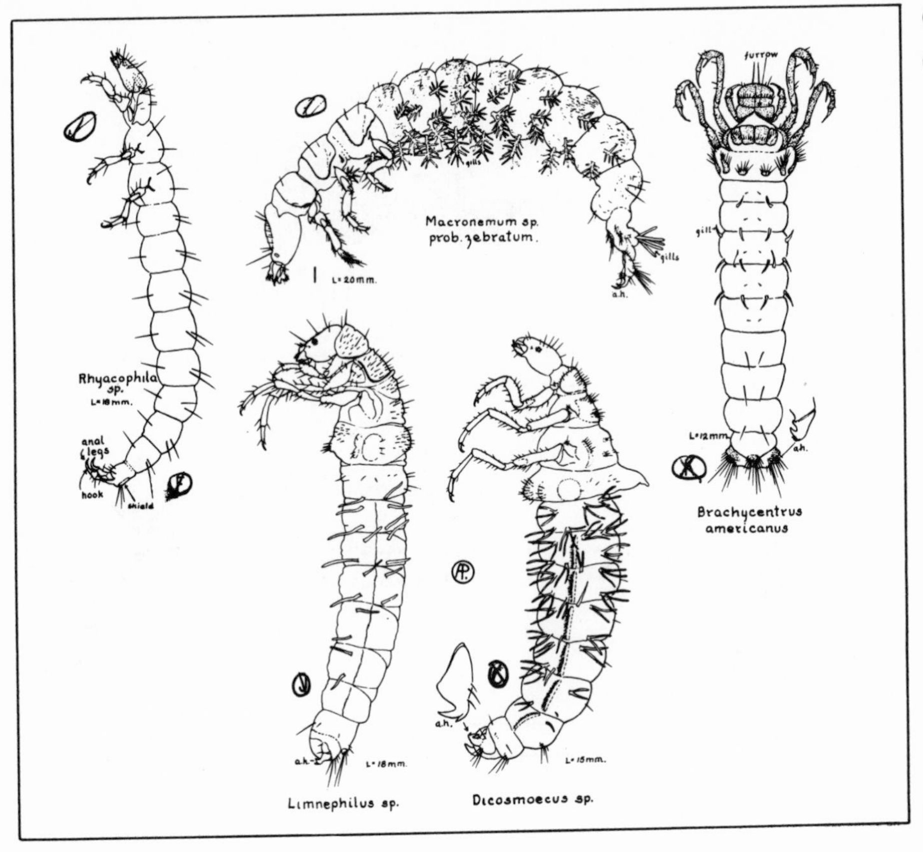

Caddis Larva and Adult

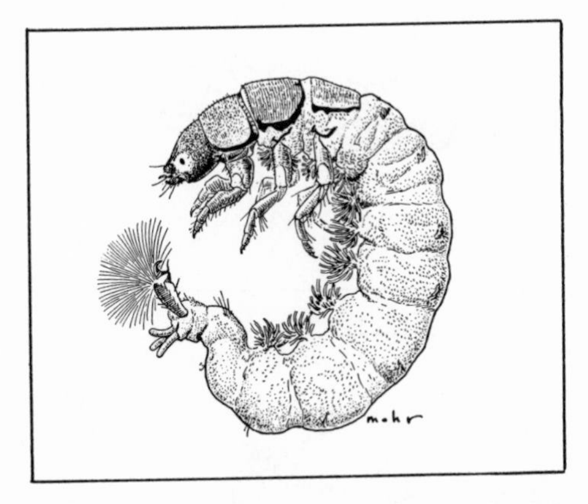

Hydropsyche simulans. Recorded from Ohio to Colorado. An abundant stream species in Illinois. Larvae reach a length of 18 mm. (from Ross).

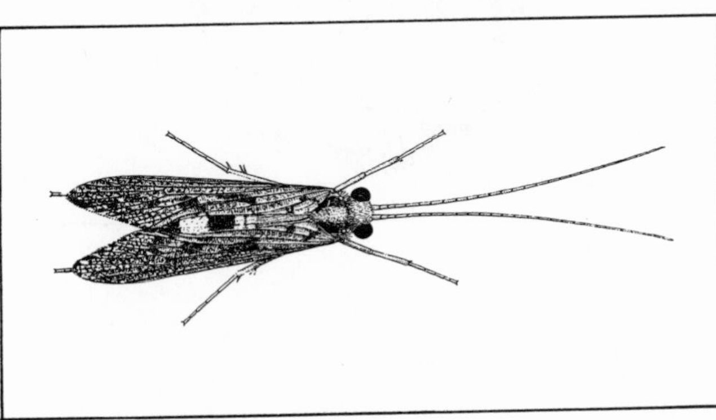

Male adult of the same species. Color pattern various shades of brown, length 13–15 mm. Adults emerge throughout the warmer months from April to September (from Ross).

Caddis Larvae in Cases

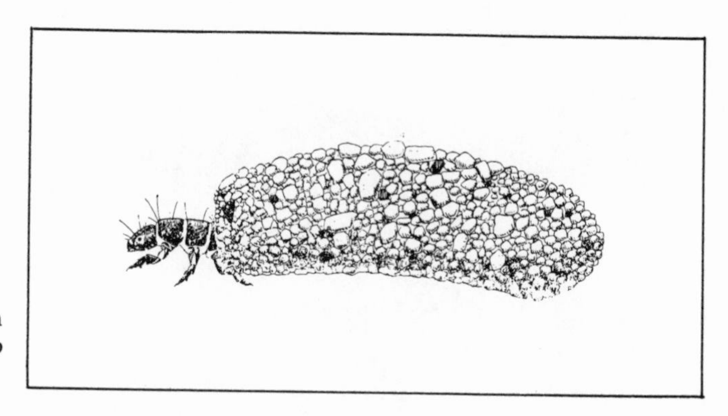

Ochrotrichia unio, a microcaddis in case. Length of larva 4 mm. Head "dark brown shading to black" (from Ross).

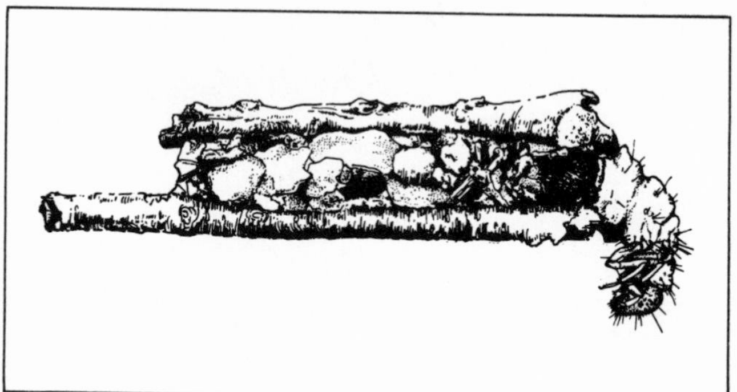

Larva and case of *Stenophylax luculentus.* Note the two "ballast" sticks that the larva has added to keep the case from rolling in the current. Length of larva probably about 22 mm. *Pycnopsyche luculenta* in Ross (from Betten).

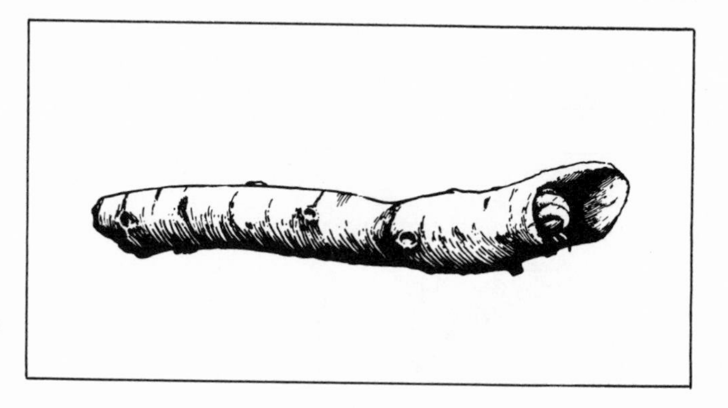

Ganonema nigrum. A twig stem hollowed out (from Betten).

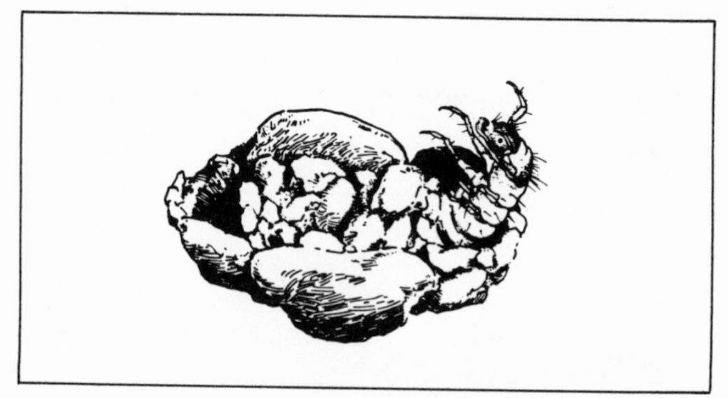

Mystrophora americana. Ross says the genus is *Glossosoma* (from Betten).

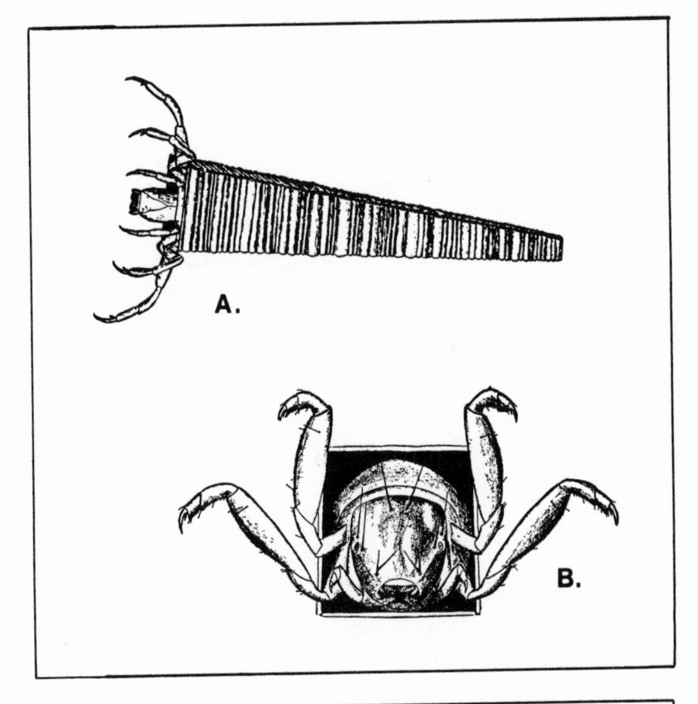

Brachycentrus nigrisoma. Fig. A: larva in case, dorsal view. Fig. B: head-on view of larva in case. From Lloyd, who describes larvae as about 12 mm. long; head black; chitinized parts dark brown, and soft body parts green. Specimens in captivity emerged in late May and early June. Betten cites Nathan Banks's description of the adult, a female: thorax deep black, abdomen brown, wings "rather darker" than the pale yellowish of *B. lutescens,* with expanse of 24 mm. Specimens reared by Lloyd had brown wings with a covering of short black hair with some yellow.

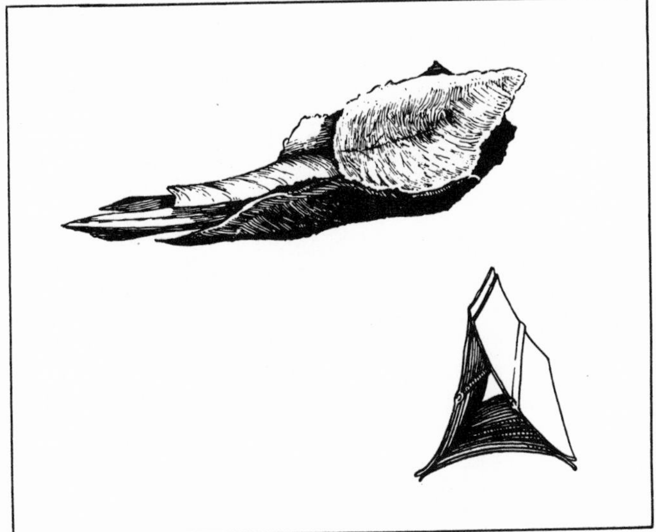

Arctoecia consocia. One type of larval case, cross section of which is shown below. Length of larva, 25 mm. (from Betten).

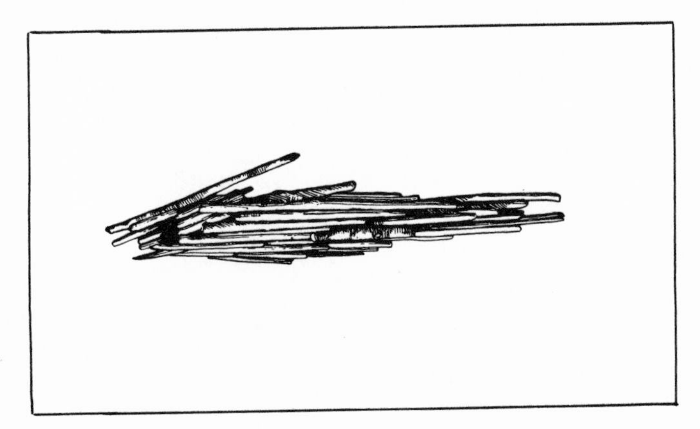

Anabolia bimaculata. Cases of vegetable material placed rather regularly, sometimes even spirally (from Betten).

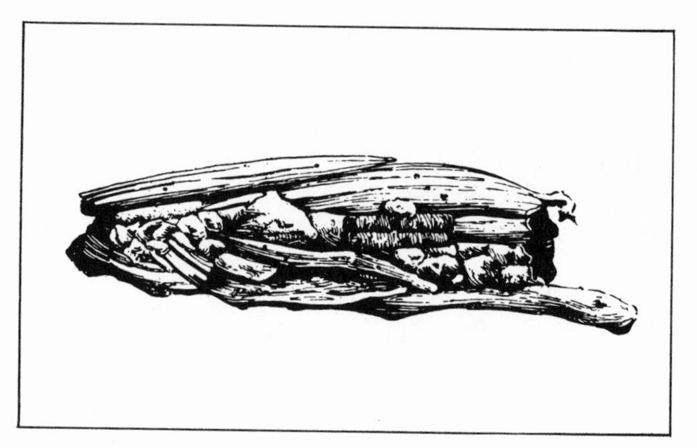

Astenophylax argus. Larvae can reach 50 mm. in length. Cases made of twigs and bark "arranged with little regard for system or symmetry," according to Lloyd. Employs ballast sticks. Head of larvae brown (from Betten).

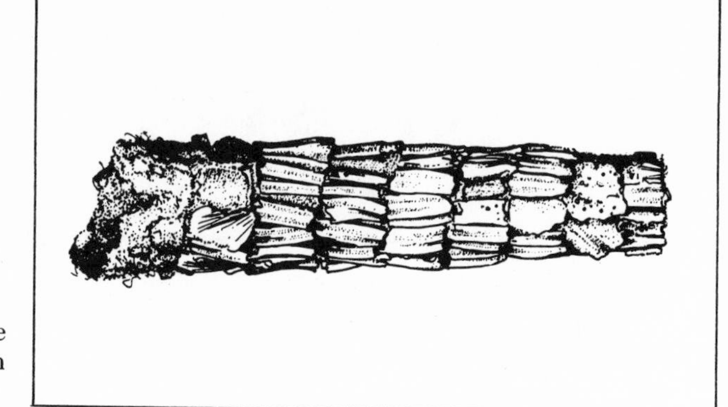

Phryganea sp. The cases are formed of vegetable material, often arranged in a distinct spiral (from Betten).

A Complex Case History

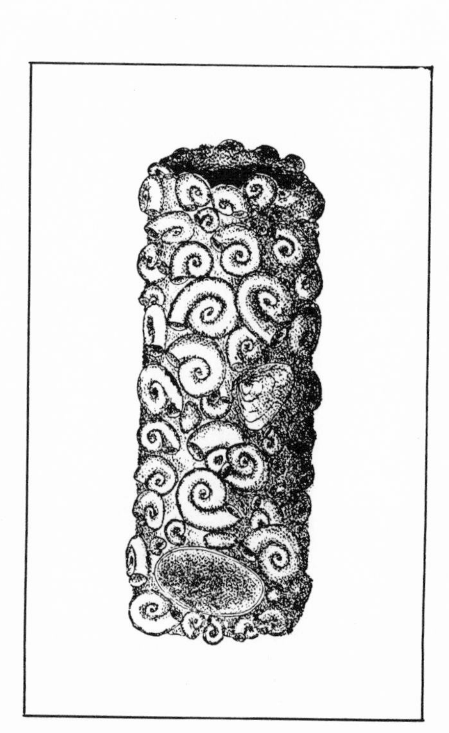

Water, snail shells, and oval seeds

Limnephilus rhombicus, two cases from Lloyd, who called the species *L. combinatus.* Lloyd describes the case as 20–25 mm. long, and he notes, most interestingly, that the young larvae make a cross-stick type of case. However, as pupation draws near, the larvae migrate away from the grassy shoreline of a stream, and the case takes on a new appearance. The building materials might now consist of the shells of water snails and oval seeds, while farther up the same stream, where thickets overhang, the larvae use chunks of bark in their cases.

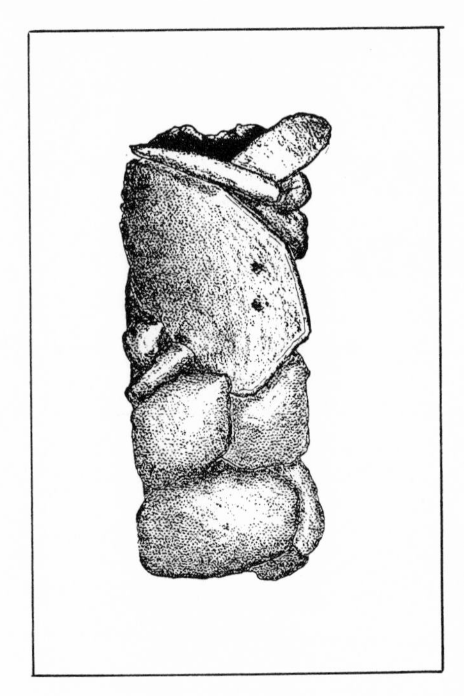

Chunks of bark

Betten writes of the adult, "Dr. Lloyd tells me that the adult is salmon-pink in color when alive . . ." Betten gives the length of the adult as 10–17 mm. Ross says 20 mm. and gives the color of the adult as brownish yellow, "the wings with a distinct pattern of cream color and chocolate brown arranged in somewhat oblique stripes."

Caddis Adults

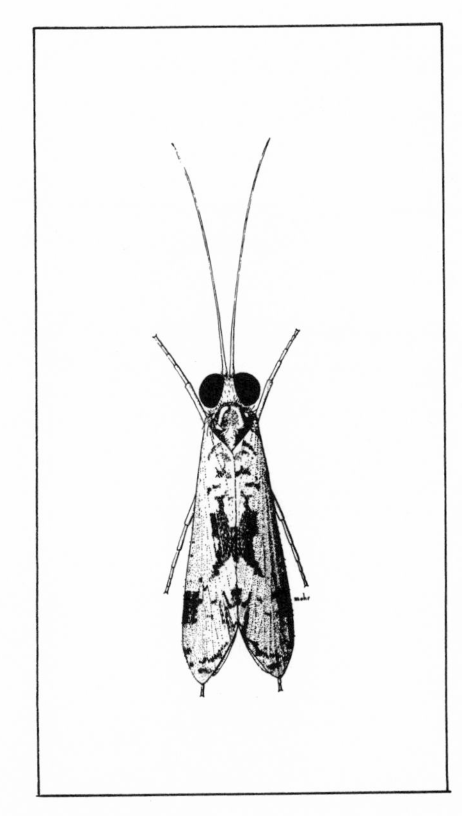

Hydropsyche aerata. This sketch (from Ross) shows the male, which is dissimilar in general appearance from the female. The male has a length of 9 mm., "head and body dark brown, antennae and legs white; wings white with definite brown markings forming a distinctive pattern; eyes very large, twice as wide as the antero-dorsal space between them." The female is slightly larger and has wings "mottled with various shades of brown." Ross notes, "All the records indicate a preference for medium-sized to large, rapid rivers." In Illinois, adults emerge from May through most of August.

Macronemum zebratum. Ranges over most of eastern North America with an isolated record from Utah. Length 15–18 mm., beautifully colored. "Color of head and thorax metallic bluish brown; antennae dark brown at base, gradually becoming lighter toward apex; mouth parts and legs yellow. Front wings brown with yellow markings" forming the pattern as shown. Emerges from late May into September. Ross encountered "large flights" of this species in midsummer; the larvae and pupae were very abundant in the rapids of the Kankakee River (from Ross).

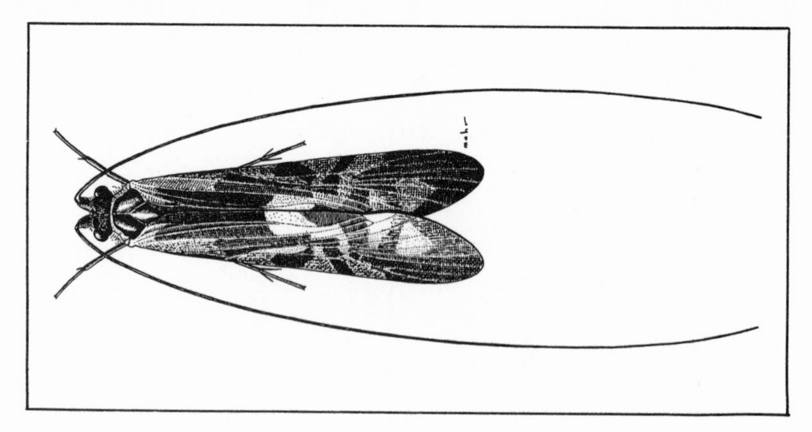

Neophylax autumnus. Length up to 12 mm. "Head and body brownish yellow; front wings fairly dark brown with irregular, small, lighter areas scattered over most the surface and with a pair of large yellow marks along the posterior margin; in repose these two yellow marks form a double, diamond-shaped mesal pattern." Recorded from various parts of the northeast, from New York to Wisconsin. "Of unique interest is the adaptation of this species to streams which become dry in summer, such as those in the Ozark Hills. In these situations, the larvae mature at least by April, fasten their cases under stones and aestivate until autumn; in September the larvae change to the pupae, and shortly thereafter the adults emerge" (from Ross).

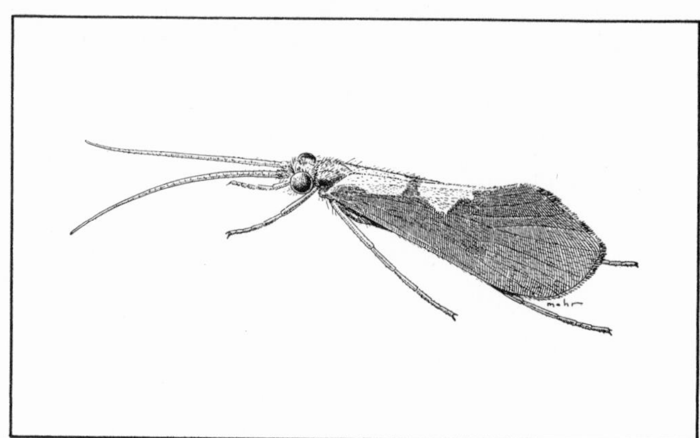

Triaenodes tarda. A widely distributed species recorded from New York, Ontario, Wisconsin, Arkansas, Oklahoma, Arizona, and British Columbia. Length 12–13 mm. "Color tawny with the same conspicuous cream and brown pattern" as shown here. Larvae found in both streams and lakes; emerges May to September (from Ross).

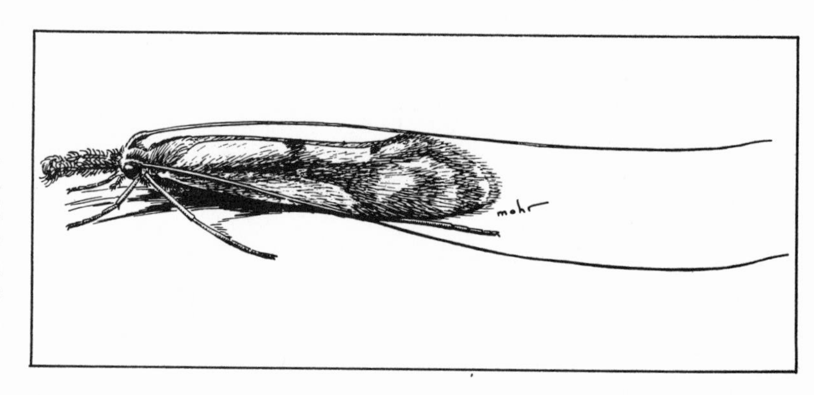

Mystacides sepulchralis. Larvae found in both lakes and streams. Length 9 mm. "Color blue-black, the wings and thorax with an iridescent metallic sheen." Species has been taken over a wide range, from New Brunswick to Saskatchewan south to the Ozarks. Adults emerge from May into September (from Ross).

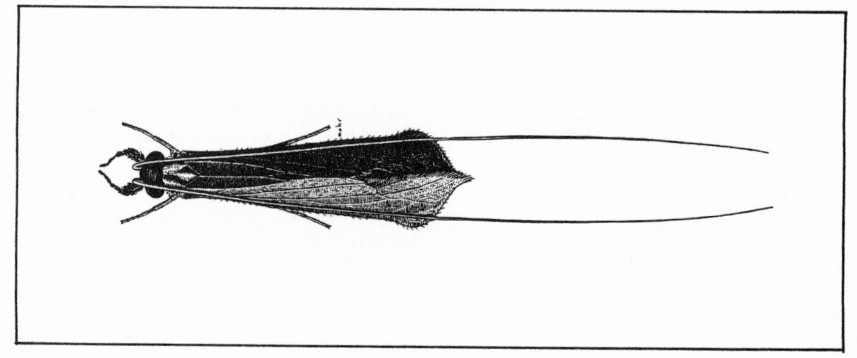

Appendixes

A Glossary of Entomology

This glossary of entomology is based on that compiled by the late Philip Garman for his study of "The Odonata or Dragonflies of Connecticut," previously cited. The glossary has been edited by us, and terms that apply only to Odonata are so indicated. For detailed drawings showing the body parts listed here for both Odonata and caddis, see pages 176–78 and 187–88. As we deal with other orders of insects in future editions of *The Fly-Tyer's Almanac* (such as mayflies, stone flies, midges, and terrestrials), we plan to enlarge the glossary by adding terms that are peculiar to those orders.

Accessory Appendages. Genital appendages on the venter of the second abdominal segment in Odonata.
Accessory Genitalia. Genital appendages on the venter of the second abdominal segment in Odonata.
Acuminate. Tapering to a long point.
Aedeagus. The penis or intromittent organ in male insects; the tip of the phallus.
Anal Appendages. Movable appendages at the tip of the abdomen in Odonata.
Anal Loop. The area including a few to many cells, between the branches of the anal vein, or between cubitus and the first anal vein in Odonata.
Anal Membrane. A semiopaque membrane in the hind wing of some Odonata beginning at the articulation of the wing and extending along the hind margin; also called "membranule" in Odonata.
Anal Vein,-s. The sixth to the ninth longitudinal vein located behind the cubitus and commonly short or abbreviated in Odonata.
Annulate. Ringed or marked with colored bands; ringlike.
Annuli. Rings.
Anteclypeus. The lower of two divisions of the clypeus in Odonata.

Antenna, -ae. Segmented sensory appendages borne one on each side of the head; "feelers."
Antenodal Cross-veins. Cross-veins between C and R (which see), proximad of the nodus in Odonata.
Anterior Lamina. Anterior part of the accessory genitalia of male Aeshnae in Odonata.
Approximate. Near or close together.
Arculus. In Odonata a cross-vein between radius and cubitus from which the median vein apparently arises.
Auricles. Earlike protuberances on the second abdominal segment in Odonata.
Austral. Belonging to the faunal region covering all the United States and Mexico, except the boreal region and tropical lowlands.
Basal Lobes. Small plates at the base of the ovipositor in Odonata.
Basilar Space. A cell at the base of the wing, bounded by radius, cubitus, arculus, and the base of the wing; also median space in Odonata.
Bifid. Divided into two parts; split; forked.
Bifurcate. Divided not over half its length into two parts; forked.
Bisinuate. With two sinuations or curves.
Boreal. Belonging to the faunal region extending from the polar sea southward to near the northern boundary of the United States, and farther south in the Rockies. *See* Austral.
Bridge. Wing vein connecting radial sector with media in Odonata.
C. Costa (which see).
Carina. Ridge.
Carinate. Ridged.
Caudad. Toward the rear or tail end.
Cephalad. Toward the head.
Cephalo-mesal. Toward the head and at the same time toward the meson.
Cercus, -i. Lateral cylindrical appendages at the tip of the abdomen.
Chitin. Substance forming the external skeleton of insects; the hard parts.
Chlorinated. Transparent yellow or yellowish green.
Claws. Hooks at the tips of the legs, commonly tarsal claws.
Clypeus. A head sclerite below the front and above the labrum.
Compound Eyes. Large eyes on the lateral surface of the head, composed of many smaller divisions.
Confluent. Running together; said of two spots that coalesce.
Contiguous. So near together as to touch.
Costa. The vein forming the front margin of the wing; first longitudinal vein.
Coxa, -ae. The segment of the leg next to the body. Pro-, front; meso-, middle; meta-, hind coxae.
Coxal Process. A point on the pleura about which the coxa rotates in its socket and which marks the ventral terminus of the pleural sutures.
Crenulate. With small scallops, evenly rounded and rather deeply curved.
Crepuscular. Active or flying at dusk.
Cubito-anal Cross-veins. Veins connecting cubitus and first anal veins.
Cubitus. The fifth longitudinal vein in an insect wing.
Cuneiform. Wedge shaped.
Declivous. Sloping downward.

Denticulate. Provided with small teeth.
Dimorphic. Differently colored in the two sexes.
Distad. Toward the outer end of an appendage, away from the body; as opposed to proximad.
Distal. Of or belonging to portions of appendages farthest from the body.
Divaricate. Spreading apart.
Dorsad. Toward the dorsum or back.
Dorsal. Of or belonging to the upper surface.
Dorsal Punctures. Punctures or spots on the dorsum.
Dorso-meson. Intersection of the meson with the dorsal surface of the body.
Dorsum. The upper surface of the body, or segment of the body.
Emarginate. Notched; with an obtuse, rounded, or quadrate section cut from margin.
Epicranial Suture. A Y-shaped suture on the dorsum of the head.
Epimerum, -a. The caudo-ventral plate of the pleurum in Odonata; same as epimeron.
Episternum, -a. The anterior or cephalic divisions of the pleura.
Exuviae. Skin cast off at molting; usually applied to the final skin cast before the adult emerges. This word is always plural in form, being similar to the English word "clothes."
Face. The front of the head below the antennae.
Falciform. Sickle shaped.
Femoral Setae. Setae on the femora.
Femur, -ora. Usually the stoutest segment or thigh of an insect leg. The fourth leg segment in Odonata, considering the trochanters as two-segmented.
Flavescent. Slightly smoky color in Odonata. Now considered incorrect, as flavescent is used to describe "a somewhat yellow color; verging on yellow."
Forcipate. Bearing forceps or similar-shaped structures.
Front. That portion of the head between the compound eyes, from ocelli to clypeus, in Odonata.
Frontal Vesicle. In Aeshnidae and others, a swelling between the compound eyes, bearing the ocelli.
Fuscous. Dark brown approaching black.
Gena, -ae. The cheeks of insects; in Odonata the sides of the face below the compound eyes.
Gills, Tracheal. Plates at the tip of the abdomen in the nymphs of Zygoptera which contain tracheae and are used for breathing.
Glabrous. Smooth, free from all vestiture; lacking setae or spines.
Gonapophysis, -es. The leaflike processes of the ovipositor in Odonata; in other insects the genitalia collectively.
Hamule, -es. A small hook; in Odonata usually forked appendages of the second segment of the male; posterior lamina.
Holotype. The single specimen selected by the author of a species as its type, or the only specimen known at the time of description. (From J. R. de la Torre-Bueno, *A Glossary of Entomology.)*
Humeral. Relating to the shoulder or humerus.
Inferiors. The lower anal appendages in Odonata.
Infraepisternum. The lower division of the episternum.
Infuscated. Smoky gray-brown; sepia.

Instar. The period or stage between molts.
Internal Triangle. Triangular wing cell behind and proximad of the triangle in Odonata.
Interpleural Suture. Suture between meso- and metapleura in Odonata.
Intersternum. A large sclerite on the sternum of the thorax just in front of the abdomen in Odonata.
Invagination. A pouch or sac formed by the infolding or indrawing of the outer surface.
Katepisternum. The lower division of the episternum; the infraepisternum.
Labial Palpus, -i. Paired, jointed appendages of the labium.
Labium. The lower lip; in Odonata a hinged appendage folded beneath the head.
Labrum. The upper lip; in Odonata the ventral flap attached to the clypeus on the front of the head.
Lanceolate. Lance- or spear-shaped; oblong and tapering to the end.
Larva, -ae. In strict entomological use, the term applied to the growth stages between egg and pupa in insect species having a complete metamorphosis. Flytyers and flyfishermen in the United States and England customarily use the word "nymph" loosely, as referring not only to the young of aquatic insects but also for small crustaceans as well, such as shrimps, scuds, sow bugs, and crayfish.
Laterad. Toward the side, away from the meson or median line.
Lateral Keel. Ridges on the sides of the abdomen in Odonata.
Lateral Spines. Spines at the caudal end of the lateral keel in Odonata.
Lateral Setae. Setae of the proximal segment of the labial palpi in Odonata.
M. Media.
Mandible. The lateral upper jaws of a biting insect.
Media. The fourth longitudinal vein in the wing.
Median Cleft of Labium. A notch or cleft in the mentum of the labium in Odonata.
Median Lobe of Labium. Same as mentum.
Median Space. Same as basilar space of the wings in Odonata.
Mental Setae. Setae on the inner surface of the mentum in Odonata.
Mentum. The central sclerite of the labium, second from the head.
Mesad. Toward the meson.
Mesepimera. Epimera of the mesothorax in Odonata.
Mesepisterna. Episterna of the mesothorax in Odonata.
Mesocoxae. Coxae of the mesothorax.
Meson. An imaginary vertical longitudinal plane passed through the center of the body of an insect, dividing it into right and left parts.
Mesopleural Suture. Suture separating episternum and epimerum of the pleura.
Mesosternum. Sternum of the mesothorax.
Mesostigmal Plates. Small sclerites surrounding the mesothoracic spiracle in Odonata.
Mesothorax. The middle division of the thorax, bearing the second (middle) pair of legs.
Metallic. Shining; opposed to dull.
Metapleural Suture. Suture separating episternum and epimerum of the metathorax in Odonata.
Metathoracic Spiracle. Spiracle of the metathorax in Odonata.

Metathorax. The third or hindmost segment of the thorax, bearing the third (hind) pair of legs.
Microthorax. A minute division at the cephalic end of the thorax in Odonata.
Naiad. The nymph of an aquatic insect, usually with an incomplete metamorphosis, such as the stoneflies, Odonata (dragonflies and damselflies), and mayflies. The term is becoming archaic, not having met with popular acceptance.
Nodus. A slight indentation in the front margin of the Odonate wing, supported by a heavy cross-vein.
Notum. The dorsal or upper part of a segment, usually applied to the thorax.
Nymph. In strict entomological sense, the term applied to the life stages of insects having incomplete metamorphosis, that is, the period between egg and adult. Anglers use the term widely to describe a variety of underwater life.
Occipital Horn. Chitinous horns just below the occipital ridge on each side of the head in Odonata.
Occipital Ridge. A ridge extending between the compound eyes on the caudo-dorsal angle of the head in Odonata.
Occipital Spine. Spine on the caudo-dorsal surface of the head between the compound eyes in Odonata.
Occiput. Region of the head between the compound eyes and behind the transverse suture in Anisoptera.
Ocellar Ridge. A ridge just behind the ocelli in Odonata.
Ocellar Stripe. A pale stripe on the dorsum of the head behind the ocelli in Odonata.
Ocellus, -i. Simple eyes of adult insects. There are three on the dorsum of the head of adult Odonata.
Ochraceous. Yellow with a slight tinge of brown.
Ovate. Egg shaped.
Ovipositor. The tubular or valvelike structure by which the eggs are placed.
Palpus, -i. The mouth feelers on insects; in Odonata, the jointed appendages attached to labium.
Paraptera. Small plates at the bases of the front wings.
Pile. Very fine hairlike setae; velvety or furry in appearance.
Pilose. With pile; velvety.
Pleura. The lateral sclerites between the dorsum and sternum of a segment.
Pollinose. Covered with a pollenlike dust.
Postclypeus. In Odonata the proximal division of the clypeus.
Postcoxal Areas. Areas on the venter of the thorax behind the metacoxae.
Posterior. Hind or hindmost; opposed to anterior.
Postgenae. Sclerites on the rear of the head on either side of the occipital foramen.
Postnodal Cross-veins. Cross-veins between C and R (which see) and between nodus and stigma in Odonata.
Postocular Spots. Pale spots on the dorsum of the head in Zygoptera behind and usually laterad of the ocelli.
Precoxal. Before or in front of the coxae.
Preocellar Band. A dark pigment stripe immediately in front of the ocelli in Odonata.
Prescutum. Front division of the scutum.
Proepimerum. Caudal plate in the pleura of the prothorax in Odonata.
Proepisternum. Cephalic plates in the pleura of the prothorax in Odonata.

Pronotum. Dorsal shield of the prothorax.
Propleura. Pleura of the prothorax.
Prothorax. That division of the thorax bearing the first (forward) pair of legs.
Proximad. Extending toward the body.
Proximal. Situated near the body; opposite of distal.
Pruinose. Hoary, as if covered with a fine frost or dust, like the bloom on a plum.
Pterostigma. A dark, opaque spot on the front margin of a wing near its tip; same as stigma.
Punctae. Small spots on the dorsum of Aeshna nymphs.
R. Radius.
Radial Sector. A branch of radius which crosses media; supposed to combine several branches of radius.
Radius. The third longitudinal vein of the wings.
Rugose. Wrinkled; with irregular, waved, elevated lines.
Sclerite. A body plate bounded by sutures; what flytyers seek to demark by spiraling with thread or tinsel.
Serrate. Saw toothed; the teeth set toward one end.
Seta, -ae. A pointed, movable bristle or stiff hair.
Setiform. Resembling a seta.
Setigerous. Bearing setae.
Setose. Bearing setae.
Sigmoid. S shaped.
Spatulate. Sounded and broad at top or end, attenuate at base.
Spine. A heavy, immovable bristle.
Spinigerous. Provided with spines.
Spinule. A small spine.
Spinulose. Provided with small spines.
Spiracle. A breathing pore or external opening of the air tube or trachea.
Spurious. False or accidental.
Sternites. Sclerites of the sternum.
Sternum, -a. Ventral plates of a body segment.
Stigma. *See* pterostigma.
Striated. Marked with parallel, fine, impressed lines.
Stylus, -i. A small rod-shaped projection at the tips of the lateral gonapophysis of the ovipositor; in the male Odonata nymph, short acute processes on ventral surface of segment nine.
Sub. A prefix frequently meaning almost; used in such words as subcircular, subtriangular.
Subcosta. The second longitudinal vein of the wing.
Subcostal Cross-vein. A single cross-vein between subcosta and radius next to the body or proximad of all other antenodal cross-veins; present in Progomphus.
Submentum. The segment of the labium next to the head.
Subtriangle. The cell in the wing behind the triangle in Odonata.
Sulcate. Grooved or furrowed.
Superiors. Dorsal anal appendages in Odonata.
Supertriangle. The wing cell just in front of the triangle in Odonata.
Supraepisternum. Same as anepisternum.
Suture. A depressed line between two sclerites.

Tarsus, -i. The last two or three short segments of the leg of an insect, forming the foot.

Tenerals. Adult insects not having their full coloration or not entirely hardened after emergence.

Terete. Cylindrical, or nearly so.

Tergite. Applied to tergum when occupied by a single sclerite.

Tergum, -a. Dorsal surface of any body segment; refers mainly to abdominal segments.

Tibia, -ae. The fifth segment of the leg or second long segment in dragonflies, bearing the tarsus at the distal end and attached to the femur at the proximal end.

Tibial Setae. Setae on the tibiae.

Trochanters. The second and third segments of the leg in dragonflies; usually short and closely united.

Trochantins. Small sclerites at the base of an appendage.

Truncate. Cut off squarely at tip.

Venter. The lower surface of the whole body or of a division of the body.

Ventro-meson. Intersection of the meson with the ventral surface.

Vertex. An indefinite area on the dorsum of the head, next to the front and between the compound eyes.

Vitta. A longitudinal colored line or stripe.

Vulvar Lamina. Reduced gonapophyses of the female in Odonata, usually consisting of two small plates, one on each side of the vaginal opening.

Vulvar Spine. Spine on venter of abdomen immediately in front of the ovipositor or vulvar lamina in Odonata.

Wing Cases. Envelopes enclosing the wings in nymphs.

Basic Scientific Books and Papers on Aquatic Entomology

Basic Books (in order of importance):

Pennak, Robert W. *Fresh-Water Invertebrates of the United States.* New York: The Ronald Press Company, 1953, 769 pages. Pennak's compendium is the bible. Well worth the purchase price ($15). With keys and excellent illustrations.

Edmondson, W. T., ed. *Fresh-water Biology.* New York: John Wiley and Sons, Inc., 1959, 2nd ed., 1,248 pages. A standard reference work. The chapter on Trichoptera is by Herbert H. Ross. Outrageously priced at $45.

Frey, David G., ed. *Limnology in North America.* Madison: University of Wisconsin Press, 1966, 734 pages. A marvelous book, chock full of information on aquatic research in the various regions of North America.

Hynes, H. B. N. *The Ecology of Running Waters.* Toronto: University of Toronto Press, 1970, 555 pages. No fly-fisherman who takes stream life seriously should be without this massive, informative book which Professor Hynes undertook "in an attempt to provide a comprehensive and critical review of the literature on the biology of rivers and streams." Hynes consulted some 2,500 references, and the bibliography contains more than 1,500 entries of scientific papers cited in the text of the book. Extremely valuable, with a deep, wide range and written in an admirably clear style. In addition to chapters on such subjects as aquatic insects, the chemical and physical characteristics of algae, plankton, and flowing water, there are several on the fishes of running water, the ecological factors affecting them, and their feeding habits. The book should prove of assistance to the flytyer, angler, and conservationist seeking to save a stream, hopefully one and the same person. Understandably expensive: $25.

Needham, James G. and Paul R. *A Guide to the Study of Fresh-Water Biology.* San Francisco: Holden-Day, Inc., 5th ed. revised and enlarged, 1966, 108 pages. This little paperback is designed to "facilitate the recognition of fresh-water organisms both in the field and laboratory." Only organisms commonly found in fresh water are included.

Morgan, Ann Haven. *Field Book of Ponds and Streams.* New York: G. P. Putnam's Sons, 1930, 448 pages. Now out of print, but a book to pluck off the secondhand dealer's shelf, for it is a sturdily bound, pocket-sized volume crammed with information that is easily carried to stream- or pond-side.

Klots, Elsie B. *The New Field Book of Freshwater Life.* New York: G. P. Putnam's Sons, 1966, 398 pages. The successor to Miss Morgan's book above. Numerous illustrations and color plates. Helpful keys to families.

Usinger, Robert L., ed. *Aquatic Insects of California, with Keys to North American Genera and California Species.* Berkeley, Los Angeles, and London: University of California Press, 1971, 508 pages. The Pennak-style bible for the West Coast flytyer.

Lubell, Winifred and Cecil. *In a Running Brook.* New York: Rand McNally & Co., 1968, 64 pages. It may seem odd listing this children's book, but there is no better general introduction to stream life for the novice than this slender volume. The Lubells do not name the stream, but it is Hunter Brook, which flows into the New Croton Reservoir in Yorktown, New York.

Linsenmaier, Walter. *Insects of the World.* New York: McGraw-Hill Book Company, 1972, 392 pp. Originally published at $25, this book is now being remaindered at the bargain price of $12. It is a masterwork. A resident of Switzerland, Linsenmaier is a gifted entomologist, artist, and photographer of worldwide reputation, and the book includes 160 full-color paintings and photographs. The text covers a wide range, dealing with such varied subjects as the insect body, development, mimicry, and classification. There are chapters on water insects, mayflies, caddis, Odonata, stone flies, aquatic moths, and others.

Odonata

Garman's "The Odonata or Dragonflies of Connecticut," from which the Chapter 20 selection was extracted, can usually be purchased from out-of-print booksellers specializing in natural history at from five to ten dollars. There are, however, other Odonata studies that should prove of great interest to those who wish to pursue the subject, which is fascinating in its own right. We have tried to limit the bibliography to books, but have cited a couple of papers because of their excellence and singular interest. The authors are listed alphabetically, with comments.

Bick, G. H. 1941. Life History of the Dragonfly, *Erythemis simplicicollis. Ann. Entomological Soc. Am.* 34 (1): 215–30.

Byers, C. Francis. 1930. A Contribution to the Knowledge of Florida Odonata. Univ. of Florida, *Biological Science Series* I (1): 327 pp. Should be right up the alley for the Southern bass bugger who wants to match the hatch.

Corbet, Philip S. 1957. The Life History of the Emperor Dragonfly *Anax imperator* Leach (Odonata: Aeshnidae). *Journal of Animal Ecology* 26: 1–69. Separately bound in paper by Blackwell Scientific Publications, Oxford. A British species, but a model life history for those flytyers who eventually may give up fishing in favor of studying and collecting dragonflies.

———. *A Biology of Dragonflies.* London: Witherby, 1962. 247 pp. A world view of the order concerned with ecology, physiology, and behavior. A must for the serious reader.

———, Longfield, Cynthia; and Moore, N. W. *Dragonflies.* London: Collins, 1960. 260 pp. A serious but very well written volume, with numerous illustrations and color photographs. One of the "New Naturalist" series published by Collins, the aim of which is "to interest the general reader in the wild life of Britain by recapturing the inquiring spirit of the old naturalists." Of necessity, *Dragonflies* concentrates on species in the British Isles, but we recommend it without hesitation for the flytyer-entomologist seeking information on general life history and behavior. There is an interesting and valuable appendix on wing venation, long a subject of argument among specialists, in which Miss Longfield adjures the American James G. Needham for his "pretracheation" theory.

Gardner, A. E. 1952. The Life History of *Lestes dryas* Kirby. *Entomological Gazette,* 3: 4–26.

Hutchins, Ross E. *The World of Dragonflies and Damselflies.* New York: Dodd, Mead & Co. 1969. 127 pp. A popular but basic book. Most highly recommended. Written in clear language, it provides a simple but helpful key to families and is illustrated with excellent black-and-white photographs by the author, a professor emeritus of entomology at Mississippi State University. A clever man, Hutchins uses a squirt-gun oil can filled with ordinary liquid soap to capture dragonflies. The can will shoot a jet of liquid ten feet or more, knocking a dragonfly from its perch, a very effective way of capturing species that are very wary of collectors with nets.

Kennedy, Clarence Hamilton. Notes on the Life History and Ecology of the Dragonflies (Odonata) of Washington and Oregon. 1915. *Proceedings of the United States National Museum* 49: 259–345.

———. Notes on the Life History and Ecology of the Dragonflies (Odonata) of Central California and Nevada. 1917. *Proceedings of the United States National Museum* 52: 483–635.

Kennedy is unsurpassed for his lovely and realistic sketches of nymphs and adults (some of which we have reproduced here), and his narratives also are often of interest, since he occasionally used a shotgun to collect dragonflies that eluded his net.

Kormondy, Edward J. 1959. The Systematics of *Tetragoneuria,* Based on Ecological, Life History, and Morphological Evidence (Odonata: Corduliidae). *Miscellaneous Publications, Museum of Zoology,* University of Michigan 107: 79 pp. Part of a four-year study submitted for a doctoral dissertation.

Needham, James G. and Heywood, Hortense Butler. *A Handbook of the Dragonflies of North America.* Springfield, Ill., and Baltimore, Md.: Charles C. Thomas, 1929. 378 pp. A scarce book dealing with both damselflies and dragonflies, but only for the very serious student. The material on Anisoptera has been superseded by the volume below.

———, and Westfall, Minter J., Jr. *A Manual of the Dragonflies of North America (Anisoptera).* Berkeley and Los Angeles: University of California Press, 1955. 615 pp. The standard reference work for the United States.

Snodgrass, R. E. 1954. The Dragonfly Larva. *Smithsonian Miscellaneous Collections* 123 (2): 38 pp.

Tillyard, R. J. *The Biology of Dragonflies.* Cambridge University Press, 1917. 396 pages. The classic work—complex, scarce, and expensive in the out-of-print market.

Walker, Edmund M. *The Odonata of Canada and Alaska.* 1: 292 pp.; 2: 318 pp. University of Toronto Press, 1953 and 1958. A detailed study of the damselflies and four families of dragonflies by an ardent student of Odonata for more than fifty years.

Editor's Note: Tombo, a semiannual scientific journal devoted solely to damselflies and dragonflies, is published by the Society of Odonatology (Japan), c/o S. Asahina, Totsuka III–123, Shinjuku-ku, Tokyo, Japan. *Tombo* is printed in both Japanese and English. A subscription costs $2 a year.

Trichoptera

Balduf, Walter Valentine. *The Bionomics of Entomophagous Insects.* Pt II. St. Louis: John S. Swift Co., 1939. 384 pp. An associate professor of entomology at the University of Illinois, Balduf surveyed more than one thousand scientific articles and papers published throughout the world over a fifty-year period to prepare this valuable work, the title of which means, in everyday language, "the life histories of insects that eat other insects." Trichoptera are treated (pp. 102–86), and inasmuch as the entomophagic (insect-eating) proclivities of caddis are inseparable from their scavenging and phytophagic (plant-eating) tendencies, all biological aspects of the order are dealt with in succinct detail. Other orders treated in the book are Lepidoptera, Mecoptera, and Neuroptera. Long out of print, *The Bionomics of Entomophagous Insects* was scheduled for reprinting in 1974. The first volume by Balduf (1936) dealt with beetles, *The Bionomics of Entomophagous Coleoptera.*

Betten, Cornelius. The Caddis Flies or Trichoptera of New York State. 1934. *New York State Museum Bulletin* 292: 576 pp. An important sudy, with special chapters by Blenda L. Kjellgren, Alfred W. Orcutt, and Mrs. Marion B. Davis, the last most winningly on the habits of caddis. There is a rather amusing prefatory note written in 1934 by Charles C. Adams, director of the New York State Museum: "The present report by Doctor Betten calls for a special apology on account of the long delay in its publication. The report was originally written in 1906–17, and has since been revised and brought up to date several times. After this prolonged delay it was considered that, in justice to the author, the report should be published, even at the sacrifice of delaying reports from other fields which have so long been given precedence." Still in print at the bargain price of $3.

Denning, Donald G. 1937. The Biology of Some Minnesota Trichoptera. *Transactions Am. Entomological Soc.* 63: 17–44. Useful for techniques in rearing larvae.

Dodds, G. S., and Hisaw, F. L. 1925. Ecological Studies of Aquatic Insects. III: Adaptations of Caddisfly Larvae to Swift Streams. *Ecology* 6: 123–37.

Elkins, Winston A. 1936. The Immature Stages of Some Minnesota Trichoptera. *Ann. Entomological Soc. Am.* 29: 656–81.

Flint, Oliver S., Jr. 1960. Taxonomy and Biology of Nearctic Limnephelid Larvae (Trichoptera) with Special Reference to Species in eastern United States. *Entomologica Americana* 40: 1–117. This exhaustive study, which contains numerous keys and illustrations dealing with larval forms, was modified from a doctoral thesis at Cornell. Dr. Flint, now at the Smithsonian, is one of the leading students of caddis.

———. 1962. Larvae of the Caddis Fly Genus *Rhyacophila* in Eastern North America (Trichoptera: Rhyacophilidae). *Proceedings of the United States National Museum* 113 (3464): 465–93.

———. 1966. Notes on Some Nearctic Psychomyiidae with Special Reference to Their Larvae (Trichoptera). *Proceedings of the United States National Museum* 115 (3491): 467–81.

———. 1968. The Trichoptera (Caddis flies) of the Lesser Antilles. *Proceedings of the United States National Museum* 125 (3665): 1–85.

Hutchins, Ross E. *Caddis Insects, Nature's Carpenters and Stonemasons.* New York: Dodd, Mead & Co., 1966. 80 pp. A popular work, and Hutchins is always well worth reading.

Lloyd, John Thomas. 1921. The Biology of North American Caddis Fly Larvae. *Bulletin of the Lloyd Library of Botany, Pharmacy, and Materia Medica.* Cincinnati: Entomological Series No. 1 (21): 124 pp. Working at Cornell, Lloyd based his study on caddis larvae found in the vicinity of Ithaca, New York. Very informative and detailed on the habitat, habits, and food of the larvae, their periods of emergence, and descriptions of the larvae, pupae, and cases for a number of species. See also Sibley, below.

Milne, Margery J. 1938. Evolutionary Trends in Caddis Worm Case Construction. *Ann. Entomological Soc. Am.* 32: 533–42. This paper discusses the adaptation of different case-building techniques in relation to habitat and food preferences.

Milne, Lorus J. and Margery J. The Arctopsychidae of Continental America North of Mexico (Trichoptera). 1938. *Bulletin, Brooklyn Entomological Society* 33: 97–110.

Noyes, A. A. 1914. The Biology of the Net-Spinning Trichoptera of Cascadilla Creek. *Ann. Entomological Soc. Am.* 7: 251–72.

Peterson, Alvah. *Larvae of Insects.* Part II. Columbus, Ohio: privately printed, 1960. 416 pp. The larvae of Trichoptera are dealt with (pp. 366–73). There is a key to families modified from Ross (see below). Other orders in this work are Coleoptera, Diptera, Neuroptera, Siphonaptera, and Mecoptera.

Ross, Herbert H. 1944. The Caddis Flies, or Trichoptera, of Illinois. *Bulletin of the Illinois Natural History Survey* 23: 326 pp. Regarded as the classic work, this book belongs in the library of any serious flytyer. Copies are occasionally offered for sale by out-of-print booksellers, but Entomological Reprint Specialists (see pages 214–16) have been offering a reprint at $9.95.

———. A Review of the Nearctic Lepidostomidae (Trichoptera). 1946. *Ann. Entomological Soc. Am.* 39: 265–90.

———. 1947. Descriptions and Records of North American Trichoptera with Synoptic Notes. *Transactions, Am. Entomological Soc.* 73: 125–68.

———. 1948. New Nearctic Rhyacophilidae and Philopotamidae (Trichoptera). *Ann. Entomological Soc. Am.* 41: 17–26.

———. 1949. A Classification for the Nearctic Species of *Wormaldia* and *Dolophilodes* (Trichoptera, Philopotamidae), *Proceedings, Entomological Society of Washington* 51: 154–60.

———. 1950. Synoptic Notes on Some Nearctic Limnephilid Caddis flies (Trichoptera, Limnephilidae). *Am. Midland Naturalist* 43: 410–29.

———. 1951. Phylogeny and Biogeography of the Caddis flies of the Genera *Agapetus* and *Electragapetus* (Trichoptera, Rhyacophilidae). *Jour. Wash. Acad. Sci.* 41: 347–56.

———. *Evolution and Classification of the Mountain Caddisflies.* Urbana: University of Illinois Press, 1956. 213 pp. A very technical survey of the phylogeny (racial history) and geographic dispersal of three families of caddis—the Philopotamidae,

Rhyacophilidae, and Glossosomatidae—on a world-wide basis over the span of geologic time. Probably of interest to only those most advanced students of caddis who have a compelling drive to know as much as possible about these families, particularly in the Appalachians and the western mountain region of North America.

———, and Merkley, Don R. An Annotated Key to the Nearctic Males of *Limnephilus* (Trichoptera, Limnephilidae). 1952. *Am. Midland Naturalist* 47: 435–55.

Sibley, C. K. 1926. Special Studies on Trichoptera, in "A Preliminary Biological Survey of the Lloyd-Cornell Reservation," *Bulletin of the Lloyd Library of Botany, Pharmacy, and Materia Medica.* Cincinnati: Entomological Series 5 (27): 247 pp. A follow-up to the J. T. Lloyd entry above.

Sleight, C. E. 1913. Relations of Trichoptera to Their Environment. *Jour. N. Y. Entomological Soc.* 21: 4–8.

Vorhies, Charles T. 1909. Studies on the Trichoptera of Wisconsin. *Transactions, Wisconsin Academy of Sciences, Arts and Letters* 16 (I): 647–739. A pioneering work that holds up.

Dealers in Books, Periodicals, and Out-of-Print Books

The editors have dealt with the following specialist booksellers (listed alphabetically), and we recommend them to readers searching for an old favorite, an elusive study of caddis larvae, or an out-of-print book.

Angler's and Shooter's Bookshelf
Goshen, Conn. 06756

Out-of-print and rare hunting-and-fishing books; also sporting art. Prices often high, but a bargain now and then. Without question the best stock in the country of out-of-print angling works. Send $1 for catalog, rebated against the first order of $10 or more—worth it, because the catalogs themselves are becoming collector's items.

E. W. Classey, Ltd.
Park Road, Faringdon
Oxon, SN7, 7 DR.
England

Publications on natural history, rare and antiquarian, new titles, and a small number of Classey's own publications. There are occasionally books for the angler, but the Classey catalog is must reading for entomologists and other serious students of natural history. The 1974 spring catalog offered wide and varied fare: a 1969 reprint of McLachan on European Trichoptera at £18; an autograph letter by Darwin concerning sexual and protective coloration in butterflies, £60, and a shop-soiled copy of the 1972 reprint of Needham, Traver, and Hsu's *The Biology of Mayflies* for £9.50.

E. B. & H. A. Darbee
Livingston Manor
N. Y. 12758

Out-of-print and new books on angling.

Entomological Reprint Specialists
P. O. Box 77224
Dockweiler Station
Los Angeles, Calif. 90007

In addition to publishing books, Entomological Reprint Specialists offer for sale any insect book in print. Write for the list on Aquatic Entomology. ERS is offering a complete reprint of Ross's 326-page study on caddis flies for $9.95. To quote from the list on another offering, "Merrill, Mary. Chaoborus. Vols. 1 & 2, bound together. 2nd ed. 1973. 35p., illust. Mimeographed, hideously bound. The illustrations, mostly without captions, are awful. The subject is an aquatic insect, and we offer it only as an excruciating example of our efforts to provide any insect book in print. Of particular interest to bibliographers of entomological minutiae and scurrilous pamphlets. Some aquatic entomologists may want it as a curiosity. Apparently an elaborate joke—but can anyone be that clever? (Vol. 3 due shortly.) . . . 15.00."

Fly Fisherman's Bookcase
Route 9A
Croton-on-Hudson, N.Y. 10520

Fly-fishing and fly-tying books in print at approximately a 15 percent discount from the published price. Fast service a specialty.

E. Chalmers Hallam
Earlswood,
Egmont Drive,
Avon Castle, Hampshire,
England

Out-of-print books on angling and fishes, mainly British. An excellent stock, judging from the catalogs. Hallam also sells books on cockfighting and falconry, dogs, travel, shooting, and wildfowling, among other subjects.

John Johnson
R.F.D. 2
North Bennington, Vt. 05257

Out-of-print natural history, including entomology and fishes. The catalogs bear reading for hard-to-find books, although there usually is not much on fly-fishing or fly-tying. A fine bookman.

Kraus Periodicals Co.
Route 100
Millwood, N.Y. 10546

An enormous, modern warehouse in the countryside, absolutely stuffed with runs and odd volumes of periodicals dealing with entomology, fishes, and just about any subject you can name. Kraus may be out of what you want, but then again the company might just have the item, such as J. T. Lloyd's study "The Biology of North American Caddis Fly Larvae," which we bought for $3. The company was started by H. P. Kraus, the rare bookseller in Manhattan, who recently offered a Gutenberg Bible for sale at $2 million.

Eric Lundberg
Augusta, W. Va 26704

Out-of-print natural history, including entomology and fishes. Catalogs can be extremely interesting, especially when Lundberg devotes one solely to entomology. He also reprints or publishes works for the dedicated specialist, such as T. B. Mitchell's *Bees of the Eastern United States* (2 vols, 268 illus., 1,095 pages, $20).

Julian J. Nadolny
35 Varmor Drive
New Britain, Conn. 06053

Natural history books, occasionally some really good ones on entomology and fishes.

Henry Tripp
92-06 Jamaica Avenue
Woodhaven, N.Y. 11421

Out-of-print books on natural history, strong in entomology (including individual papers) and fishes, occasionally angling. Tripp usually has sets, runs, or odd volumes of scientific periodicals for sale. Very helpful.

Rudolph Wm. Sabbot
5239 Tendilla Avenue
Woodland Hills, Calif. 91364

Out-of-print and antiquarian books on natural history. A catalog can come on strong on fishes or marine invertebrates. You can never be sure what you're going to find, and the same goes for the prices.

Larry C. Watkins
Natural History Books
R. F. D. #1
Dolgeville, N. Y. 13329

A newcomer to the field, Watkins started out strong in mammalia, but is moving into fishes and related subjects, and his catalogs bear scrutiny.

Periodicals of Interest to Flytyers

The Roundtable
United Fly Tyers, Inc.
Room 603 59 Temple Place
Boston, Massachusetts 02111

Membership in UFT, a nonprofit international organization founded to preserve, promote and develop the art of fly-tying, includes a subscription to the bimonthly magazine.

Fly Fisherman
Circulation Division
P. O. Box 2947
Boulder, Colorado 80303

Editorial correspondence should be sent to *Fly Fisherman,* Manchester, Vermont 05254

Trout
Editorial Office
737 South Sparks Street
State College, Pennsylvania 16801

The official magazine of Trout Unlimited, published quarterly. Annual TU membership includes a subscription to *Trout.*

Salmon Trout Steelheader
P.O. Box 02112
Portland, Oregon 97202

Often describes how to tie best western patterns.

The Flyfisher
4500 Beach Drive, S.W.
Seattle, Washington 98116

The official magazine of the Federation of Fly Fishermen, published quarterly. Membership in FFF includes subscription to magazine.

Natural History and Scientific Supply Houses

Flytyers looking for useful materials, equipment, insect specimens, and various knick-knacks, such as larval forceps, that may come in handy will find a happy hunting ground roaming through the catalogs issued by firms dealing in natural history and scientific supplies. The latest Ward's catalog, to cite just one company, is as thick as a good-sized phone book.

American Biological Supply Company
P. O. Box 3149
Baltimore, Md. 21228

Bio-Quip Products
P. O. Box 61
Santa Monica, Calif. 90406

Carolina Biological Supply Company
Burlington, North Carolina 27215

Gulf Specimen Company, Inc.
Panacea, Fla. 32346

Specializes in marine specimens, living and preserved. The proprietor, Jack Rudloe, is a fine writer. Saltwater tyers will enjoy such books of his as *The Erotic Ocean.*

LaPine Scientific Company
6001 South Knox Avenue
Chicago, Ill. 60629

Turtox/Cambosco
8200 South Hope Avenue
Chicago, Ill. 60620

Ward's Natural Science Establishment, Inc.
P. O. Box 1712
Rochester, N. Y. 14603
or
P. O. Box 1749
Monterey, Calif. 93940

Scientific Institutions

Lists of available publications can be procured from:

Connecticut Geological and Natural History Survey
Wesleyan Station
Middletown, Conn. 06457

The Lloyd Library and Museum
917 Plum Street
Cincinnati, O. 45202

Illinois Natural History Survey
Natural Resources Building
University of Illinois
Urbana, Ill. 61801

New York State Museum and Science Service
Albany, N. Y. 12224

Dealers in Fly-Tying Materials

When ordering fly-tying materials that you have earmarked for specific patterns (saltwater hackle streamers, bass-bug tails, tails and legs for nymphs, No-Hackle spinner-wing hen hackle, and so forth), it is always best to include this special information on the order blank or in an accompanying letter. Most materials dealers will understand more clearly what you need with this directive. The order-and-hope technique will create problems for both you and the dealer, whereas customized ordering will help your supplier both to choose material you really want and also to order future stocks accordingly.

If you cannot find a particular material, color, or size listed in these catalogs, don't hesitate to write or call the firm and make known your need. Often, dealers will actually have the material or be able to get it, or will refer you to another source. Some available items are simply not practical to catalog.

We advise each tyer to supply himself with a complete library of material catalogs, for they are both useful and informative, and are the best means for the average tyer to keep abreast of fly-tying. No one shop will have everything you might need, but you will surely find certain dealers particularly geared to your kind of tying.

The following shops are all reliable. We have commented on those with which we have had first-hand experience.

American Anglers
P.O. Box 521
Bethlehem, Pa. 18015

Angler's Roost
141 East 44th Street
New York, N.Y. 10017

Jim Deren holding forth as usual amid extraordinary clutter. A must stop for anyone passing through New York City.

Dan Bailey's Fly Shop
209 West Park Street
Livingston, Mont. 59047

Free catalog. Retail and wholesale. A very reliable source for flies, fly-tying tools, hooks, limited selection of materials. Complete stock of fly-fishing tackle and accessories. Western specialists. Excellent in-shop customer service and prompt, efficient mail-order services.

The Barbless Hook
23 N.W. 23rd Pl.
Portland, Ore. 97210

Quality retail materials and West Coast flies.

Black's Custom Flies
Idleyld Route, Box 95
North Umpqua Highway
Roseburg, Ore. 97470

Raleigh Boaze, Jr.
P. O. Box 115
Brunswick, Md. 21716

Latex sheets.

Bodmer's Fly Shop
2404 East Boulder
Colorado Springs, Colo. 80909

Free catalog. Shop and retail mail-order service. Good personalized service by George Bodmer. Regular newsletter to customers. Good assortment of flies, fly-tying materials, tools, hooks, and fly-fishing tackle and accessories for the Rocky Mountain area.

Buz's Fly and Tackle Shop
805 West Tulare Avenue
Visalia, Calif. 93277

Free catalog upon request. Retail and wholesale. An up-to-date complete stock of highest-quality hand-selected materials and tools, flies, popular fly-fishing tackle, and angling books. Extremely high-quality, fast, personal service (by Mickey Powell and Virginia Buszeck) in the shop, and mail order. Direct importers. All-country specialists.

Len Codella's Anglers' Den, Inc.
5 South Wood Avenue
Linden, N. J. 07036

Creative Sports Enterprises
2333 Boulevard Circle
Walnut Creek, Cal. 94595

Free catalog. Wholesale and retail. An up-to-date, complete stock of high-quality standard and unusual fly-tying materials, flies, and quality tackle. Fly-tying school. Good custom service in shop and mail order, managed by Dave Inks and Andre Puyans. Many items available that are not listed in catalog. Direct importers. West and West Coast specialists, and arrangers of foreign fly-fishing trips.

E. B. and H. A. Darbee
Livingston Manor, N. Y. 12758

An excellent source of flies and materials. (See profile.)

Fireside Angler, Inc.
P. O. Box 823
Melville, N.Y. 11740

Free catalog. Retail and wholesale. Under new management since 1974. A complete line of up-to-date fly-tying materials, tools, hooks, fly-fishing books, flies, tackle, and accessories. Good custom shop (managed by Glen Mikkleson) and mail-order services. Direct importer. Eastern fly-fishing specialists.

Fly Fisherman's Bookcase and Tackle Service
Route 9A
Croton-on-Hudson, N.Y. 10520

Retail and wholesale. Discount prices. Direct importers. A fast-expanding service that carries a complete stock of tying materials, tools, hooks, fly-tying accessory items, flies, the widest selection of in-print angling books and fly-fishing tackle. High-quality in-shop and mail-order service, directed by Sam Melner, assisted by Eric Leiser and Phil Pirone. Seasonal catalogs provide fast updating of new inventory information to customers.

The Fly-fisher
315 Columbine Street
Denver, Colo. 80206

The Flytyer's Supply Shop
P. O. Box 153
Downington, Pa. 19335

The Hackle House
P. O. Box 505
Oakville, Ontario, Canada

Catalog 50¢, refunded on first order. Discount prices and wholesale. Importer and exporter. A new Canadian fly-tying mail-order service that is specializing in custom-service orders and a wide choice of standard and unusual tying materials, tools, imported quality English hooks, and many unusual accessory items. Managed by Don McGregor. Eastern and midwestern Canadian and United States specialist.

Hackle & Tackle
553 North Salina Street
Syracuse, N.Y. 13208

Free catalog. Broad supply of fly-tying tools, materials, and equipment, at discount prices. Managed by Frank Vadalla.

Herter's Inc.
R. F. D. 2, Interstate 90
Mitchell, S. D. 57301

Retail, discount, wholesale. Large catalog, $1.00. Importer. Impersonal shop and mail-order customer service. A very wide selection of fly-tying materials, Herter's fly-tying tools, Herter's imported hooks, fly-tying accessories, lure-making components, Herter rod blanks, Herter fly-tying kits, Herter fly-fishing tackles, Herter flies, and all other types of Herter hunting and fishing goods. Seasonal catalog issues and management policy provide up-to-date merchandise.

E. Hille
815 Railway Street
Williamsport, Pa. 17701

Retail and wholesale. Free catalog. A complete shop and prompt, reliable mail-order service. A very wide stock of quality fly-tying materials, hooks, tools, and an unusually large and complete selection of lure hardwares, rod blanks, and fly-fishing accessories.

Joe's Tackle Shop
186 Main Street
Warehouse Point, Conn. 06088

Kaufman's Streamborn Flies
P. O. Box 23032
Portland, Ore. 97223

Shop and mail order service. Quality selection of materials.

Ed Koch's Yellow Breeches Fly Shoppe
Box 205
Boiling Springs, Pa. 17007

H. L. Leonard
25 Cottage Street
Midland Park, N. J. 07432

Free catalog. Retail and wholesale. A new and expanding quality service to flytyers and fly-fishermen by this old, renowned company. Fly-tying materials, tools, hooks, Leonard rods, fly-fishing tackle and accessories, books and flies. Eastern specialist.

Bud Lilly's Trout Shop
West Yellowstone, Mont. 59758

Free catalog. High-quality service. Good selection of tools and materials, excellent selection of fly-fishing tackle. Western specialist. First-rate information on flies and fishing for West Yellowstone area.

Ojai Fisherman
218 North Encinal Avenue
Ojai, Calif. 93023

The Orvis Company, Inc.
Manchester, Vt. 05254

Free catalog. Retail and wholesale business. An up-to-date, complete stock of high-quality fly-tying materials, tools, hooks, fly-rod kits, tying accessories, fly-fishing books, wide selection of flies and Orvis fly-fishing tackle. Fly-tying schools. A very high quality in shop and mail-order service. Fly-fishing information and travel specialist for this and other countries. Interesting and elaborate seasonal catalogs and regular news bulletin that allows customers to keep well informed on schools, trends, sales, and new products.

Price's Discount Feathers
P. O. Box 53
Three Rivers, Calif. 93271

Rangeley Region Sports Shop
Box 850
Rangeley, Maine 04970

Free catalog. Good selection of tools, materials, books, tackle. Eastern specialist.

Reed Tackle
Box 390
Caldwell, N. J. 07006

Free catalog. Retail and wholesale. Very independent shop service and excellent mail-order service. High-quality, complete, up-to-date stock of materials, tools, hooks, lure-making parts, accessories, rod blanks, books. Eastern specialist.

Hank Roberts
1035 Walnut Street
Boulder, Colo. 80302

The Rod & Reel
P. O. Box 132
Leola, Pa. 17540

Raymond C. Rumpf & Son
P. O. Box 176
Ferndale, Pa. 18921

Hank Shotwell
Box 3761
New Haven, Conn. 06525

Sierra Tackle
Box 373
Montrose, Calif. 91020

Free catalog. Wholesale and retail. An up-to-date stock of quality fly-tying materials, tools, large stock of hooks, books, and complete line of fly-fishing tackle. Managed by Ned Grey. Pacific Coast fresh- and saltwater fly-fishing specialist. An excellent shop and mail-order service. Direct importer.

Streamborn Flies
P. O. Box 23032
Portland, Ore. 97223

W. W. Swalef & Son
P. O. Box 5574
Fresno, Calif. 93755

The Trout Shop
Box 2158
Missoula, Mont. 59801

Universal Imports
P. O. Box 1581
Ann Arbor, Mich. 48106

E. Veniard, Ltd.
138 Northwood Road
Thornton Heath, England CR4 8YG

A complete stock of common and rare fly-tying materials, most foreign books, hooks, tools, dyes, and accessory items. Excellent mail-order service. Specialist in world fly-tying material market.

Notes on the Contributors

DARWIN ATKIN has been providing fly-fishermen of the West with some of the most beautiful, well-tied flies possible. His patterns reflect his warm manner and his love for fly-fishing. Darwin's steelhead flies are his masterpieces, and the variation he makes here with marabou may set a whole new style for steelheading in the West. Darwin Atkin is also the inventor and patent holder for Waste-Trol, a highly effective waste control system for tyers.

Darwin Atkin. *Photo by R. S. Kilburn*

Dan Blanton. *Photo by Bill Rhodes*

DAN BLANTON, one of the fly-fishing pioneers of the San Francisco Bay Area, has originated several highly successful West Coast saltwater fly patterns, including the Sea Arrow and the Whistler series. The salt is his true love; Dan has fished extensively in the Pacific off California and Mexico, and Costa Rica's Caribbean coast, the waters of the giant tarpon. He is a director of the Federation of Fly Fishermen and West Coast advisor to the Striped Bass Fund. Dan and his wife live in San Jose, California.

Raleigh Boaze, Jr.

RALEIGH BOAZE, JR., at the age of twenty-seven opened up a new dimension in fly construction by using strips of latex to create larval and pupal imitations. The success of Ral's Caddis launched him into a part-time fly-tying business, and thousands of his flies are used all over the country now. Ral also makes stone-fly and mayfly nymphs out of latex. Besides fishing and hunting, Ral's life is enriched by his wife Janet and their daughter; they live near Brunswick, Maryland.

Bob Boyle. *Photo by Dean Brown*

Robert Boyle, a senior writer for *Sports Illustrated,* has contributed articles to numerous sporting anthologies and authored several books, notably *The Hudson River: A Natural and Unnatural History.* He holds a scientific collector's license to seine fishes from the Hudson, and many of the specimens he has collected are in the American Museum of Natural History. He is a director of the American League of Anglers, the Striped Bass Fund, and the Hudson River Fishermen's Association. Bob and his three children live near the Hudson at Croton, New York.

Bill Charles

BILL CHARLES is an extremely personable and gifted flytyer. His generosity and dedication to the discipline of tying are well known to fly-fishermen in the Midwest. The liquid-latex method of building wet fly and nymph bodies Bill discovered is the result of many years of development. It is a major fly-tying breakthrough. Bill now lives in Chicago, Illinois.

Thom Green

THOM GREEN, a petroleum geologist by profession, is an expert and enthusiastic fly-fisherman. He is also that rare breed, the reluctant tyer. When Thom does sit down to his bench, however, he comes away with original and effective patterns. Thom's Leech, which has taken many trophy-sized trout from western lakes, is his favorite. When he is not fishing Arkansas's White River or Henry's Lake in Idaho, Thom lives in Tulsa, Oklahoma.

T. Donald Overfield

T. DONALD OVERFIELD, of Solihull, Warwickshire, is one of England's foremost angling historians. He is also a talented angling artist, and he combines these two attributes in many articles on fly-tying history in the American angling press. His work reflects tradition but also shows a flair for innovation and modern methodology. It was fitting that he be directly involved in the development and testing of the New Yorkshire Fly-Body Hook.

Larry Solomon

LARRY SOLOMON began his angling career in his boyhood summer home in Rockland County, New York, where he caught his first trout on the famous string, pin, and worm combination. During the course of the normal progression through lures and bait, Larry witnessed a hatch on the Beaverkill; he has been an active fly-fisherman ever since. Larry is an enthusiastic tyer, sharing the tyer's basic love of experimenting with new patterns. He still lives and works in the New York City area.

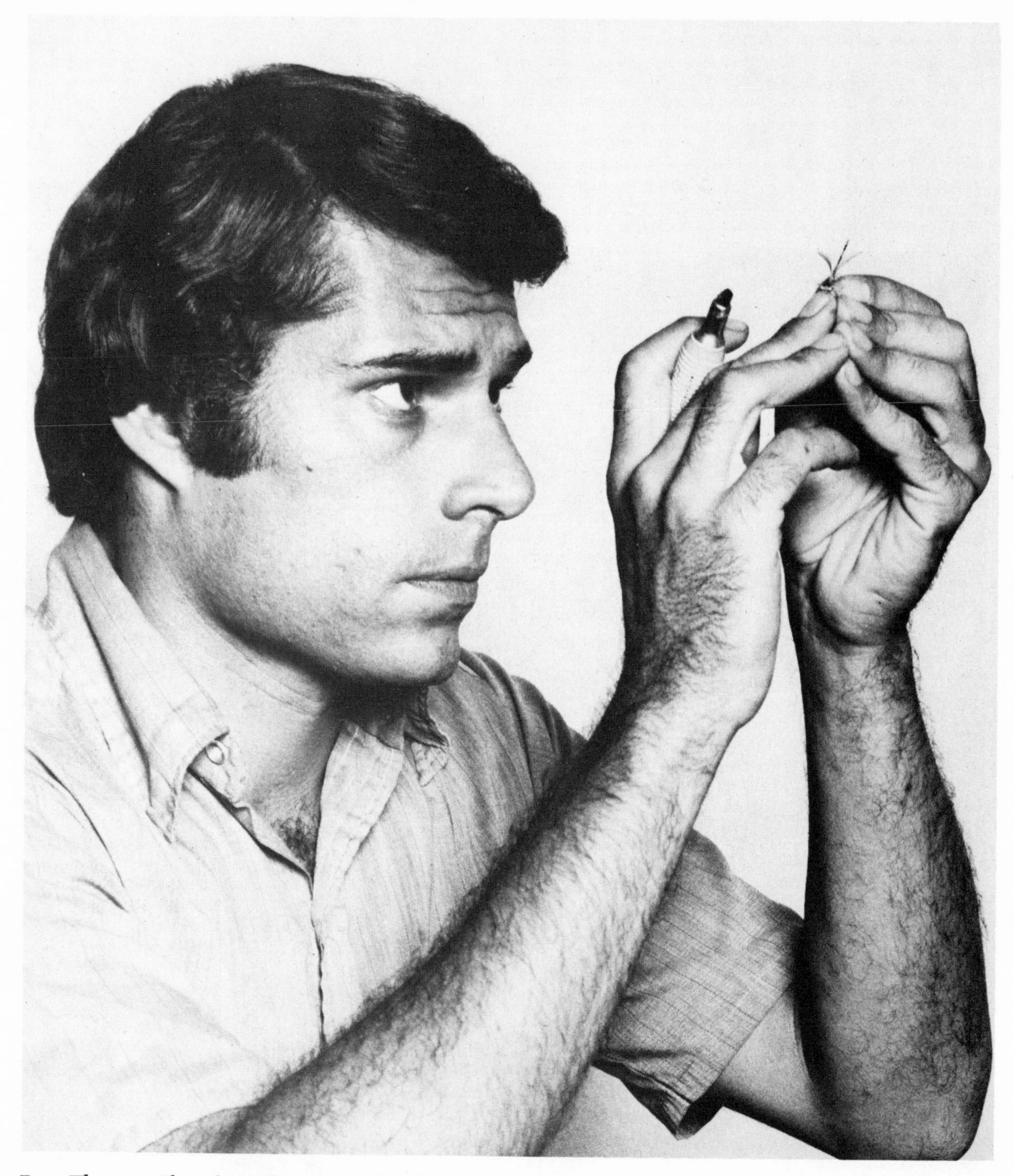

Russ Thomas. *Photo by Nakamoto Art Studios*

RUSS THOMAS, one of angling's free spirits, is a hard tyer to pin down. His patterns, nonetheless, are exact and effective, including his tie for the difficult adult damselfly. Russ follows the Western fishing circuit.

Dave Whitlock

DAVE WHITLOCK is a particularly gifted tyer and angling artist, specializing in western patterns. Besides illustrating many angling books, Dave has been a contributor to ***Art Flick's Master Fly-Tying Guide*** and *The Stream Conservation Handbook.* His original patterns, such as the Whitlock Sculpin, have attracted national attention. He has a special interest in adapting new materials and in the tools of fly-tying. Dave and his family live in Bartlesville, Oklahoma.

WHYGIN ARGUS, a descendant of stock that settled colonial Newfoundland, moved to the Hudson Valley at an early age. There he pursued nature in the raw in wood, field, and river with vigor sufficient to prompt notice in *Sports Illustrated* and *Field Trial Retriever News.* A bachelor and enthusiast of aquatic life, he has made field studies in Lake Superior, the rivers of New Brunswick and the Gaspé, and the Chesapeake. Now middle-aged and prematurely gray, he expressed no interest in being photographed for the first issue of *The Fly-Tyer's Almanac.*

Index

Page numbers in *italics* indicate illustrations.

C

D